Religion in Western Society

SOCIOLOGY FOR A CHANGING WORLD
Series Editors: Graham Allan and Mary Maynard
Consultant Editor: Janet Finch

This series, published in conjunction with the British Sociology Association, evaluates and reflects major developments in contemporary sociology. The books focus on key changes in social and economic life in recent years and on the ways in which the discipline of sociology has analysed those changes. The books reflect the state of the art in contemporary British sociology, while at the same time drawing upon comparative material to set debates in an international perspective.

Published
Graham Allan and Graham Crow, *Families, Households and Society*
Rosamund Billington, Annette Fitzsimons, Lenore Greensides
  and Sheelagh Strawbridge, *Culture and Society*
Lois Bryson, *Welfare and the State*
Frances Heidensohn, *Crime and Society*
Stephen J. Hunt, *Religion in Western Society*
Mike Savage and Alan Warde, *Urban Sociology, Capitalism and Modernity*
John Solomos and Les Back, *Racism and Society*
Andrew Webster, *Science, Technology and Society*

Forthcoming
Kevin Brehony and Rosemary Deem, *Rethinking Sociologies of Education*
Gordon Causer and Ray Norman, *Work and Employment in Contemporary Society*
Jörg Dürrschmidt and Graham Taylor, *Globalisation, Modernity and Social Change*
Philip Gatter and Jeffrey Weeks, *Changing Sexualities*
David Morgan, *Men, Masculinities and Society*
Julie Seymour, *Social Research Methodology*

Series Standing Order

If you would like to receive future titles in this series as they are published, you can make use of our standing order facility. To place a standing order please contact your bookseller or, in case of difficulty, write to us at the address below with your name and address and the name of the series. Please state with which title you wish to begin your standing order. (If you live outside the United Kingdom we may not have the rights for your area, in which case we will forward your order to the publisher concerned.)

Customer Services Department, Macmillan Distribution Ltd
Houndmills, Basingstoke, Hampshire RG21 6XS, England

RELIGION IN WESTERN SOCIETY

Stephen J. Hunt

palgrave

First published 2002 by
PALGRAVE
Houndmills, Basingstoke, Hampshire RG21 6XS and
175 Fifth Avenue, New York, N.Y. 10010
Companies and representatives throughout the world

PALGRAVE is the new global academic imprint of
St. Martin's Press LLC Scholarly and Reference Division and
Palgrave Publishers Ltd (formerly Macmillan Press Ltd).

ISBN 0–333–94591–3 hardback
ISBN 0–333–94592–1 paperback

This book is printed on paper suitable for recycling and made from fully managed and sustained forest sources.

A catalogue record for this book is available from the British Library.

Library of Congress Cataloging-in-Publication Data
Hunt, Stephen, 1954–
Religion in Western society/Stephen J. Hunt.
p. cm.—(Sociology for a changing world)
Includes bibliographical references and index.
ISBN 0-333-94591-3 – ISBN 0-333-94591-1 (pbk).
1. Religion and sociology—Developed countries. I. Title. II. Series.
BL60.H84 2001
306.6¢09182¢1—dc21

10   9   8   7   6   5   4   3   2   1
11   10   09   08   07   06   05   04   03   02

Transferred to digital printing 2005

Contents

To Nikki

1 Religion in the West – A Sociological Perspective

The sociology of religion has several enduring themes. These might be usefully stated in terms of answering a number of broad questions. What is religion; how might it be defined? To what extent is religion a product of society? Conversely, to what degree does religion impact upon the social order? Then there is the related question: Is religion inevitably and discernibly experiencing a marked decline? This book considers these key questions and addresses them within the context of contemporary Western societies and with reference to contrasting sociological perspectives. In doing so, it attempts to show that the sociology of religion endures as a vibrant sub-discipline of considerable relevance to the wider remit of sociology in analyzing and accounting for the richness of social life.

The continuing relevance of the sociology of religion

Despite their theoretical divergences, the earliest sociologists identified religion as a central concern for their discipline. The reason why this was so seemed obvious. Both cross-culturally and historically, all social institutions were self-evidently founded on religious belief and practice. Social life in the pre-industrial world – ranging from tribal to agrarian societies – was saturated in religion. In turn, this social prominence that religion universally seemed to enjoy had the consequence of placing the sub-field of the sociology of religion at the core of the sociological discipline itself. Its prestige and relevance were undisputed.

For these early writers, however, this central place of religion appeared to be increasingly less the case in the industrializing

societies of the West. Those such as Auguste Comte
(1798–1857), Emile Durkheim (1858–1917) and Max Weber
(1864–1920) therefore orientated much of their sociological work
to describing and accounting for the profound social changes
engendered by modernization and its implications for religion
from the eighteenth century to the early twentieth century.
Pluralism, the breakdown of traditional communities, social
mobility, specialization, differentiation, the development of the
'free' market and a growing faith in reason and progress all had
profound implications for social life, including religiosity. The
modern world, so it was argued, would bring human progress,
while the advance of science and rationalism inevitably
conquered religion and superstition.

If these prophets of the doom of religion are now proved
correct, then the continuing relevance of the sociology of religion
may, at first, scarcely seem obvious. Indeed, it might be argued
that the evidently increasing marginalization of religion in
Western societies renders the sub-discipline, and many of the
questions that it traditionally addressed, now irrelevant.
Increasingly fewer people today discernibly subscribe to the historically dominant religion, Christianity. Surveys in Western Europe
and, to a lesser extent, the USA, point towards an identifiable drop
in church membership and attendance. The number of people
married in church, or having their infants baptized is also declining. While these trends vary from one country to another, the
secular society has, it can be argued, arrived in earnest. Yet, the
picture is far more complicated than the simple assumption
concerning the decline of religious faith might suggest. Paradoxes,
contradictions and ambiguities related to religion in the West
today are clearly evident and if there is a general demise then it is
by no means a straightforward or linear process.

For one thing, it was evident by the 1970s that some forms of
Christianity were still resisting the social changes that had challenged them for at least two centuries. As elsewhere in the world,
the more conservative expressions of religion have come to exhibit
considerable political assertiveness. This is certainly the case in the
USA where the so-designated Christian New Right has attempted
to conquer the heights of political life and thereby sought to
enforce a Christian morality on the nation by contending such
issues as pluralism, abortion and the decline of the family as a social

institution. By the end of the twentieth century religion had undoubtedly become a more and more politicized topic and, at least as far as conservative Christianity in the USA was concerned, the subject of acrimonious debates surrounding such issues as the teaching of religion in public schools. All this suggests that if traditional forms of religion are disappearing then they are not going without a struggle.

If we do accept, for the moment at least, that older forms of religiosity are experiencing a demise, then this has been parallelled by the emergence of new and sometimes innovative 'alternatives'. From the middle of the twentieth century there appeared to be an increase in the *variety* of religious activity. Evidence of this was the rise of the so-called 'New Religions'. The popularity of the Unification Church, the International Society for Krishna Consciousness and the Church of Scientology, often displaying seemingly bizarre beliefs and practices, all provided evidence that decline was not a forgone conclusion. Moreover, today there are totally new expressions of religiosity which, in many respects, are not obviously 'religious' in the conventional sense but nonetheless may serve the same function as more traditional faiths in providing belief systems and the foundation of meaning in life for an increasing number of people. These include what has come to be known as the 'self-religions' that are synonymous with many aspects of the New Age movement that began to attract adherents from the 1980s. In addition there are what are frequently referred to as quasi-religions where such social phenomena as sport, or the cult of rock or film stars provide, arguably, innovating expressions of religiosity which give a whole new dimension to what has been traditionally regarded as religious belief and practice. These, and other emerging forms, suggest that religion is far from being an irrelevant part of social life in the West.

While the form and expression of religiosity may have changed, the fundamental endeavour of sociology remains to further the understanding of the role of religion in society, to analyze its significance in and impact upon human history and to understand its diversity and the social forces which shape it. Above all, it offers an on-going recognition that religion is a social phenomenon. While the emergence of new forms of religiosity in the West confirms that the human capacity for religious belief and practice is virtually limitless, they also provide markers of current social change and cultural transformation. Similarly, if we wish to understand the apparent upsurge in conservative Christianity then we must look at wider social trends and developments. To put it succinctly, contemporary religion is telling us something about contemporary society.

Although all sociologists share these broad assumptions regarding the social origins of religion, the discipline has always been identified by contrasting traditions and perspectives that diverge on precisely how the subject could be best approached. This is as true today as it ever was. The early pioneers of sociology sought to find patterns in what they assumed was the irrationality of religion and to establish its principal social underpinnings. It was an approach that had its roots in the rationalism and positivism of the eighteen and nineteenth centuries that assumed that religion is a natural phenomenon which can be objectively and scientifically studied and explained in much the same way as other aspects of social life. This amounted to a reductionist approach that was very much a product of the Enlightenment. At the beginning of the twentieth century this was exemplified by the work of Durkheim (1915) who identified religion as primarily performing the vital social function in bringing a social integration and solidarity that was derived from a system of shared beliefs and practices. Religion, according to Durkheim, is a means of worshipping society itself. Irrespective of the type of society and irrespective of the beliefs and practices it embraced, religion had the same universal function. Although Durkheim's writings appear less relevant to Western society today, his broad endeavour to discover trends and regularities in religious life, and to identify it fundamentally as social in origin, is still retained.

While it would be helpful to stylize all sociology of religion in these reductionist terms, things have never been quite so simple. This reductionist approach has been rivalled by others. Until relatively recently, the phenomenological perspective has proved extremely influential. It had its own distinctive characteristics and assumptions that were often in opposition to the reductionist account. Here, the work of Peter Berger and his writings with Thomas Luckmann are particularly noteworthy since much of their work addressed the changing nature of contemporary religion. According to Berger (1967), the provision of meaning, especially channelled through religious worldviews, was of great importance because of the way in which meaning linked the individual with the larger social group and provided a source of social stability. Religion, therefore, not only provided meaning for the individual, but created order through a shared worldview of the nature of reality and man's place in the cosmic realm. In this way the phenomenological approach could subsume the sociology of religion under the broader category of the sociology of knowledge. The subject matter of both was the legitimate intellectual and moral structures of society. This marked a recognition that humans beings have the distinct capability to make sense of the world, including the social world. Only human beings could ask 'ultimate' questions: What is the purpose to life?, Why is there suffering?, Is there life after death?

In this quest to understand religion in Western society at the beginning of the twenty-first century however, the 'classical' approaches briefly considered above are increasingly less able to account for recent developments. Not that they are entirely redundant, and what they have to offer will be considered in this volume. Nonetheless, they appear more and more inadequate in accounting for many contemporary expressions of religious life and what seems to be its growing diversity. The speed of technological and cultural transformations renders any enquiry into social life a difficult task and ensures that future predictions are equally problematic. Sociology has attempted to come to terms with the rate of change and adapt its theoretical frameworks accordingly. New perspectives have been developing for several years in order to make sense of where Western culture is going and what the implications are for religious belief and practice.

Changes in religious orientations over the last few decades have engendered something of a sociological revolution in the theoretical frameworks by which the subject is now studied. At times, much of the recent theorizing seems to reflect nothing more than the fads and fashions in mainstream sociology, yet the developing approaches do mark a serious attempt to analyze major social transformations. A number of these changes, particularly cultural and technological, have profound implications for the sphere of religious activity. The more obvious are theories related to post-modernity which are gaining legitimacy in the field of the sociology of religion. Although works related to post-modernity are complex and wide-ranging, they are part of a new paradigm that considers the rapid changes that have occurred in Western societies. One of the principal changes has been in the cultural realm. Since religion is closely linked to aspects of culture, it has gained a special interest amongst sociologists – one enhanced by the apparent increasing diversity of religious life and the possibility of a religious revival in the West.

A second developing theoretical framework, particularly in North America, is that of rational-choice theory and the consumer aspects of religion. From this perspective religion is best understood in terms of the spiritual 'seeker's' individual search for a suitable faith in the 'religious marketplace'. For many rational-choice theorists the freedom to choose one's religion has brought about not only new and innovating forms of religion, but an increase in religiosity *per se* – an assumption which, in turn, has been forcefully rejected by their critics. These evolving theories, along with those related to post-modernity, will be considered in a number of the chapters of this book, allowing us to understand changes in mainline religion as well as the more innovating and 'alternative' forms.

There is another evolving approach to consider, if 'approach' is the correct terminology. It is that of globalization. Although this book focuses on religion in Western societies today, it necessarily recognizes that recent developments mean that the sociology of religion is now characterized by a broader frame of reference. In fact, this volume necessarily has an international dimension. In the context of globalization no nation is immune from events and developments elsewhere. Any examination of the nature of religious change in the West, even in private expressions of belief and practice, must invariably be grounded in an understanding of major global trends and transformations.

Globalization has allowed foreign religious imports to the West which, although they are by no means unprecedented, impact in numerous different ways. One obvious example is the faiths of ethnic minorities. Their public profile has been elevated in the West not only because ethnic diversity now characterizes many Western societies, but because of the steady demise of traditional Christianity. Yet, the impact of 'foreign' religions has less obvious ramifications. Many new forms of religiosity are inspired by the ancient world religions, transforming their beliefs and practices in line with Western cultural idioms. Hence, those particularly related to Eastern mysticism have merged with aspects of Western culture to create the syncretic forms that are exemplified by the New Age movement.

What is religion?

Old and new theoretical approaches to religious life struggle with a number of conceptual, analytical and methodological problems. One of the more enduring is the broad philosophical question: How exactly should religion be defined? This has become a particularly pertinent question in the context of contemporary religion and inherent in the above suggestion that the cult of the film or rock star could conceivably be interpreted as a form of religion. In fact, the debate as to what exactly constitutes religion is perhaps more pertinent than ever since how religion is perceived, described and analyzed in contemporary society depends to a large extent on how it is defined. Above all, the matter of definition has a direct bearing on whether religion is understood as enjoying a new lease of life or experiencing a long-term decline.

In the nineteenth century some anthropologists such as Edward Tylor proposed what he called a 'minimum definition' of religion; that is, religion constitutes a 'belief in spiritual beings' (Tylor, 1903, p. 424). It is a narrow 'substantive' definition. At its simplest, religion is the belief in the supernatural – a belief which, although extremely varied, is apparently present in every known society. Although this definition has a comparative edge, allowing a survey of religion in different societies and over time, it fails to incorporate the idea that spiritual forces have some influence or control over the world, a notion that always accompanies belief in the supernatural. Substantive definitions have, therefore, generally come to embrace such criteria. Roland Robertson (1970, p. 47), for example, states that religion 'refers to the existence of supernatural beings that have a governing effect on life'.

Substantive definitions tend to be embraced by those who identify a demise of religion in Western societies. In many respects this is understandable. If religion is identified in terms of religious beliefs related to the supernatural, then it is possible to speak of the 'Golden Age of religion' in pre-industrial societies and the apparent increasing secularity of the West. This is also why some current sociologists would see new expressions of religiosity, particularly those without a supernaturalistic frame of reference, as not 'real' religion at all. Substantive definitions are also inclined to correspond more closely to common-sense notions of religion primarily because they are based on Western ideas, and this usually means specifically Christian dogma since the faith places relatively great emphasis on a formal belief system and range of doctrines. Thus if we limit the discussion to the decline of Christianity, then a religious decline may well be taking place.

Other sociologists have been unhappy with substantive definitions and prefer a 'functional' definition. Their charge is that there is far too much emphasis on beliefs and not on what religion *does*. For instance, according to Durkheim, this meant in a positive and 'functional' way the well-being, stability and integration of society. Religion promotes unity and social cohesiveness. This has implications today in surveying religiosity in Western societies. If it could be shown that various social manifestations, while not obviously 'religious' in the conventional sense, performed this function, then religion may still be flourishing. Hence, secular ideologies, ethos and value systems, worldviews, interpersonal relations, leisure activities, voluntary association and other social phenomena that substantivist theorists identify as non-religious could be defined as such. In doing so, the functional definition is predisposed towards affirming the endurance of religion in the West, albeit in non-supernaturalistic forms and embracing many of the new expressions of religiosity.

The functionalist approach, as typified by the work of Durkheim, has not been unique in embracing a broad interpretation of religion. Phenomenological viewpoints could also offer a wide definition and have shown that they are able to enforce either side of the decline of religion debate. Since sociology has been redefined by phenomenologists as the study of the nature of subjective reality or of the way in which the world appears to human beings, religion is what individuals and societies say it is. This is particularly so in the case of so-called quasi-religions. Thus, for example, if a soccer fan regarded the support of his team as a form of 'religion', who could legitimately question the claim? The implications for the study of religion in the contemporary Western context are therefore radically rephrased. Whether religion was declining, increasing, or expressed in different ways depended on what was meant by the term and that, in turn, depended on how 'believers' defined it. The complexity of the discussion of religion in the Western world, particularly in its emerging expressions, thus comes into clear relief and is endorsed, as we shall see, by more recent approaches – particularly those which explore notions of post-modernity.

The functional definition is not without its problems and two are worth mentioning since they have a bearing on contemporary forms of religion. The first is that such definitions have the problem of encouraging a tautology by eliding what is to be demonstrated (that religion has certain functions) with the identification of religion itself. Put another way, how do we know what a religion is? The answer being that it is identified by certain positive social functions. Secondly and relatedly, by claiming that a social phenomenon is 'religious' it is possible to apply the definition to social groups who would categorically deny that they have a religious element. For example, it has been claimed that Alcoholics Anonymous operates as a kind of religious sect. Several commentators have stressed AA's strict set of beliefs, strong moral codes, and its rather vague higher 'transcendental' aim that makes it a religion of sorts (Greil and Rudy, 1984). Needless to say that the organization itself would reject such assertions.

The problem of objectivity

Although sociological approaches may come and go out of fashion, another perennial problem that they have all faced is one especially relevant to the sociology of religion and is related to the subject matter of religion itself. This is as true today as it ever was and is related to the importance of objectivity and the question of how sociologists should approach the specifically 'religious' element. A small minority of sociologists have preferred to limit the scope of the subject to the sympathetic description and interpretation of different belief systems, ruling out causal generalizations. Thus, Eliade (1969), for example, believed that a comparison of religions would be allowed only in so far as it did not seek to go beyond the perception of religion by those who have a religious faith themselves. Here, religion is seen as understandable only in its own terms. It cannot be reduced to social or psychological factors. This necessarily restricts our approach to religiosity to a rather narrow exercise and is of very limited application in an attempt to understand religion in contemporary Western societies.

Few have taken such a restricted and seemingly neutral approach as that advanced by Eliade. Indeed, some have been particularly hostile to religion. Karl Marx (1818–83) who was, strictly speaking, an economist and philosopher, saw a sinister side of religion. This was a lesson of history. For Marx, religion was, above all, a tool for ideological domination in oppressive class-based societies and simultaneously provided the oppressed with a way in which they could come to terms with their dehumanizing condition. Marx, although bringing his unique understanding of religion, typified three elements of classical sociology. First, in explaining religion scientifically, sociology tended to have the intended or unintended consequence of explaining it away. To understand it sociologically was to dismiss it. Secondly, and relatedly, many of the early sociologists insisted that religion was something that human beings could best do without since it was so much irrational superstition. Thirdly, Marx espoused the rather ethnocentric view that the underdeveloped countries would in the future undergo a similar process of modernization that Europe and North America had experienced first. A decline in religion would invariably follow. Thus Western societies showed other nations what they would eventually become and this included all the alleged virtues of modernity and cultural attributes of the West.

Others have been more accommodating. There were those classical sociologists, typified by Max Weber who, while maintaining that religion was likely to decline in the modern world, believed that as a value-free science sociology cannot side for or against the truth claims of religion. This may be the approach that most sociologists today endorse and a good deal of sociological ink has been spilt in considering the 'proper' position to take. In this search for neutrality perhaps the most currently respectable stance now taken is that of 'methodological atheism' (Berger, 1973, p. 106). This holds that it is necessary to 'bracket' aside the question of the status of religious claims, reserving judgement on whether they are ultimately founded upon some irreducible and inexplicable basis. Moreover, it is now quite legitimate for sociologists to hold a faith of their own, to be an atheist or agnostic.

Such an approach, however, does not do away with all the problems related to objectivity. For example, in attempting a survey of contemporary cults and new religious movements (NRMs), there is a tendency for sociologists to be sympathetic towards them in the sense that they are often oppressed religious minorities subjected to negative labelling by government agencies and the public at large and where beliefs are viewed as bizarre techniques of winning converts and tantamount to 'brain-washing'. Hence, sociology has, sometimes by default, frequently sided with the 'underdog' as a consequence of attempting to understand why some forms of contemporary religion attract 'bad press'. On the other hand, in accounting for conversion to such religions, as we shall see, the sociological enterprise starts with social or social–psychological factors. Hence, conversion is explained in terms of personal crisis, social backgrounds and social trends. In fact, it is explained by any other variable apart from the convert's own accounts of their conversion.

At the same time that a more accommodating standpoint is at least idealized, the broad sociological approach to religion is in stark contrast to others, above all, the discipline of theology. The latter, especially in its more conservative traditions, regards religion as closely akin to 'true' spirituality and is essentially a supernatural phenomenon that, by its very nature, can never be defined nor for that matter wholly comprehended. The theological approach examines religion but is primarily concerned with understanding the essence of the divine. Society may change but the nature of the divine does not. Such an approach often assumes that 'true' religion is not amenable to sociological analysis. Religion is not just another social institution or human product like any other. It is not something that can be objectively and rationally explained since it has a non-naturalistic or spiritual character which cannot be conceived in any other way than in religious or spiritual terms. A rather extreme view is that belief can only be explained and truly understood by the believer. However, it is a sign of the endurance of the sociology of religion, and perhaps a mark of secularity, that today many theological colleges supplement their courses with modules that espouse the virtues of the sociology of religion. It is a recognition that even if there were some irreducible element in religious experience, the observable expressions it takes may well be mediated by social and cultural processes.

Summary and overview

So far, we have attempted to define what religion is, what is unique about the sociological enterprise, how old and new perspectives might inform our discussion of religion in the West, and some of the enduring problems related to the study of religion. All of these themes will resurface in the subsequent chapters and will be considerably elaborated upon in the exploration of contemporary religion.

We have also recognized that at the beginning of the twenty-first century religious life in the West is substantially more complex than the early sociological theorists would have predicted. Few sociologists today now subscribe to the simplistic view that secularization equals the demise of religion. Certainly, most would probably argue that the earlier assumption regarding the decline of religion within *modernity* cannot now be substantiated given the evidence of the advanced industrial societies of Europe and North America. Indeed, the current orthodoxy in sociological thinking seems to be that although there appears to be a decline in institutional expressions of religiosity, most obviously of Christianity, religious activity is far from completely marginal and that there is an observable growth of parallel, yet contrasting, types of religion. These are issues which clearly need to be explored more comprehensively.

Each chapter of this volume covers substantive topics, although some of the concerns invariably overlap. Those of secularization and the debates surrounding the so-called 'decline of religion' are perhaps the most apparent. At the same time, there is a focus on some familiar themes such as the fortunes of Christianity, changes in mainline religion, the locus of belief and belonging, and sectarianism and fundamentalism. Nonetheless, given rapid social transformations and accompanying developments in sociological theory, there is also room for exploring fresh and emerging themes.

One, as already suggested, is that of the many implications of globalization for religion in the West, and the repercussions of the global exportation of Western religion. Another is an analysis of the new expressions of religiosity – exploring the controversies surrounding them and, more broadly, whether they are reversing the alleged decline of religiosity in the West. Yet another theme is the significance of ethnic religions that complicates the debate of the place of religion in the contemporary West. The volume concludes with more 'hidden' aspects of religious life, which must also be added to the equation of 'decline' or 'resurgence', through an overview of popular forms of religiosity ranging from superstition to the quasi-religions. This survey, then, is a wide one. Yet, it presents a sociological framework by which to approach and comprehend developments in the field since about 1960, although some historical background is inevitably included alongside an examination of recent trends and contemporary theorizing.

2 Secularization and the 'Decline' of Religion

As a survey of the literature would suggest, the sociology of religion has been preoccupied with the debate surrounding the secularization thesis. In turn, this debate is hedged in by the problems of definition. The popular assumption is that it simply denotes the decline of religion. However, this is to oversimplify a complex area which needs to be addressed in more detail. This chapter and Chapter 3 consider the theme of secularization, overview the problems associated with it, and examine the evidence that points to a possible decline, resurgence or, alternatively, the increasing plurality of religiosity.

Secularization: myth or ideology?

As we shall see, some sociologists have argued the so-called decline of religion is something of a myth and cannot be substantiated by either historical or contemporary evidence. Others have argued that there are good reasons for arguing that sociological speculations related to secularization cannot themselves be divorced from their wider social context. Hence, the problem of objectivity disussed in the opening chapter is also encountered in the core debate regarding secularization. Indeed, Bellah (1971) suggests that the insistence of the decline of religion is itself a notion generated by modernity and, therefore, cannot be separated from its Western cultural roots. Stemming from the Enlightenment, the hope for a secular society began as an academic response to the dominance of the Christian Church and continued as a reaction to religious authority by those who are inclined towards atheism. In good tradition, many sociologists have since viewed religious belief as an intellectual error, which the progress of science and rationality would ultimately weaken to the point of disappearance. In his early work, David Martin (1965), argued that the failure of sociology to be objective in this respect meant that the term secularization had strong ideological overtones. Moreover, secularization was so contentious a concept that it should be abandoned entirely.

Despite the controversies surrounding the term, secularization, conceptually speaking, can at least be recognized as an interpretive paradigm which allows us to describe and comprehend the inter-related themes of social and religious change in the West. Nor should the numerous contrasting theories of secularization distract from acknowledging their overlapping concerns. In this regard, a not untypical appraisal of theories of secularization is advanced by Olivier Tschannen (1991) who argues that, while many are not compatible at the abstract level, they nevertheless share a very broad set of assumptions of modernity and include:

First, *the advance of rationalization*. Here, perceptions of reality lose their sacred character to be replaced by a rational–causal explanation of the world whereby human knowledge, behaviour and institutions, once thought to be grounded in divine power, are recognized to be merely human creation.

Secondly, *differentiation*: the disengagement of society from religion. Religion draws into its marginalized enclave and becomes primarily of private concern. In doing so, religious symbols, doctrines and institutions lose their prestige and significance.

Thirdly, *increasing worldliness*, including a greater conformity to this world and attendance to worldly problems at the expense of belief in the supernatural, even by forms of traditional religiosity.

Around these core 'concepts' revolve a number of subordinate themes, most notably atomization, privatization, generalization and pluralization. These will form the background to our discussion of secularization.

Rationalism and the decline of religion

The idea that science and rationality would eclipse religion has been an enduring theme. The most influential work in this respect has proved to be that of Max Weber (1958), who stressed the growth of rationality as the primary mode of motivation, particularly in the

West, as a result of unique historical conditions including urbanization, technological advances, communication and the growth of the capitalist economy. Weber predicted that the world would no longer be charged with the mystery of the 'magical garden' that had infused the consciousness of pre-modern man. Writing at the beginning of the twentieth century, he foresaw social existence as increasingly dominated by rational motivation, meaning and action which involved a deliberate and precise calculation of means and goals orientated to this world. Religiously motivated behaviour, such as the search for other-worldly salvation, would be eclipsed. Ironically, Weber had identified this cognitive shift as partly attributable to certain internal factors related to Christianity, particularly Protestant varieties. Ascetic Protestantism largely provided the motivational spark responsible for the work ethic that was to herald the emergence of large-scale capitalism which, in turn, enhanced the march of rationalism through its calculated pursuit of profit. With a twist of irony, Weber predicted that rationalism would subsequently turn back and erode its Christian foundations and bring a 'disenchantment of the world'.

A similar theme has been developed by Peter Berger (1973). His view is that, along with a number of other social and economic factors, Protestant Christianity contained within it the seeds of secularity. The key factor for Berger, as with Weber, is the increasing disenchantment of the world in the West as a result of distinct historical developments. Some of these explicitly 'religious' causes could be traced back to ancient Judaism with its rejection of magic and mysticism in favour of an ethical rationalism that, within centuries of its emergence, was adopted by Christianity. Bursting through during the Reformation, this innerworldly ethic was to influence Western civilization or at least its Protestant expression. Disposing of the mystical, sacramental and ritual aspects of Catholicism, Protestantism radically separated the sacred and profane spheres – undermining the sacred relationship between God and man. Secularization, as defined by the eclipse of a supernatural view of the world, was therefore inadvertently advanced. At the same time, according to Berger, the Church-type organization with its specialized religious functions, particularly discernible in Protestantism, pointed in the direction of secularization. This form of organization carried an inherent potential institutional specialism of religion that was rare in the history of religion. The major implication was that the other areas of social life were gradually reduced to the profane realm and subject to the impact of rationalization, knowledge and science.

The Wilsonian perspective

Other sociologists such as Bryan Wilson (1966) have focused on the significance of rationality as central to secularizing impulses but have identified it as an external factor to religion, rather than uniquely internal to Protestantism. The key variables are primarily associated with the growth and development of modes of thought and worldviews which are not supernaturalistic in outlook. Wilson's argument is that the autonomous growth of scientific knowledge and method has undermined the credibility of religious interpretations of the world. Of particular importance is the application of scientific approaches to man's endeavours. Increasingly, Western consciousness has come to understand that human destiny is in human rather than divine hands, and that human problems have human solutions. Wilson argues that this is a tendency which was enhanced in the last half of the twentieth century. Much was typified by the victory of the Allies in the Second World War, especially with the development of atomic weapons, which showed man as master of his own world and destiny.

For Wilson, rationality alone would not hasten secularization. A process of institutional differentiation was taking place which meant that the various institutional domains in society became separated from each other because they performed specialized functions. The implication for religion is that specialized religious institutions have merely religious functions. The contrast here is with religion in simpler, non-industrial societies where beliefs, values and practices of religion directly influence behaviour in all spheres of human life. In modern society, suggests Wilson, religion is reduced to marginalized areas with the minimum of significance and authority in any given realm of social existence.

Another consideration advanced by Wilson (1976) is the decline of community from which religion ultimately stems (a theme earlier developed by Durkheim). The decline of community in modern industrial society results from high levels of social and geographical mobility and consequent changes in the nature of social control. In well-integrated communities authority has a moral and religious basis. By contrast, in the modern, rational and bureaucratic world control is impersonal and removed from its former religious and ethical foundation. Religion loses its significance in such a setting, as do communal values which traditionally receive expression in the form of collective rituals. The Western world of today is, therefore, in marked contrast with the Middle Ages when the Church was at the height of ecclesiastical and political power in Europe and largely responsible for identifying and punishing perceived deviant social and religious behaviour by excommunication and the threat of hell, together with the sanctioning of physical punishment on behalf of the community.

Religious pluralism

A contrasting approach to the theme of secularization has focused on the pluralist dimensions of Western society. Here, Peter Berger's work (1970) has been particularly influential and, until relatively recently, appeared to be the prevailing paradigm in sociological accounts of secularization. Berger concurs with Wilson in accepting that rationalizing tendencies erode a supernaturalistic worldview. However, there is more to the equation, and of overriding significance is the pluralistic nature of the modern world. Modernization and industrialization aid the social fragmentation of society which creates a plurality of cultural and religious groups. Berger, writing with Luckmann (1967), points out that instead of one religious tradition with a single, unchallenged worldview of the supernatural, there are now many divergent views. No longer is a single universe of meaning, passed on from one generation to the next, provided for all members of society. In some respects this is close to Wilson's view in that it assumes that religion can no longer express and reinforce the values of society or sanctify its social institutions, and in which the state is unable to support a single religion without causing conflict with different social groups.

Berger, like Wilson, therefore argues that religion ceases to perform its traditional function of promoting social solidarity. However, Berger's emphasis is on the decline of religion in the sense of offering a shared comprehensive explanation of the world and at the level of human significance and meaning.

The plurality of religion, Berger also suggests, reminds individuals that their beliefs are a personal preference, a matter of choice, and no longer part and parcel of their membership of society. It follows that the condition where one can choose between one religious interpretation and another, and where rival interpretations and organizations compete in the 'marketplace' of religions, is likely to result in a devaluation or loss of authority for the religious world-view generally. In short, the pluralist situation relativizes competing religious worldviews and their matter-of-fact acceptance. Moreover, the pluralistic situation where one can choose one's religion is also a situation where one can choose to disbelieve. (Berger and Luckmann, 1967, p. 151).

Evidence of religious decline

Such approaches as those considered so far remain compelling and influential. However, the notion of an inevitable decline of religion in the wake of modernization was always an unconvincing assumption for some commentators. One plank of the argument that is critiqued is the assumption by advocates of the secularization thesis that there was once some Golden Age that has somehow been lost. Shiner (1966), who refutes the secularization thesis, argues that the problem is 'of determining when and where we are able to find the supposedly "religious" age from which decline has commenced'. Certainly the anthropologist Mary Douglas (1973) does not see religion as always integral to the life of small-scale, pre-industrial societies. Even in tribal communities, she maintains, alongside spiritual fervour there are frequently many of the expressions of scepticism and materialism that are familiar aspects of contemporary Western societies. It is, therefore, wrong to draw a sharp distinction between the past and the present. There is no simple parallel between the supposedly 'religious' pre-industrial society and the Western world typified by secularity.

According to Bruce (1997a), who actually supports the secularization thesis, the 'Golden Age of Faith' is something of a caricature. However, he maintains that there is nothing in the secularization thesis that requires that such an age existed. All that the argument requires is that previous generations were more religious than people are today. Bruce argues that much depends on what is meant by 'religion'. In the choice between functional definitions (what religion does) and substantive ones (what religion is in terms of beliefs related to the existence of supernatural powers and beings), he opts for the latter in adopting a historical perspective. In countries where Christianity was strong, ordinary people saw religion in terms of a set of beliefs and practices related to the supernatural. This being so, the evidence shows that the history of the Church, as an institution deeply embedded in social, economic and political life over the centuries in Europe, experienced periods of popularity and decline. For example, it lost popular support during the upheaval of the Reformation. In some parts of Western Europe it soon recovered, in others it did not. Nonetheless, the general trend is that of the decline of an all-pervasive religious worldview whether that was predominantly Christian or the magic and superstition that frequently gained greater popularity when the faith experienced periods of decline.

What then is the historical evidence for some Golden Age of religion in the West? Some believe that the testimony often advanced is unreliable. For instance, the historian K.V. Thomas (1974) points out that, in the case of sixteenth- and seventeenth-century England, little is known of the religious practices and belief which prevailed at the time – certainly insufficient to draw conclusions. Indeed, what evidence does exist of religiosity in Europe over the centuries tends to be limited to the more visible and better documented religion of the ruling social elites rather than that of ordinary people (Douglas, 1983).

It may well be that religion was not that significant for much of the population of Western societies in previous centuries. Even Marxists, such as Bryan Turner (1983), have sometimes taken a revisionist stance by suggesting that at the so-called height of religiosity and ecclesiastical power of medieval Catholic Europe, peasant communities were largely untouched and indifferent to the faith in their daily struggle for survival. Thus, the significance of religion may have been merely a concern for the nobility where it was, above all, an ideological prop for the dominant system of property rights and inheritance. This kind of assessment has, in turn, been contested. For instance, evidence suggests that the cult of the Virgin Mary and the saints does appear to have had great popular significance for the masses in terms of belief and practice in medieval Europe (Hamilton, 1995, p. 168).

While the evidence of the impact of Christianity is inconclusive, there remains the problem of putting too much emphasis on the evidence of a Golden Age of Christianity and its subsequent demise. As Wilson (1982) argues, in his decline-of-religion thesis, we should not place overdue stress on the dissolution of Christianity in the West. Secularization is not the same as de-Christianization. A whole range of pagan beliefs and practices, superstition and 'folk' religion permeated Christian Europe and even influenced the Christian faith. Nonetheless, according to Wilson, it is these expressions of religiosity, as well as the more pronounced Christian aspects, which have also discernibly diminished.

Measuring decline

Belief

Even today the attempt to measure religious decline by so-called hard empirical evidence is a notoriously hazardous enterprize. Two of the usual indices advanced are those of religious belief and belonging. We may take the matter of belief first by exploring a few examples through the findings of opinion polls which probably supply the simplest type of data related to religious belief.

Several European Values surveys conducted from the 1980s to the year 2000 (Harding, Phillips and Fogarty, 1985; Cook, 2000) have found that under 60 per cent of Europeans regularly define themselves as 'a religious person', some 50 per cent claim that God was significant in their life and around 50 per cent believe in an existence after death. At the same time, however, only some 20 per cent admit to a religious experience sometime during their life. In addition, evidence from Britain suggests that the number of people who would describe themselves as atheists or agnostics remained fairly constant at just under 27 per cent (Brierley, 2000).

Clearly, these statistics are very much open to interpretation. It might be suggested that a sizeable majority of the population of Britain retains religious belief and, therefore, could be used as evidence against secularization even if only a minority attend religious institutions and perform religious ceremonies with any regularity. This kind of approach has been endorsed by Davie (1994), who argues that, at least in the case of Britain, there has occurred a separation of belief and belonging. Widespread belief remains but it is not expressed by institutional allegiance. Nonetheless, it may be argued that the data produced by the European Systems Study also supports the secularization theory since only half those sampled purported that God was significant in their lives.

Belonging

Belonging to a religious institution or collective is perhaps the most obvious and visible way of measuring the extent of religiosity. Leading secularization theorists such as Wilson are influenced by what may appear to be the popular view that a religious individual is one who regularly attends church and displays other discernible outward expressions of religiosity. However, the empirical evidence of a decline of such outward commitment is difficult to substantiate and is tied up with the problem of measuring the extent of the personal and private religiosity of those who practice religion. Even those measurements of personal faith that have been carefully constructed, such as that of Glock and Stark (1969) which include knowledge of one's faith, claims to a religious experience and regularity of ritual observance, are impossible to apply in any meaningful way to the measurement of religious decline in large-scale nation states.

Certainly, a good deal of statistical evidence concerning religious practice does seem to point towards religious decline, despite the problems of validity and reliability. Church membership and attendance figures are often provided as a measurement, as are the rates of the performance of special Christian ceremonies such as baptisms and marriages. In England there were 428 per 1000 baptisms per live births in 1976 compared to 554 in 1960. The basis on which baptism figures are calculated changed after 1976 but the decline has continued up until today. There has similarly been a noticeable drop in the number of marriages conducted in church. In 1929, 56 per cent of marriages in England and Wales were carried out in the Church of England compared with 37 per cent in 1973. Church membership has also diminished. In 1990, only 14.6 per cent of the population were members of a church – a fall of 4 per cent over the previous five years. In 2000, the figure was closer to 7 per cent with the projected figure for 2020 a mere 1 per cent (Brierley, 2000, p. 12).

A prevailing point of view is that such statistics are unreliable. Nineteenth-century church attendance figures, to which today's data is often compared, arguably pose special problems because the methods of data collection do not match present standards of reliability. More recent figures can also be hard to verify. Attendance and membership data may be distorted by the concealed designs of those who produce them. Roman Catholic churches tend to underestimate the size of their congregations in order to reduce the capitation fees they have to pay to central church authorities. Others may overestimate statistics to generate impressive totals, particularly where there may be a chance of a church with a small congregation being closed down.

This approach which doubts the validity of statistics can, however, be countered. While there are undoubtedly difficulties of interpretation, these are probably no greater for religious data than for any other subject area that the historically minded sociologist has to contend with. Areas of apparent unreliability can also be checked. The Catholic Church, for example, also issues annual attendance rates which can be set against total community size.

The complexities of secularization

If we accept that there is a general decline of religion, it is clear that the process is extraordinarily complex. First, there is evidence of considerable variation of its demise in different Western societies. Secondly, even within individual societies the alleged decline appears to be occurring to different degrees in different spheres of social life. Thirdly, there is the debate as to whether decline is a global phenomenon, or merely a distinct characteristic of the West.

Variations in the West

The institutional decline of religion seems to be an unequal one in advanced industrial societies. In terms of church attendance, decline appears more marked in the Protestant countries of Northern Europe than in the Catholic countries of the Mediterranean region. Church attendance is minimal in Scandinavia with countries such as Sweden displaying attendances as low as 5 per cent. In the Benelux countries, declining attendance is somewhat less obvious, while in Northern Ireland, for distinct historical reasons, church membership remains high at over 50 per cent.

Also complicating the picture are developments in the USA – arguably the most advanced industrial nation on earth. The *Yearbook of American Churches* states that from 1940 to 1957, church membership increased from 49 per cent of the population to 61 per cent, while average weekly attendance rose from 37 per cent to 40 per cent. Though there was a minor decline in attendance during the 1960s and early 1970s, according to survey statistics published in 1987 by Roof and McKinney, 46 per cent of the American population attended church at least once a week, while a further 21 per cent were occasional attenders. Their data also showed that only just under 7 per cent of Americans claimed no religious preference. However, more recently, the findings of Hadaway Marler and Chaves (1993) suggest that such statistics are misleading. This is not because of the way they are calculated but the way they are collected. The attendance figures among Roman Catholic and Protestant churches may be only 50 per cent of what they are commonly held to be. This is because of the way people exaggerate their frequency of church-going with statistics noticeably higher than those recorded by church bodies.

Even if we acknowledge that church attendance in the USA is far higher than in most European countries, this could be due to unique cultural variables and may not necessarily be bound up with impressive levels of religiosity. This was possibly also the case with the relatively high nineteenth-century attendances in Victorian Britain which may have been influenced by non-religious factors – a sign of middle-class respectability rather than deep religious conviction. In line with this conjecture, the influential work of Herberg (1956) suggested that in the USA church affiliation was very much historically tied up to membership of Protestant, Catholic or Jewish communities, and was also a badge for adhering to the broad values of American society and nation. For Herberg, this represented a thorough-going secularization and a largely superficial form of religiosity. A similar conclusion is also advanced by Luckmann (1967, p. 36) who argues that in the USA many mainline churches and denominations have been subject to an 'internal secularization'. In short, they have become this-worldly in their orientation, and accept the mainstream values of secular American society, rather than focusing on the fundamentals of the faith with its emphasis on directing belief and practice towards the next life.

Levels of secularity within societies

Even the most vehement supporters of the decline-of-religion thesis have not viewed it as a uniform or inevitable process, while others have identified both forces of secularizion and resistance or even counter-secularizing forces. There have been attempts to grapple with this complexity and in this respect one of the more impressive works is that of Dobbelaere (1981). Dobbelaere uses the term 'laicization' to refer to the complementary social process of differentiation, de-sacrilization and transposition. They may be understood as follows:

- *Differentiation*: the disengagement of society from religion. Religion becomes merely another (rather marginalized) social institution.
- *Transposition*: a reference to religious change or changes in the structure of religious organizations and their beliefs. Frequently, it denotes an increasing adaptation to, or growing conformity with, the contemporary world.
- *De-sacrilization*: the level of religious involvement on the part of the individual – measured in terms of declining religious activity.

There is no reason, Dobbelaere argues, to suggest that secularization may not occur at these different levels at one and the same time. Hence, religion may simultaneously be confined to the private sphere, may lose social significance, or itself become worldly orientated. Secularization in various social contexts must be carefully examined at each of these levels:

Richter (1994) has attempted to do just this by applying Dobbelaere's framework of laicization in his analysis of the liberalization of Sunday trading in Britain and the public debate surrounding it. Developments can be appreciated at the social, private, and specifically religious level.

1. *Social level* (differentiation): social change in most Western societies is primarily intimately connected to technological and commercial advances. Those advocating Sunday trading are capitalist companies motivated by worldly commercial interests. Arguments to support it are advanced in rational terms; for example, that Sunday shopping is a matter of consumer choice and optimizes economic growth.

2. *Religious change* (transposition): Britain, like other Western societies, is now essentially pluralistic with public opinion and even some expressions of Christianity ignoring the Third Commandment of keeping the sabbath holy. There are vociferous opponents to Sunday trading from conservative Christians. However, the prevailing consensus is in favour.

3. *The private sphere* (de-sacrilization): religious involvement is now a voluntary activity and is itself unlikely to be affected by Sunday shopping. People may choose church or Sunday shopping. Nevertheless, as evidence from the USA suggests, both practices are not exclusive of each other. For example, some of the larger churches actually have their own shopping malls.

Universal trends

There have been attempts by some sociologists to show that religious decline is not only associated with Western countries, but that a global trend is observable. For example, Acquaviva (1979) concluded from a survey of data in North America, Europe and Latin America that in the industrialized and industrializing Christian world at least, there was a widespread weakening of ecclesiastical religiosity and belief. A conviction that religion is declining in the nominally Christian countries is not however to suggest a broad global or inevitable decline. Others such as Wilson (1966, 1982), by contrast, see secularization as a long-term process occurring in all human societies, although the precise pattern of decline might be culturally and historically specific to each context.

Alternatively, some, including David Martin, see the nature and extent of the changes in the role of religion varying to such a degree globally that it is misleading to see secularization as anything like a single process. Comparing Europe, North America and the Middle East, Martin (1991) concludes that secularization is largely a European phenomenon and relates this to the struggle between the churches and secular forces in the history of Europe and the early modern era which discredits religion to an extent not experienced elsewhere.

Martin has also drawn attention to the contrasting fate of religion in different countries in the developing world. For example, in Latin America there are plenty of examples where the Roman Catholic monopoly has been broken by new waves of Protestantism in the form of Pentecostalism – a dynamic form of Christianity with an emphasis on primal spirituality and expressive worship. Evidence in Islamic societies suggests that religious change also varies from country to country. As far as Tunisia and Egypt is concerned, the state has become somewhat secular. In other countries, Islamic fundamentalism has taken hold. Given the global evidence, Martin concludes that 'There is no inevitable tilt to history down which every society is sociologically fated to fall' (Martin, 1991, p. 87). Secularization then, is not a universal or inevitable process.

The debate nonetheless continues with those such as Steve Bruce (1992) reinforcing the more traditional interpretation of secularization. While he accepts that the pattern of religious change varies from society to society, Bruce concludes that 'The modern Western world is not a religious place.' Technological advances reduce religious perceptions of the world. This has given individuals a greater sense of control over the natural environment and less need to resort to supernatural explanations or remedies. Moreover, low church attendance rates, the increasing worldliness of the churches, decline in the political significance of religion and the complexities of pluralism all point to religion becoming little more than a leisure pursuit and lifestyle preference, and of no great social significance.

Bruce argues that in parts of the world where religion still appears strong, it does so largely because it constitutes a form of cultural defence. Perhaps, above all, it is used by ethnic or national groups to protect their identity from external threats. This has proved to be the case in Northern Ireland, in Poland where it aided resistance to Communism and in Yugoslavia where it has enhanced the cultural distinctiveness of conflicting ethnic factions. Bruce also argues that in other circumstances religion remains resilient since it provides a means of coping with cultural transition. It is, in short, a way of dealing with social change. For example, for new immigrant groups and their descendants it provides a reassertion of identity often denied them in their new surroundings. However, the overall long-term, global trend is clearly towards secularity.

Religious transformation

There has always been a contrasting set of theories which has stressed the endurance of religion in Western societies. For example, Durkheim anticipated that religion in its traditional form would be of declining social significance. However, he insisted that there was 'something eternal in religion'. One of the ways that he believed this would be expressed was in the emergence of secular forms of religiosity, including 'religious' status being given to the principles of modern society and an allegiance to the overarching values of liberal democracy, social justice and the free market. At the same time, Durkheim surmised, there would develop the 'cult of man' – an almost 'divine' recognition of human progress and what man was capable of (Durkheim, 1915, p. 336) – a prediction which Westley (1978) believes has come true and is encapsulated in the contemporary human potential movement. It is clear that in such conjectures a more functional definition of religion is preferred which necessarily gives an account of contemporary religion a far broader scope.

One other popular theme among commentators developing Durkheimian arguments is that, rather ironically, science has itself become a form of religion. This notion is not entirely new. Comte, in the eighteenth century, fervently argued that science would emerge as the new religion, while a belief in the supernatural declined. More recently, Ellul (1976) has maintained that religious conviction has been replaced by a faith in science and technology. In short, the latter has become a form of religion and can be understood 'as a power both as usable and incomprehensible, terrifying and redeeming, liberating and dominating' but, above all, it provides a new order of meaning. In turn, this kind of speculation, which obviously includes a very broad definition of religion, has been challenged. For Boudin, Dain-Cricq and Hirschhorn (1982), the advance of such a faith in science must primarily be seen as a clear indication of the retreat of supernaturalistic forms of religion in Western societies.

The individualization of religion

Another concern of those commentators who would stress the endurance of religion is the increasingly individualistic nature of religious faith, which is invariably linked to the wider processes of social differentiation in Western societies. Many of those opposed to the decline-of-religion thesis tend to accentuate the alleged prevalence of numerous private and individual practices in contemporary society outside of organized, traditional religious institutions. Bellah (1964), for instance, denies that Western man should be seen as essentially secular, materialistic, dehumanized and fundamentally areligious. Void of institutional and social pressures, individuals are now free to follow a personal quest for meaning rather than embrace a collective act of religious involvement. In this sense religion has undergone a process of individuation whereby people work out their own salvation and follow their own path to 'ultimate meaning'. The key point is that the importance of religion has not declined. Rather, its form of expression has changed and this may be a truer expression of religiosity since it is not enforced by established religious institutions or social pressures. From this point of view, religion will not lose out in the face of rationalism, and the scientific and technical basis of modern society. Indeed, the endurance of religion results from 'the limits of rationalism'. In short, rationalism fails to provide for all human emotional and intellectual needs and, above all, the search for meaning. Religion therefore continues many of its erstwhile functions.

A similar view has been adopted by Luckmann (1967) who denies that secularization is taking place at all. It is simply that traditional forms of religion have been transformed into new expressions. Luckmann has characterized contemporary societies as having no need for an overarching system of values framed in religious terms. Subsequently, religion becomes an aspect of private life, of individual choice from a variety of alternatives which can be constructed into a personally satisfying system of beliefs. This leads Luckmann to conclude, however, that modern societies are witnessing a profound change in the location of religion, away from the 'great transcendences' concerned with other-worldly matters, of issues of life and death, and towards new forms expressing 'little transcendences' of earthly life which involve self-realization, self-expression and personal freedoms (Luckmann, 1990).

For Luckmann, the important point is that a great deal of hidden religiosity exists and is not expressed in institutional form. This 'invisible religion' that he observes, particularly to be found among the middle classes, obviously stretches definitions of religiosity far more than other sociologists would accept.

The kind of approaches advanced by Bellah and Luckmann have been criticized on several grounds. First, that their arguments are based in part on a broad view of religion as defined by a search for ultimate meaning and that is synonymous with new forms of religiosity. However, these seem to be lacking in all the vital ingredients of religion including a supernatural reference, strict codes of morality and focus upon what they can do for believers in this world rather than preparing them for salvation in the next (Bruce 1992). Secondly, there is no proof that this search for meaning is a widespread sentiment. Thirdly, the alleged religiosity underlying such private activities as personal prayer and meditation, does not find expression in any institutionalized or collective form and in itself testifies to the precarious position of religion. This loss of an institutional basis may be a stage in the ultimate demise of even private religiosity. Moreover, Wilson (1976) sees no real endurance of religion in the emergence of new forms. He argues that these tend to be short-lived, faddish and rather superficial forms of religiosity.

Summary

So far we have approached the theme of the decline or otherwise of religion through a discussion of the definition of secularity, the ideological significance of the term and its relevance in the context of Western society. The brief survey above also shows that speculations regarding religious decline in Western societies to a great degree depend upon how religion is defined. As Shiner (1966, p. 211) has stated; 'It is evident that part of the difficulty in measuring the decline of religion is the definition of religion itself.' It is fairly evident that those who adopt a functional approach are inclined to deny the secularization thesis, whereas those who take a substantive approach are likely to support it.

In some regards all of the themes related to secularity so far discussed have been rather oversimplified. Nonetheless, many of these themes will be elaborated in the substantive topics that constitute subsequent chapters. For instance, the link between ethnicity and the endurance of religion will be considered in

Chapter 10. More, however, needs to be said about contrasting theories and developing paradigms which allow us at least to consider the secularization debate in sometimes radically different ways. This is the subject matter of the next chapter.

3 The Resurgence of Religion?

Much of what we have considered in the previous chapter relates to the classical theories of secularization and their defence or refutation by renowned commentators in the area. Some of the historical evidence that supports or, alternatively, tends to disprove the different sides of the debate has also been taken into account.

Recent developments within the realm of religiosity has engendered the growth of new sociological frameworks. These evolving paradigms would seem to run counter to much that we have overviewed so far. This is not to suggest that earlier writings are now superfluous. However, the emerging theories do ask us to look again at the evidence, or at least consider much of it from a different approach. Over the last decade or so sociologists, either wedded to theories of rational-choice or, by contrast, working within post-modernist paradigms, have come to challenge, in their own distinctive ways, many of the long-standing assumptions related to secularization.

Rational-choice and consumer religion

In terms of rational-choice theory and the growth of a 'religious marketplace' in Western societies, the work of Rodney Stark and his associates is perhaps the most influential, especially in North America. Not all of those who have stressed the alleged significance of a religious marketplace have gone as far as Stark's rational-choice model. Nonetheless, the link between choice, religious 'markets' and the alleged resurgence of religion has developed into what has been termed an emerging 'new paradigm' (Warner, 1993).

Much of Stark's theory regarding the nature of religion in

contemporary society can be seen as rooted in his general theory of religion, developed with William Bainbridge (1987). For Stark and Bainbridge, the origins of religion begin at the individual, rather than social level, although society invariably shapes many of the key variables. It is the universal psychological need for religion which ensures that it survives in advanced industrial societies. Profound social changes do not undermine this basic human necessity.

Stark and Bainbridge commence their broader theoretical framework with the conviction that human beings are rational actors who are primarily motivated by 'rewards' and try to avoid what they regard as 'costs'. 'Rewards' are those things which humans desire and are willing to incur some cost to obtain. These may be specific goals such as good health or material enrichment, or they may be more general, including answers to questions of ultimate meaning. However, individuals are often unable to achieve what they desire, especially wealth and status which are always in short supply. They may then turn to 'compensators'. A compensator constitutes the belief that a reward will be obtained in the distant future or in some other context which cannot be verified. It amounts to a kind of 'IOU'. In short, individuals believe that if they act in a particular way they will eventually be rewarded. This is the essence of religious belief – it provides an unverifiable future – especially after death, and compensates for what cannot be obtained in this life. At the same time, this particularly religious desire answers the ultimate questions which have plagued humanity from time immemorial. What is the purpose of life? Why is there suffering? Is there an existence after this life? This constitutes a search for meaning to life which only a belief in supernatural entities with the power to influence human existence can provide answers to.

In their work on contemporary religion, Stark and Bainbridge argue that secularization should not be seen as a smooth and continuous process. Historical evidence shows that religion has its peaks and troughs of decline and revival. Moreover, there is no inevitable spiralling demise of religiosity. While acknowledging that the rise of science stimulated an unprecedented, rapid degree of secularization, Stark and Bainbridge argue that science itself cannot fulfil many of the core needs and desires that religion provides. It is unable to remove all the suffering and injustice of the world or man's mortality, and fails to give significant meaning to human existence. Religion today still provides for these needs by answering the 'ultimate questions' of human existence.

For Stark and his co-writers religion is now increasingly 'marketed' and likewise 'consumed', and there subsequently exists the endless potential for religious growth in terms of satisfying personal spiritual, material and psychological needs. The model therefore suggests that the individual exercises considerable volition, and makes rational choices, in subscribing to a particular religion. At the same time a growth of the 'supply-side' of religion can be discerned whereby traditional religious structures, namely Christianity, adapt to the needs of religious 'consumers'. Should they fail to do so, new religions in the form of cults and sects, may emerge to 'fill a gap in the market' (Stark and Iannaccone, 1993).

It follows that secularization is a self-limiting process and a new revival of religious consciousness is emerging. Principal evidence for this is the appearance of new cult movements which, generally free of the deficiencies of the older religious traditions, are in line with the needs of individuals in Western societies. Stark and Bainbridge (1985) argue that the fact that their survey evidence proves that those who report no religious affiliation or belief are more likely to show interest in some form of unorthodox or fringe supernaturalism such as astrology, yoga and transcendental meditation, and is an indication of the endurance of religion. These new religions and cults are not superficial and insignificant forms of faith. Rather, they have meaning and relevance in supplying the universal functions of religion. At the same time, although the more secularized American denominations are in decline, the least secularized or more conservative are not since they provide more meaningful expressions of Christianity. Stark, Finke and Guest (1996) maintain that, free of ecclesiastical monopolies or state involvement so evident in European history, the religious marketplace of today increases religious activity as 'consumers' are now liberated to express their religious requirements in a variety of ways. Now, de-regulation has stimulated a free market and the activity of the new religious entrepreneurs in an ever-expanding religious marketplace where market forces have produced 'a supermarket of faiths; received, jazzed-up, home spun, restored, imported and exotic' (Stark and Bainbridge, 1985, p. 437).

Stark and Iannaccone (1994) suggest that the USA has largely proved to be historically more religious than many European societies. Unimpeded by an established state 'monopoly' religion, as was the case with the Anglican church in England and the Roman Catholic church in Spain, the USA had permitted a level playing-field for religious groups to compete and hence it has always generated a greater degree of religious activity. With regard to Britain, Stark contends that the decline of a civil religion has likewise encouraged the proliferation of a religious marketplace. Therefore, the underlying assumption in the dominant North American version of the religious market model is that such developments have encouraged growth in the religious sphere by stimulating a latent spiritual quest.

Criticizing the rational-choice model

The work of Stark *et al.* has, in turn, been forcefully criticized. While rational-choice theory has proved to be influential in the USA, its popularity has perhaps already begun to decline. In recent years there has been a spate of books and articles that have offered quite damaging criticism of the rationale upon which it is based and, secondly, the evidence that is produced to support it. Some of the criticism has been orientated to the general theory of religion developed by Stark and Bainbridge. For instance, Wallis (1984) undermines the whole notion of a religious 'compensator'. He points out that it is not at all clear in Stark and Bainbridge's writings why many religious beliefs should constitute compensators of some kind and in what sense belief in morality is a compensator for anything. While beliefs may give comfort in the face of the meaningless that death presents, this is very different from the alleged purpose of a compensator for the fact that human beings do not live forever or the significance that it might otherwise have. Secondly, the human need of religion might begin at the individual and psychological level. However, Stark *et al.* (1996) fail to appreciate the extent to which society shapes and forms our needs and desires and that it is society that also restricts their fulfillment.

There are also a number of telling criticisms aimed at the alleged growth of religion in the contemporary West that Stark and his associates promote. Among the more vociferous opponents is Steve Bruce (1999). Bruce accepts that religious behaviour may be

rational in the most general sense of being reasoned and reason-
able. In short, people have always adopted religion for fairly
common sense reasons. However, rational action in the religious
sphere is not illuminated by the application of rational-choice and
market orientated models. Indeed, such an approach would be
meaningful only in a society that was entirely secular and 'rational'.

In criticizing the supply-side argument, Bruce argues that there
is little indication of the supposed increased religious activity in the
majority of Western societies. This also brings us back to the historical testimony advanced by Stark *et al.* (1982) in suggesting that the
past was not a Golden Age of religion, while religion today is
enjoying something of a revival. Bruce maintains that the weight of
historical evidence simply does not substantiate such a claim.
Moreover, two 'master trends' of modernity continue to work
against a revival of religion: cultural diversity and individual autonomy. The first, cultural diversity, suggests that even if existential
questions are some how biologically given, the answers are not.
Rather, they are culturally produced. The second, individuality,
means that we are at liberty to choose our answers. Thus, contemporary man cannot agree on the formulations of these essentially
'religious' questions or what would count as acceptable answers.
This is indicative of the fact that the common values and assumptions which give legitimacy to a divine authority, and upon which
a truly religious society is built, have gone (Bruce, 1999, p. 185).

Post-modernity and religion

The distinctive tone of USA-style market theories of religion,
particularly those of rational-choice, is one which, almost by definition, focuses on some of the key distinguishing features of
advanced industrial society, above all rational instrumentalism and
individualism. However, a rival approach, particularly in Europe,
has recently developed which locates a consideration of contemporary religion in post-modernity.

As we have seen, theories of secularization have been fashioned
largely with reference to the profound effects of *modernity*. The
notion of post-modernity suggests that the Enlightenment, and the
modernity to which it gave birth, have been overtaken by new

cultural developments that have repercussions for religion as well as other aspects of social life. Theories related to post-modernity, above all, tend to abandon the secularization thesis and seek to find ways of explaining the perseverance of religion and its relevance in contemporary Western societies into the twenty-first century, especially in its new and innovating forms.

Post-modernity defined

Theories of post-modernity generally, and of contemporary religion more specifically, are predicated on the belief that Western societies have moved beyond what was previously understood as modernization and industrialization and most of what that entailed. This is by no means easily accounted for. If modernity is a heavily contested concept, this is even more so with post-modernity. Yet, despite the complexities, post-modernism has become an increasingly fashionable approach in academic circles.

Inglehart (1997, pp. 22–5) suggests that post-modernist theories can be divided into three broad schools of thought:

1. *Post-modernism is the rejection of modernity*; that is, of rationality, authority, technology and science. Within this school, there is a widespread tendency to equate all these components with Westernization. Post-modernism is thus a rejection of Westernization.
2. *Post-modernism is the revalorization of tradition.* Since modernization drastically devalued tradition, its demise opens the way for this revalorization. An integral part of this development is the end of the notion of human progress. This has allowed tradition to regain status and has engendered the need for new legitimating myths. Tradition now has positive value, although this tends to be in a rather selective way.
3. *Post-modernism brings the rise of new values and lifestyles*, with greater tolerance for ethical, cultural and sexual diversity, and individual choice concerning the kind of life one wants to lead. There is an emphasis on human autonomy and diversity instead of the hierarchy and conformity that are central to modernity. Although post-modernization *does* involve a downgrading of modernity and a revalorization of tradition, the emergence of a new culture is even more significant.

It would be too easy to state that all writers on post-modernity fit into one of these schools and that this is so for those who have offered a commentary on contemporary religion. Yet, despite the different accounts offered by sociologists on post-modernity, there is some common ground. Most commentators specializing in the area agree that, with post-modernity, a new worldview is gradually replacing the outlook that has dominated industrializing societies since the Industrial Revolution. It is transforming the core norms, circumventing politics, economic life in production and especially consumption, the family, sexual behaviour and religion. However, there are considerable overlaps between these schools which means that religion in Western societies is sometimes discussed in a contradictory way and the trajectory taken has varied considerably. We may consider some examples.

One leading theorist of post-modernity is the French writer Lyotard (1984), who argues that post-industrial society and post-modern culture began to develop at the end of the 1950s, although the rate of development and the stage reached varied between and within countries. These transformations essentially related to technology, science and a number of social developments, but most importantly they were connected with changes in language and meta-narratives.

According to Lyotard, meta-narratives of human emancipation and social progress are undermined by the advent of post-modernity. Everything becomes relative which, from one point of view, aims a critique at religious absolutes since there is a widespread willingness to abandon the search for overarching or triumphant myths, narratives, or frameworks of knowledge. However, as part of the same condition, people no longer believe that human reason can conquer superstition. The Enlightenment 'project' of perpetual progress and optimism has been abandoned in contemporary societies. There is no longer belief in the inevitability of progress, the power of science to solve all problems, the perfectibility of humanity, or the possibility of organizing societies in a rational way. There is now a profound pessimism about the future and much less willingness to believe that the truth can be found in grand theories or ideologies.

For Lyotard, the collapse of modernist social and cognitive structures means that post-modernity also includes a desire to combine cultural symbols from disparate codes or frameworks of meaning, perhaps from different parts of the globe, even at the cost of dysjunctions and eclecticism. In addition, post-modern culture includes a celebration of spontaneity, fragmentation, superficiality, irony and playfulness. It follows that for post-modernist theorists, like Lyotard, contemporary forms of religion would embrace many of these features. At the same time, diversity of discourse and the abandonment of unitary meaning systems would allow syncretic elements of religion to flourish – a tendency enhanced by the collapse of the boundaries between 'high' and 'popular' forms of religion which mirrors the disintegration of distinctions between different cultural systems in Western societies.

Other writers have put the emphasis on a new vitality permitted to religion that results from the uncertainty of meaning produced by the post-modern condition. The collapse of all-embracing religious worldviews and traditions leaves a vacuum. For Bauman (1992), this constitutes a 'crisis' of meaning for the atomized individual who may increasingly search for the ultimate significance to life that only religion can satisfactorily answer. Thus questions pertinent to religion endure. If they cannot be answered in the context of traditional religion, namely Christianity, then questions are likely to be satisfied mainly in the form of quasi-religious movements or new forms of religion which display a strong moral content. According to Bauman, the crisis of post-modernity is also crucially related to the self and identity. In contemporary society individuals struggle to find a sense of identity, self, belonging and meaning. New expressions of religiosity can restore a concept of self and identity by linking them to a moral system and a cosmic order.

In post-modernity, the variety of cultural life and the pursuit of meaning may bring, rather paradoxically, the perseverance of traditional forms of religiosity and may give rise to expressions of fundamentalism which will attempt to impose ancient systems of morality (Flanagan and Jupp, 1996). This recourse to older forms of religion, often through a mythological revalorization, are precipitated by the collapse of mega-narratives, such as an all-embracing Christian worldview. This has also meant that new forms of religion, such as the New Age or feminist spirituality, have arisen in an increasingly fragmented culture where all cultural styles are deemed as equally 'valid'. Moreover, with the decline of religious monopolies, religious activity is enhanced in a culture where 'anything goes'. Thus, practically anything can be transformed into an expression of religion or grafted on to more traditional forms.

The resurgence of religion?

At the same time, it is frequently argued by post-modernist writers that the resurgence of religion in post-modernity may result from the fresh emphasis on culture and its dominant consumer ethic (Lyons, 1996). Consumerism, with its preoccupation with taste, and the accompanying aestheticization of social life, constitutes a new appreciation of the symbolic realm and a quest for transcendental meaning. The post-modern era is one where belief has become fragmented, a matter of personal preference and a commodity to be packaged for the spiritual marketplace. In this regard much will be linked, according to post-modernist thought, to spiritual considerations related to identity, notions of the self and the body, all of which are cognate with choice of lifestyle and constructions of the self.

Paul Heelas (1998) argues that the disintegration of the certainties of modernity has left a situation in which post-modern religion – particularly, mystical or New Age spirituality and what he terms 'self-religions' – has emerged to fill a spiritual vacuum and satisfy the need for meaning. This emphasis on self in this context is particularly significant. Post-modernity brings a utilitarian selfhood – an expressive form of being, an emphasis on 'experience' and an 'off-the-shelf' image. It establishes the freedom for individuals to create and sustain the self-image of their choice. Hence, traditional forms of religion give way to those congruent with contemporary culture, above all, consumerism.

Related to the growth of the consumer culture is the tendency of religion in the emerging age to be expressed in terms of individualistic religious 'experience' in line with contemporary culture with its attraction to the fleetingly dramatic, titillating, and exotic (Roof and McKinney, 1987). Such an emphasis on experience may be at the expense of the codified beliefs that informed traditional religion. Much may be typified by the New Age movement. York (1996, p. 56), for instance, argues that many expressions of New Age and neo-paganism come to assert that belief *per se* is not essential to religious orientation. In short, it is experience, through various forms of mysticism, which is central.

Consumerism in the post-modern condition is also said to be one which is primarily conducive to the growth of innovating new religions which often constitute a mix 'n' match religiosity, many of which develop belief systems enhanced by reconstructing past religious myths. This tendency towards syncretic forms of religion, according to Fenn (1990), has been enhanced in the post-modern world by the speed of social change and the decline of cultural continuity that has brought an ignorance of history, including religious history. In turn, religious chronicles may be re-invented through new narratives with religious collectives frequently perceiving themselves as restoring, reforming, or reviving the true faith.

Theories of post-modernity are, it seems, varying and often contradictory. Such is the nature of the post-modern world. A common assumption, however, is the belief that the emergence of post-modernity is significant because it may suggest the resurgence of religion. This is a theme developed by David Lyons (1996) who argues that this resurgence is global and expresses itself in different forms: civil religion, fundamentalism and innovating new cultist expressions. Despite their variety and increasing fragmentation, it is clear that in the West, as elsewhere in the world, religion is emerging with a new vigour and in new forms. Partly this assumption is based on the belief that there is a widespread opposition to the rationalizing tendencies of modernity. People seek a mystical and meaningful spirituality beyond the limitations of the secular and rational world. Writers such as Milbank (1990) speculate that in post-modernity the death of religion ironically allows people to discover and develop new traditions. It is a world in which the relativizing tendency of modern thought undermines rationality. What appears to be a very firmly irreligious and secular culture is in fact a very fragile ideological construct that can easily be replaced by a religious counter-culture.

Not all sociologists, however, are convinced of the link between post-modernity and the resurgence of religion. Thus, according to Inglehart (1997), post-modernity should be understood in its relationship to prosperity and security. Post-modernity and the values that it engenders rests, above all, on a new stage of economic development – the shift towards post-modern values is based on a rising sense of mass security. For one thing, there appears to be a near universal connection between increasing prosperity and a decline in conventional religion. This does not mean that there is not a search for meaning in this new cultural order. On the contrary, the key question is how *widespread* this religious searching is and the *depth* of its expression. Both may be doubted. Moreover, the *way* that religion is expressed in post-modernity is through values linked to self-improvement, identity construct and therapeutic techniques. This invariably brings us back to the universal questions: how do we define religiosity and how might it be measured?

Summary

While theories of rational-choice and those of post-modernity have different philosophical underpinnings and even appear contradictory, they do converge with their emphasis of consumerism and the implications for religion. In the post-industrial society, consumerism, rather than production, has become the dominant economic and cultural mode. Religion comes to partake of the consumer ethic. It becomes a matter of choice, fashion and lifestyle. Certainly, from both a rational-choice and post-modernist approach, the implications of consumerism are immeasurable and the potential for fresh speculations as to the nature of religion today now seems endless.

The key premise advanced, particularly by rational-choice theorists, is that increasing choice stimulates the amount of religious activity. This is a forceful claim which, however, calls for a constructive appraisal. From the onset, it has to be acknowledged that the increasing marketability of religion and its consumerist aspects have been recognized for some time. It is, for example, to be found in such earlier works as that of Wilson (1966) and Berger (1973). Nonetheless, there is a far greater emphasis placed on these aspects of religion in current sociological thinking. Consumerism is now believed to be central to contemporary religion, not just a facet of it.

There are, nonetheless, problems with this stress on consumerism. For one thing, religion is not like other social phenomena. There are too many dimensions of religion which, by its very nature, cannot simply be reduced to the marketplace and consumerist forces (Heelas, 1996, p. 102). To conjecture otherwise is to profoundly limit our understanding of religion. Secondly, it may also be that those who equate religious growth with the expansion of a spiritual marketplace have missed an essential point. People may choose the religion they wish. Indeed, this is likely to be the case with the decline of the primary associations such as the extended family and the local community which, in the past, had enforced religious socialization. Yet, most significantly, people may elect, in a profoundly materialistic world, not to choose a religion at all. It may be argued that this is increasingly the case and that choice is subsequently bringing about, in essence, the religiousless society.

If we do accept that religion has become primarily a commodity, along with practically everything else in the contemporary world, the leading question becomes; what *kind* of religion is being generated by contemporary Western society? Much can be surmised from Bocock's definition of consumerism (1993, p. 50). He suggests that it constitutes 'the active ideology that the meaning of life is to be found in buying things and prepackaged experiences'. Given this definition, it may be argued that little of what now passes as religion, particularly in its new forms, has any great substance, any great degree of spirituality. As Bocock goes on to surmise, consumerism, as the ideology of the future, locates meaning not in the things held sacred but in the profane pursuit of self-gratification. Religion is thus reduced to what it does for individuals in this world and not the next. It will tend to advance a philosophy of human potential, health, and wealth – whatever the spiritualized clothing it is dressed up in. It will be void of an abstract system of morality imposed by divine beings which demand human obedience. The tendency will be to play down beliefs that the divine impinges its will upon this world. If this appraisal is correct, then traditional religion in the West, that is Christianity, will continue to decline, and new forms of this-worldly religions will continue to proliferate.

4 Western Religion in the Global Context

'Globalization' has become something of a 'buzz' word in recent years – and not just in sociological circles since the term now enjoys common usage. This is understandable given the profound changes which have taken place internationally and their significance by way of economics, culture and, as far as we are concerned here, the sphere of religion. However, as a key concept in sociological thinking, there remains some debate about how globalization should be defined and what its principal ramifications are.

While acknowledging the complexities, it is increasingly obvious that a discussion of religion in any particular society or indeed any political–geographical region of the world, including the industrialized nations of North America and Europe, will be valid only with reference to the globalized context. There is no attempt in this chapter to offer a comprehensive discussion of all the issues raised by globalization. While core theoretical perspectives will be considered, the focus will be limited to certain aspects of globalization in as much as they are relevant to religion in societies in the West. This still ensures wide-ranging areas of analysis, including the ways that Western forms of religion have impacted globally and how, conversely, non-Western religions have impinged on the West, as well as the link between globalization and the resurgence of religious fundamentalism.

Globalization defined

In recent times, even the most distant reaches of the world have become more easily accessible through economic networks and rapid advances in technology and communication. Thus, it is

44

necessary to look beyond the boundaries of any given society for the full implications of what may be understood as an extension of the changes brought about by modernization. Now there is a global interconnectedness of what McLuhan (1962) has referred to as the 'global village' which implies that the world is now a smaller place and that national, political and cultural boundaries are breaking down. Multinational corporations, international financial markets, transnational communications systems (such as satellite TV) and transnational political organizations (including the United Nations) all function outside the jurisdiction of individual nation states, yet have a significant influence on them.

The dynamics of globalization are far from new; they have been impacting for several centuries and there has been no straightforward line of development. However, many aspects of globalization are increasingly marked by their scale and intensity. Religion is a case in point. Although for centuries the major religions such as Islam and Christianity have had an influence which transcends national boundaries, globalizing forces have brought numerous other consequences. Hence, Roland Robertson (1993) maintains that while religion may, at first glance, appear to be peripheral to globalization, it is, in fact, at the heart of it. Recent history suggests that what Robertson refers to as 'national societies' are related to different cultures and traditions as the economic and power structures of these societies become interdependent at a global level. This is true of religious culture and tradition as much as any other social dimension.

Religion and economic hegemony

Undoubtedly, one of the principal forces behind globalization has been economic development. The assumption of many theorists of globalization is that global interdependence results from the process by which the entire world has gradually become part of a single economic system. In the past, so it is argued, most economic activity was local or regional. Today the increasing scope of economic interdependence has broadened – to whole societies, whole continents, and ultimately the entire world. In turn, these economic transformations have become enthused with political, cultural and, indeed, religious significance.

Most of the early influential work that stressed the economic consequences of globalization tended to be written by neo-Marxists working within the 'hegemony' paradigm that was developed by Immanuel Wallerstein (1980). This theory states that the nations of the world are subject to the power and influence of the Western industrialized nations; economically, culturally and politically. Thus, the disproportionate global impact of Western forms of religion can best be appreciated as little more than an appendage of economic denomination and is connected to cultural hegemony – the ideas, values and ethos that sustain and justify capitalism. This is certainly a factor that is deemed to have implications for the spread of one form or another of Western Christianity – particularly those with a strong evangelical thrust.

The global spread of Western religion is by no means novel. Christian missionaries have taken their gospel message across the world for centuries and often followed military conquest, colonialism or the trade routes opened up by merchants. The growth of the USA as the world's dominant economic power is of particular significance. Whilst Europe once exported her religions to North America, the pattern has now been reversed with the USA being the home of various forms of evangelical Christianity – a development that came with the increasing global activity of the USA. This is most clearly demonstrated by Wilson (1970), who has traced the largely one-way exportation of numerous North American Christian orientated sectarian movements over the last 150 years. Hence, the Holiness Movement, the Church of the Latter-Day Saints, Christian Science, Seventh-Day Adventism, Jehovah's Witnesses and Christadelphianism, to name but a few expressions, have all made their way across the Atlantic from 'God's backyard' in the USA, to Europe and beyond.

By the end of the twentieth century, new forms of Protestant evangelicalism had come to the fore and subsequently have substantially increased the global importance of USA-style religion. It is apparent that the peoples of the world, in a more rigorous and systematic way than ever before, are now exposed to the beliefs and ways of life espoused by North American Christian fundamentalism. This is largely because the contemporary evangelizing ministries have utilized state-of-the-art technology and communication rapidly to disseminate their fundamentalist dogma and enhance their penetration of very different global cultural localities. Satellite television and multi-million-dollar sponsored ministries have therefore engendered what has been called the 'mass marketing of God' (Smark, 1978). For example, in 1990 the USA evangelist, Pat Robertson, launched his 'Project Light', a television revival directed at all of Central America. Broadcasting on Guatemalan television with a programme put together at the Christian Broadcasting Network in Virginia, the campaign reached over 60 per cent of the Guatemalan audience, a record for any kind of programming. In the next six months, the revival engaged thousands of evangelical and Pentecostal churches throughout Central America. Sometimes such ministries are inspired by 'Last Days' scenarios – the belief that mass conversions will hasten the return of Christ. Hence, the American evangelist and healer, Morris Cerullo, has beamed his distinctive gospel message to the people of Israel in the belief that conversions will fulfil Biblical prophecies before the end of the world.

Exporting the American gospel

A recent detailed account of the global spread of USA evangelism is *Exporting the American Gospel* (Brouwer, Gifford and Rose, 1996). Here, it is argued that Western, at least nominally Christian, countries have come to control the world's productive resources, manufacturing, banking and commercial institutions. For Brouwer, Gifford and Rose, the global diffusion of new forms of Christian fundamentalism largely results from distinct economic developments. Such transformations amount to what they call 'fundamentalist Americanism' – the belief peculiar to USA Christianity that simultaneously sanctifies American nationalism and the American 'gospel' of success, wealth and prosperity.

At the same time, this transnational religious culture is meeting a common need in the large urban areas of different parts of the developing world, in the slums that surround them, and the outlying agricultural districts as well. There is then, considerable international receptivity to a fundamentalist Christian message particularly when simultaneously promising worldly success and heaven in the next world – a message disseminated by a sophisticated and powerful network for spreading the Word. As Brouwer *et al.* cogently put it

While the leaders of the new Christian faith come from various
nations, the message is predominantly American. When believers enter a church in Africa, Asia or Latin America, they participate in a form of worship that can be found in Memphis, or
Portland, or New York City. Perhaps it will be Pentecostal, or
Southern Baptist, or a ubiquitous charismatic product marketed
by Bible schools in places such as Tulsa and Pasadena. These
Protestants disseminate beliefs that can comfort middle-class
businessmen at a prayer breakfast in Rio de Janeiro and inspire
the poorest of the world's would-be consumers. (Brouwer *et
al.*, 1996)

The hegemonic paradigm is particularly impressive when
deconstructing the teachings and practices of North American
evangelical ministries. This is perhaps most convincingly exemplified by the so-called 'Faith' movement and its prosperity gospel.
The global significance of these ministries cannot be doubted.
Across the world hundreds of thousands of people subscribe to
those centred in the USA that are identified by their vast scale of
organizational structure and financial resources. Hence, the characteristic tenets of the Faith ministries have been successfully
exported to very different global cultural environments ranging
from the advanced economies of Western Europe, to the emerging economies of Latin America, the Pacific Rim and Third
World Africa (Gifford, 1990).

There is much in the teachings and practices of the Pentecostal-
style Faith ministries which is obviously congruent with USA-style
religion. Marvin Harris (1990) argues that as far as the principal
beliefs are concerned, there is an indication of the increasing secularization of religion which is directed towards this world and
material gain, and that they are best understood as an attempt to
fulfil America's dream of worldly progress by magical and supernatural means. To the fore is the doctrine of the assurance of
'divine' physical health and prosperity through faith; in short, that
health and wealth is the automatic divine right of all Bible-
believing Christians.

It may be argued that largely through its prosperity gospel, the
Faith movement should be interpreted as representing the justification of the Western economic free market. Indeed, the principal doctrines espoused can be understood as the cultural and

ideological underpinning of both components of capitalism: the ethic of consumerism and the entrepreneurial spirit. On the 'entrepreneurial' side, the Faith gospel may be accounted for in terms of the expansion of Bourdieu's 'cultural capital' (Bourdieu, 1977). Briefly, the dominant cultural value of the pursuit of endless profit and material gain that permeates all aspects of life – including the religious. This is exemplified in some of the teachings of the leading exponents of the Faith gospel which argue that neither Christ nor his disciples were poor. Rather, they were hard-working artisans who, through faith in God, achieved the proper fruits of their labour and therefore provided the model lifestyle for all true believers. At the same time, the consumer element, apparently congruent with advanced Western economies, is present in that the Faith teachings insist that the blessing is showered upon the *individual* believer, rather than the corporate Church. This brings prosperity doctrines firmly in line with a culture which renders the individual as the subject of consumerism.

The Faith ministries have made some inroads into Western Europe. Their expansion, especially since the 1980s, can be attributed to economic changes and accompanying cultural transformations. In his work on the USA ministries in Sweden, Simon Coleman (1991) speculates that they can primarily be understood as a carrier of the North American capitalist ideology. In the case of Sweden, throughout the 1980s, the success of the Faith ministries was largely due to the spread of the business ethic. According to Coleman, this has occurred at a time when the social democratic political consensus was collapsing and free enterprise increasingly encouraged by the state, alongside the growing cultural emphasis upon consumerism and individualism.

Where the Faith teachings have appeared to carry cultural capital more effectively is in many of those nations which constitute the world's emerging economies. For example, over the last decade the Faith ministries have enjoyed a prolific growth in the wake of the collapse of Soviet domination where the free market has increasingly replaced the state economic monopolies. Poland, the Czech and Slovak Republics and Hungary, in particular, have been receptive to the new gospel. For the relatively deprived peoples of Central and Eastern Europe, the attraction might seem obvious. Religious and free market ideals are merged into one package of spiritual and economic liberty. Hence, 'cultural capital' is discernible in the theology and activities of numerous Faith ministries active in the region (Hunt, 2000).

McDonaldization and glocalization

McDonaldization has become an important term that is intrinsically linked to the economic aspects of globalization. First coined by George Ritzer (1996), it denotes the global patterns of consumption and consumerism and is a process of rationalization exemplified by the American fast food company McDonald's. On a global scale, McDonald's is a major stakeholder in the burger and French fries market, and what is produced is a fairly standard package. The McDonald's burger purchased in London is very likely to be the same bought in New York, Tokyo, or Moscow. It follows that the market dominance of McDonald's, as the 'supply side' of the burger enterprise, dispels the myth that a free global economy brings endless variation and upholds consumer choice through competition. It is the same all over the world – the same image and the same product.

In *The McDonaldization of Society*, Ritzer describes how the principles which lie behind McDonald's are spreading throughout the world and into every area of life:

> McDonaldization affects not only the restaurant business, but also education, work, health care, travel, leisure, dieting, politics, the family, and virtually every other aspect of society. McDonaldization has shown every sign of being an inexorable process by sweeping through seemingly impervious institutions and parts of the world. (Ritzer, 1996, p. 1)

The application of ideas of McDonaldization to aspects of religion, both nationally and internationally, are attractive. This is not least of all in the exportation of evangelical forms of Christianity from the West. We may again cite the example of the Faith ministries from the USA in that they not only preach a fairly standard range of core doctrines which are promulgated throughout the world, but the organizational structure of the various ministries also tends to be very alike in form, direction and genre. They are typically based on well-trained pastors, congregations, bible schools which annually turn out hundreds of graduate ministers who extol the central tenets of the Faith gospel across the globe, and world-wide systems of communication with believers through mass-produced publications and audio and visual tapes.

Clearly, theories which link globalized religion primarily to economic causes and subsequent cultural developments have provided fruitful insights into the exportation of Western religion – particularly of distinct types of evangelical Christianity. However, this emphasis does not always sufficiently account for or describe the richness and complexity of global changes. Thus, in recent years, alternative approaches have been advanced, many of which have adopted post-modernist perspectives or themes closely akin to them. As with the hegemonic model, there is a stress placed on cultural, economic and political concerns in that the shift of local, and even personal contexts of social experience, are increasingly influenced by events and developments in diverse parts of the globe. These forces nonetheless range across a fairly level playing-field so that even the most remote local culture and lifestyle habits become universally consequential. It is not, by any means, all one-way traffic from the West across the globe. What happens in even the most remote part of the world has repercussions for Western societies as well.

As a result of these multi-dimensional aspects of globalization, religion becomes a 'cultural site' since any society, including those in the West, can be influenced by the ebbs and flows of various expressions of religiosity across the world which subsequently generate infinite variations and localized expressions of faith (Albrow, 1995, p. 20). This analysis is significant because it argues that although there might be cultural migration of religions from the West, this exportation is not only in one direction – far from it. Moreover, even if a system of belief originates within the Western context, it cannot be assumed that it will be given the same meaning as originally attributed to it, since people in different places look at the world through their own cultural 'lenses'. In short, there is a process of glocalization; that is, the ways in which global phenomena are responded to varies considerably in different local cultures (Featherstone, 1990).

From this perspective it would be wrong to see North American evangelical ministries simply imposing their theological constructs upon an unsuspecting world. The evidence does not always square up to the cultural dominance model. Infinite complexities, contradictions and paradoxes remain. Hence, the acceptance of health and prosperity teachings are only partly inspired by the exported USA Faith movement. To some extent, at least, they also appear to have arisen to give articulation to internal cultural aspirations. One illustration relates to the impact of the Faith gospel around the Pacific Rim. Korea is a good example. Here, the growing Faith churches constitute one expression of the numerous indigenous new religious movements which have developed in this part of the world. Many appear to give articulation to the emerging capitalist culture – particularly in the growing urban areas and crowded inner-cities of Korea. Much is exemplified by the church established by Paul Yonngi Cho which boasts a membership of nearly 1 million people. A form of prosperity gospel is central to the teachings of the church. However, the key doctrines show some important departures from the American variant and are obviously open to syncretic localized transformations. While the teachings take their tone from the USA ministries, they are taught alongside a shamanism and animism which has more in common with traditional indigenous Korean forms of religion than North American fundamentalism.

It appears that the hegemony model, then, has its limitations, not least of all that it may be too general and unsophisticated. Western economic and political dominance may be a reality, and religious ideas can and do reflect this hegemony. However, it is obvious that there has to be some local receptivity and this could be generated by what might be termed localized religious markets. In short, in local environments there may be significant changes in teachings that give expressions to indigenous needs. This is succinctly put in a discussion of the general cultural influence of the West across the world by Anthony Smith in his essay 'Towards a Global Culture?' He states:

> It is one thing . . . to package imagery and diffuse it . . . it is quite another to ensure the power to move and inspire. . . . Meanings of even the most universal of imagery for a particular population derive as much from the historical experiences and social status of [a] group as from the intentions of purveyors. (Smith, 1990, 178f.)

Easternization

Globalization has also ensured that religions originating outside the West have now come to exert a considerable impact. As explored more fully in Chapter 9, numerous new religious movements (NRMs) have arrived on Western shores and have brought profound changes. Again, by no means a new development, their spread has, however, increased over the last forty years or so. While the influence for NRMs comes from various sources, many are inspired by ancient mystical religions from the East; there has developed, to produce another 'ization' from the bag, the advance of Easternization.

Colin Campbell (1999) has gone so far as to argue that such a process of Easternization has meant that the traditional Western cultural paradigm no longer dominates in the West and is increasingly being replaced by an 'Eastern' one. Hence, Easternization has come in the wake of the decline of Christian culture and challenges rationalism as a dominant mode of thought.

This trend does not however, simply result from the introduction and spread of Eastern imports. There are many indications to suggest that this fundamental change has been assisted by internal indigenous developments. To generalize, these changes in Western consciousness include beliefs in the unity of man and nature, holistic views of mind, body and the spirit, the limits of science and rationality and the alleged virtues of meditation and other psychotherapeutic techniques. Campbell then argues that in many respects the Eastern paradigm is more compatible with some aspects of current Western societies with their increasing interest in environmentalism, popular beliefs related to reincarnation and human potential, as well the growth of 'life-affirming' movements. Eastern mysticism, principally expressed in Hindu and Buddhist thought, thus dovetails not only with contemporary alternative thinking, but some of the developing core values and beliefs of the West.

Something perhaps less observable has also been occurring in terms of globalization. Religion is increasingly characterized by complex diffusion and international networks with multilateral flows from diverse parts of the world. This has led to the growing tendency towards syncretic developments. Hence, elements of faiths often originating outside one cultural environment may influence or be grafted on to localized and traditional religions.

Again, there is nothing particularly new here. Religious fragmentation and syncretic forms typified a great deal of religion in the West
in the nineteenth century. Today, however, there is an even greater
interchange of cultural genres which generate complex currents of a
mix 'n' match religiosity particularly in the wake of collapsing 'grand
narratives' embedded in traditional religious systems (Featherstone,
1990, p. 10). In short, the undermining of traditional religions opens
the way to new, syncretic forms of religiosity.

Such a development is universal, although there is something
particularly significant for the West if we accept the view that religious belief and practice is best understood within an evolving
religious marketplace. The New Age movement is perhaps the
most obvious example. Among its distinguishing features are
teachings which, while clearly originating in Western forms of
occultism, are merged with Eastern mysticism, paganism and
animism (Heelas 1996). At the same time, many expressions of
Christianity are experiencing syncretic trends. Indeed, Hiebert
(1982) argues that the Western world has witnessed the return of
forms of animism which have also come to influence the contemporary Church to the extent of subverting traditional Christianity.
Cox makes a similar point in his discussion of the Neo-
Pentecostalism movement. In common with other NRM,
contemporary Pentecostalism increasingly embraces a worldview
where events are believed to be guided arbitrarily by spirits, ancestors, ghosts, magic and witchcraft and forms of shamanism that
borrow heavily from pagan and non-Christian religions (Cox,
1994, pp. 213, 281).

The ultimate development, even irony, of globalization, is that
forms of religion exported to another country are returned from
where they originated in what might be termed a process of
'reversed globalization'. Let us take the North American Faith
movement once more as an example. In some parts of Africa, the
Faith ministries have achieved some advance, particularly in countries where the contours of Christianity had already been cleaved out
by nineteenth-century missionary endeavours. In Kenya and
Nigeria, for example, the Faith message is not only an attraction to
the urban and rural poor but the ideology of the socially mobile
middle classes. Influenced by the North American gospel,
indigenous African churches have developed some of the key
doctrines for the needs of their own people.

In turn, these churches have embarked on missionary endeavours across the world, including countries of the West. In Nigeria, such churches as the Redeemed Christian Church of God (now with a global membership of some 2 million) have established congregations in the USA, Western Europe, the Far East and Australia. While seeking to win converts of all ethnic backgrounds, their main appeal, however, is to Nigerian ethnic enclaves that have settled in these countries (Hunt, 2001).

The global consequences of fundamentalism

The global order prior to 1980 largely rested on the balance of power between the USA and the Soviet empire. With the collapse of Communism, the new global structure is based mainly on the dominance of market capitalism allied to modern liberal ideas and values including, to one degree or another, a commitment to liberal democratic institutions and processes of government. What religion's relationship with this change amounts to is of major interest to the politicians and mass media of the West. In the post-Cold War world, some have come to see religion as the major threat to the new order, as a global source of division and disruption. It is the perceived threat of global religious fundamentalism which has drawn the greatest attention (Esposito and Watson, 2000).

The link between globalization and fundamentalism is also a growing theme amongst sociologists of religion. Parallel to some of the trends discussed above, and to a great degree as a result of them, fundamentalism, steeped in different traditions, appears to be proliferating. One form is that of Christian fundamentalism, particularly in the USA. This will be considered in more detail in Chapter 8. All that needs to be recognized here is that some of the causes of its growth are congruent with the rise of religious fundamentalism internationally – particularly among many of the world religions including Islam, Judaism, Hinduism and Sikhism which have had a significant bearing on world political events. The key variable appears to be the continuing tensions between tradition and modernity, although the exploration of themes more clearly associated with post-modernity is increasingly influential.

To many Westerners, the forces of Islamic revival seem the

most alarming and dangerous expression of fundamentalism because they are seen to reject and resist many of the premises of Westernization and so-called 'progress' and, secondly, because Islam is a growing religion (indeed, the fastest growing) of well over 1 billion believers. There are, of course, dangers with generalizing about Islam as some kind of 'peril' to the West, since much of the Islamic world remains largely untouched or unmoved by global developments. However, there are many currents within Islam, and some with genuinely fundamentalist traits, such as the Shi'ites in Iran, who attract a great deal of attention because of their willingness to defy the West in socio-political conflicts in the Middle East.

For some time a number of schools of sociology attributed the growth of reactionary and fundamentalist forms of religion globally to the repercussions of internal social development. Often subsumed under so-called 'cultural strain' theory outlined by Smelzer (1962), the belief was that inevitable internal progress and development precipitated the often violent response of traditional culture and, sometimes, declining social groups who had long held economic and political power. Hence, science and rationalism, secularization, pluralism, differentiation, the decline of community and the movement towards industrialized society brought a reaction to modernity that was often articulated through fundamentalist religious channels. Traditional Islam, for example, therefore becomes enmeshed in the process of modernization and globalization.

In the contemporary global context, internal societal developments can have further repercussions. Thus, some commentators have come to interpret world events as a dualistic separation of the processes of modernization and religious change into different camps – suggesting that economic globalization (the modern phenomenon) is opposed by cultural tribalism (a reversion to more primitive modes of association). This image of conflict has been cogently described as 'McWorld versus Jihad' (Barber, 1995). In short, there is now a global conflict between radically different cultures epitomized by world modernizing tendencies on the one hand, and a resistance to it on the other, identified by a rapidly expanding reactionary expression of religion epitomized by Islamic fundamentalism which has impacted as far afield as Iran, the Sudan and Afghanistan.

Kepel (1994) sees this as a fairly new development. In the

second half of the twentieth century religion was restricted to the private or family sphere. It was also a time when religion globally was trying to adapt to the modern world. From the 1970s onwards, the process went into reverse with a return to traditional forms of religiosity, away from modernism which had very often failed people in developing parts of the globe. Referring to the Moslem world, Kepel suggests that the aim was no longer to modernize Islam but to Islamize modernity. For reactionary versions of Islam, the aim is to participate in a dynamic process of spreading the faith to the whole of humanity while defending the Moslem identity that is under threat during temporary phases of weakness. The irony is that such fundamentalist movements may, in part, be attributed to Western world dominance. The Iranian Revolution of 1979 might therefore be interpreted as a response to Western dominance and as an effort to give a marginalized Third World region greater access, through a revitalization of Islamic cultural differences, to perceived global material and cultural resources monopolized by the West dependency (Gerami, 1989).

Finally, a more thorough-going post-modernist, but overlapping perspective, is offered by commentators such as Ernest Gellner (1993). Gellner argues that in the flux and uncertainty of the post-modern world there are three approaches undertaken by cultures and traditions. Each is rigorously opposed to the others. First, the acceptance of the post-modern condition and embracing of relativism, scepticism and pluralism. The next two involve distinct but opposing forms of 'fundamentalism'. Rationalist fundamentalism, with its stance in the Enlightenment, involves the firm conviction of the project of modernity and the unswerving faith in rationalism and science. Finally, there is religious fundamentalism which opposes the secularity of rational fundamentalism and the relativism of post-modernity. Thus, fundamentalist movements arise (here Gellner offers the example of the Islamic world) and are 'revivalistic' in the sense that they are a reaction primarily to the relativizing impulses which arise with the awareness of other 'truths' and the worldviews of cultural systems beyond the boundaries of their traditional societies.

The global impact of fundamentalist non-Christian religions has also influenced ethnic minorities in the West. There are, therefore, direct implications for Western societies. The Black Muslim movement in the USA was once virulently intolerant of other non-black races and religions. The beliefs and Koranic references were interpreted to form a protest against the values and attitudes of the dominant white US culture, where a dualist ideology of some Black Muslims identified the 'evil' nature of Western materialistic societies and the white oppressors (Lincoln, 1989). It was also relatively unconnected with Islam as a world religion. The spread of global fundamentalism began to change all that. Malcolm X was one of the first Black Muslim leaders to embrace a larger vision of Islam. In turn, some strands of the movement have followed his lead to greater tolerance and intense study of world Islam, becoming part of the Sunni branch of the international faith and linking with Moslems in other countries. The implications of globalization then, are seemingly endless.

Summary

In the first chapters of this book we focused squarely on the significance of religion in Western societies. This chapter has attempted to link various aspects of religion to a global context. Indeed, it is apparent that any discussion of religiosity cannot now be confined to the boundaries of nation states nor parts of the world such as 'the West' that historically have been identified by unique historical, economic and cultural variables. Perhaps above all, on the global scale, religious faith is best understood in terms of the way it integrates communities and individuals into global or localized markets. At the same time, the mix 'n' match nature of contemporary religion has been enhanced by some of the dynamics of globalization. It is this broader global reference point that will also inform a number of the themes explored in the rest of this volume.

5 Religion – Change and Stability in Western Societies

One of the central questions that has continued to concern sociology has been whether, given the historical evidence, religion tends towards enhancing social stability or, alternatively, is distinguished more by its disruptive and divisive effects. An associated debate focuses on the relationship of religion to social transformation. Here, the key consideration is whether religion is a conservative force or, alternatively, capable of instigating radical social change. These are however, rather more complex issues than are first apparent, and to appreciate the significance of religion in this respect more recent sociologists have developed and modified some of the classical sociological theorizing in order to render it relevant to contemporary society. Some of the principal themes embraced by these commentators are the subject of this chapter.

Consensus approaches revisited

The consensus approach to sociology prevailed in the early twentieth century, particularly in the USA and continued, albeit in considerably mutated form, as a significant paradigm for understanding religion in Western societies. This ranged from the structural functionalist school which dominated the sociology of religion, particularly the writings of Talcott Parsons (1951) and his work on secularization, to a substantial amount of literature on the so-called 'civil religions' of Western societies. Alternatively, this approach has been used to explain the rise of new religious movements from the late 1960s.

Durkheim's legacy – social integration

Durkheim's work (1915) constituted the earliest articulation of what has come to be termed the consensus perspective. Much of his sociology was concerned with understanding the nature of social integration and regulation and their wider repercussions. Durkheim maintained that social stability and individual well-being were underpinned by a sense of belonging and obligation to others, together with adherence to a strong moral value system. Any weakening of these social forces would have adverse consequences at both the individual and societal level. These factors were important for Durkheim in his prediction of the decline of religion in the modern world and the problems that would result from the failure of social cohesion and the concomitant reduction of the psychological well-being of its members.

Durkheim's ideas have been compelling for many sociologists. In their discussion of religion in industrialized society different themes have been developed. One is the link between religion and social conformity. For example, research on the power of religion to prevent the commissioning of crime and suicides in the USA, indicates that membership of a religious organization does promote conformity to the wishes of others and brings a measure of stability in an individual's life. It is not the religious doctrines themselves which are of significance but the importance of social bonds encouraged by integration into the religious collective as a kind of small social system (Stark, Kent and Doyle, 1982).

The ingenuity in the thinking of the consensus approach in attempting to show the integrative function of religion is evident in some interpretations of sectarianism. While, as we shall see in Chapter 8, the subject of sects is usually addressed in terms of exclusion and social deviance; some theorists speculate that sects can help integrate people into society and are themselves a source of social stability. The 'moral regeneration theory' suggests that religious sects generate the process of reaffiliation with the social order and bring conforming behaviour under the influence of new social bonds. In this regard, Akers (1977) argues that persons adrift in society, lacking ties to the moral order, are strongly re-attached to the social mainstream by virtue of their recruitment into the intensely integrated moral community constituted by the sect. It can even be argued that the very deprivations that cause people to join sects are reduced by sect membership, thus enabling people to improve their social and personal circumstances. This appears to be the case with Johnson's account of Pentecostalism in the USA (1961). While Pentecostals could be understood as a 'deviant' sectarian minority, there was evidence of strong conformity to mainstream values, particularly those which were believed to have made America great and compatible with the tenets of Christianity, including hard work and personal achievement.

Social regulation

According to Durkheim, religion is in its very essence social, since it reinforces the collective conscience. This is expressed through a series of symbolic rituals which are at the very heart of religious faith, because it is through the symbols of religion that society itself is worshipped, and the social order is expressed as having a sacred, almost god-like quality. From this point of view religious beliefs in gods, spirits and the supernatural can primarily be interpreted as collective representations of a moral order. The link between social cohesion and religion seems, however, to be more clear-cut in simple, homogeneous, pre-industrial cultures. Complex indus-trialized societies, if not completely secular, certainly cannot be associated with one single religious system. Nonetheless, recent sociologists, working within the broad consensus framework, continue to maintain that social stability rests on a shared morality and have emphasized religion's ability to survive, even if not in traditional, supernaturalist forms.

    While Durkheim believed that religion, largely expressed through ritual, would decline in modern industrialized societies, some have argued that its continuance can be identified along with its important function of enforcing a value consensus and the symbolic 'worshipping' of society. Hence, modern society is believed to provide its own collective representations by which a nation symbolizes an ideal of itself to its members – a notion not far removed from Durkheim's concept of totemism. Many civil ceremonies and festivals can be viewed as displaying a marked reli-gious quality. War remembrance days for example, and even major sporting events, although not implicitly 'religious' in the same way as a church service, may be interpreted as 'sacred' and 'set apart' from the profane, according to Durkheim's criteria. In the writings of those such as Bellah (1967) in his discussion of the USA, these ceremonies provide a set of symbols, which integrate the great diversity of American society. There may even be civic 'shrines' (such as the Lincoln Memorial), saints (such as the writers of the American constitution) and accompanying myths of American history. Thus, it is not the historic significance of civic ceremonies which is important, but their ability to symbolize the transcendence of the collective unity, that inspires awe and reverence.

While some of the studies on civil ceremonies may now seem dated, the widespread popular grief expressed at the funeral of Princess Diana in 1997, and the ritual involved, indicated that the function of civic ceremonies of this type has not been entirely extinguished. Chris Harris (1999) has, for example, drawn parallels with the 'effervescent assembly' which Durkheim, in *The Elementary Forms of the Religious Life*, claimed functions both as a reaffirmation of existing religious beliefs and the site of the emergence of new beliefs and practices. As far as the funeral ceremony of Diana was concerned, there was inherent, simultaneously, a public acceptance of the British monarchy as a national symbol but also a questioning as to whether it was in need of fundamental change in order to bring it into line with the values of a modern twenty-first century society.

Civil religion

Particularly in the USA, sociological thinking, often inspired by Durkheim's work, has attempted to explain the nature of social integration in contemporary Western society in terms of the notion of 'civil religion'. What has come to be known as 'the civil religion thesis' suggests that a form of religiosity remains with the function of expressing cohesion in even highly differentiated, advanced industrial societies. Hence, a civil religion displays the beliefs and rituals of a nation which are understood in some kind of transcendental way. From this viewpoint, civil religion is 'transcendental' because it is believed to be more significant than particular beliefs and cultures whether they be those of a social class, ethnic community or religious denomination.

Much ink has been spilt on civil religion in the USA and this is largely due to the need to explain how the country is able to weld together numerous diverse ethnic and religious groups. However, the subject has been approached in rather differing ways. According to Bellah (1967), American civil religion is related to the Judaic–Christian religion, but is given a uniquely American-style dimension. When deconstructed, therefore, American civil religion is saturated with Biblical symbolism. There is, for example, a cultural reference to the chosen people, the promised land, and a new Jerusalem. Bellah nevertheless insists that the civil religion is genuinely American and parallels the Biblical religions, rather than replacing them. This means that civil religion and Christianity are clearly divided in function so that the former is appropriate to concerns in the official public sphere, while Christianity and other religions are granted full liberty in the realm of personal belief and practice. Bellah is thus able to conclude that the existence of both a public religion and the sense of freedom of choice in personal religion brings a large degree of social cohesion and transcends the state and secular institutions.

In his principal essay, 'Civil Religion in America', Bellah also found the principal themes of a transcendental civil religion in the major public addresses, especially Presidential inaugural addresses, in the USA. Here civil religion is displayed in terms of 'an understanding of the American experience in the light of ultimate and universal reality' – the expression of America's fundamental beliefs and values. There has followed a series of subsequent works since Bellah's that focus upon the rhetoric of presidential inaugural speeches. For instance, Adams (1987) discussed the public pronouncements of Ronald Reagan in the 1980s and his emphasis on the individual's obligations to build a better society, which amounted to a kind of 'revival' of his distinct interpretation of American culture, alongside references to the 'destiny' of the American nation and the founding fathers of the US constitution as semi-divine figures.

In his account of civil religion, Bellah does not suggest that it is a conservative force or that it simply reinforces the status quo, including providing the state with legitimation. The civil religion also creates a cultural resource by which citizens can offer a critique of prevailing social and political arrangements – drawing down God's judgement on the nation. Here, Bellah distinguishes between the priestly and prophetic role of civil religion. The former provides a function in the form of a celebration of national achievements, while the latter offers a role in calling the nation to account for breaking its covenant with God. An example of the prophetic role would be Martin Luther King who, in advocating the extension of basic civil rights to Blacks, referred to aspects of the civil religion in America to identify the contrast between the nation's self-image and its actual achievements. This function of civil religion is also arguably observable in nations such as France and the Republic of Ireland where a revolutionary myth, one which has a kind of divine sanctity, constitutes a built-in point of reference for internal criticism (Stauffer, 1974).

In his later works Bellah displays an awareness that American civil religion might be undergoing a degeneration. In *The Broken Covenant* he stated that 'Today the American civil religion is an empty or broken shell' (1975, p. 145). Self-centred individualism and materialism was the greatest danger since it carried with it the prospect of social disintegration. Also, wracked by social divisions and increasing pluralism, the USA seemed to be in need of new integrated forces of religion. Bellah saw this in the emergence of the new religions, many of which gave birth to innovatory American myths as a response to the nation's general moral malaise. For Anthony and Robbins (1990), one such religion was the Unification Church (the 'Moonies') which appeared to be readily accepted in America because it placed a great deal of value on family life, anti-abortion, the entrepreneurial spirit and a belief system which holds that there is a fundamental struggle between communism and the 'God-fearing world' of which the USA is the centre.

The decline of civil religion and moral decay?

In exploring links between the decline of civil religion and moral decay Anthony and Robbins list some of the negative implications for Western society, particularly the USA, that include: a crisis of moral meaning and boundaries leading to uncertainties of how to behave; for example, sexual permissiveness, lack of faith in traditional social and political institutions, the internal dysfunctioning of such institutions – perhaps displayed in corruption in government, increase in the divorce rate and family disintegration, rising crime, and lowering voting turnout.

A more optimistic view of the continuance of religion as a national integrative force has however been advanced. Mathisen (1989) believes that in the USA civil religion declined in the 1970s, but re-emerged in the next decade in a different form – one which was in some respects more liberal in outlook regarding social issues, but one that also reinforced the prevailing entrepreneurial spirit. He argues that this was a natural state of affairs since the evidence in the USA suggested that the significance of the civil religion had advanced and declined in a series of cycles throughout the nation's history. Hence, civil religion is resilient, episodic and fluctuates in intensity. It further appeared that social integration could be generated through what can be referred to as spontaneous or popular religion, as distinct from the civil, formal, or official form. In this regard, major sporting events could be subsumed under 'quasi-religions' which represent distinct and emergent forms of religious life (Vance, 1984).

Religion and conflict

While the civil religion thesis seems to hold up in the USA, it is more difficult to substantiate in other Western societies. This appears to be the case in Belgium where linguistic, cultural, regional and indeed religious differences can be understood as divisive forces which prevent the establishment of a civil religion. Canada is another such example. Although it is an advanced industrial nation, Canada has no one civil religion that expresses its cultural and political values. For Kim (1993), it is a vast country with a population concentrated into its few major cities often separated by thousands of miles, diverse ethnic groups arriving at different historical times, together with an extremely developed basis of political power in the provinces, all of which have conspired to undermine the establishment of a civil religion. Above all, Canada is a bi-cultural society divided between Anglo and French Canadians who compete for supremacy. While, like other countries, it has national symbols, which might generally be expected to express unity and constitute elements of a civil religion, they are themselves divisive and deeply contested.

While lack of a civil religion may denote division, competing belief systems within one society may also be the source of considerable instability. Nowhere in the West is this more evident than in Northern Ireland where political conflict appears to be particularly 'religious'. Largely as a result of sectarian and terrorist activity, over 3000 people have been killed and tens of thousands injured over a period of some thirty years. In Ireland, Protestant and Roman Catholic identity cuts across class and other social cleavages. The conflict, however, is not primarily over theological debates. Religion becomes intertwined with many other issues. Distinct historical factors appear to be the key consideration. The two communities, with their Catholic and Protestant loyalties, identifying with republicanism and Irish nationalism and support of the British Union, respectively, have lived side by side while expressing their own grievances which are frequently articulated in religious terms.

One way of interpreting the situation of conflict in Northern Ireland is to identify two radically contrasting civil religions. Each has its shared history, traditions, values, beliefs and sacred symbols. Religious divides, however, coincide with and reinforce social divisions based often on profound inequalities such as the lesser opportunities in employment and education for Roman Catholics. In turn, these divisions are actively maintained and expressed in religious terms. The Catholic church endorses the continuation of separate schools for Catholic children to insulate them from Protestants as much as from secular culture. Protestant clergy refuse to enter into dialogue with their Catholic counterparts, whilst the Protestant working class struggles to maintain its dominant position in skilled manual occupations. Symbolically these religious and cultural differences are expressed by way of loyalist and republican parades (Jarman, 1997). The contrasting parades, with all their religious imagery, reinforce the sense of difference between the two communities and obscure the many similarities that exist when, rather ironically, they have more in common, by way of culture, than the rest of mainland Britain.

Religion and social change

The popular view that religion provides an anchor against social change, or is at least ambivalent towards it, is not without some substance. From one perspective there may be something innately conservative about religion. Acceptance of change, whether within society or the religious group itself, frequently revolves around the issue of acceptance of scriptural authority or tradition as literal truths and as divinely ordained. This tends to suggest that it is the conservative rather than liberal interpretation of a faith which is most at odds with the modern world. There is not, always, however, a straightforward relationship. Liberal views may focus on a range of social issues such as poverty, racial discrimination and gender inequality, that offer a critique of wider society. Despite this observation, it is conservative views of religion which are more likely to constitute barriers against 'progressive' change whether Orthodox Judaism, or Islam, some forms of Roman Catholicism, or fundamentalist Protestantism.

This tendency can be exemplified by traditional attitudes towards the position of women within several religious faiths and views of their role within wider society. Here, the interpretation of scripture is vital. The resistance of some churches to women priests results from a claim of legitimacy in biblical writings dating back some 2000 years ago together with the entrenched tradition of centuries. In contrast, liberal Christians see St Paul's New Testament injunctions to prohibit women from the ministry as merely the product of their time and place. Simultaneously, as McGuire (1992, pp. 113–14, 116–17) suggests, women's status in many religious groups is determined by traditional male views of gender rather than theological or spiritual qualifications. This view is exemplified in the prohibition against women performing certain rituals such as carrying the Torah in Judaism or consecrating the communion elements of the Christian faith. In this respect, McGuire interprets the position of women in Orthodox Judaism as a form of caste – they have few ritual duties to perform while many, such as the ritual bath after menstruation, symbolize a low social and religious status.

The response of some religious groups to modern secular and pluralist societies is an attempt to restore what is perceived as a kind of mythological moral state of affairs. This response can be radical and sometimes violent. Spurred by a distinct worldview, one based on dualistic conspiratorialism, patriarchal misogyny, inner-worldly asceticism and millenarianism, the Christian Patriotism movement in the USA typifies Right-wing Christian identity movements, that have sometimes turned to violence in order to further their ends against perceived social evils (Aho,

1990, pp. 166–75). However, although religious views appear to be the motivation, they often mask hidden interests or conservative perceptions of the world. Religion, then, is often a powerful and attractive vehicle for the articulation and mobilization of other interests. Himmelstein (1986) concurs with this interpretation and sees religion as a source of traditional images of women and the family and as a network from which political traditionalist movements can be mobilized to resist change in these areas. Religion therefore becomes confused with many other issues and interests. On the other hand, religious traditions may become connected with conservative and reactionary movements. This was the case in the McCarthyite witch-hunt for communists and communist sympathizers in the 1950s where Roman Catholics and fundamentalist Protestants supported the movement as part of their objection to secular and pluralist society.

Religion can, however, induce social change. The link between particular forms of religiosity and the emergence of modernity has been advanced by consensus theorists such as Talcott Parsons, as well as the classic work of Weber. Parsons argued that specific Christian values not only bring social change but enhance modern value systems. In his work, *The Social System* (1951), he suggested that Christianity generated and legitimated the values and norms which were essential for the stability and economic development of modern societies.

In his own interpretation of civil religion in the West, Parsons insisted that Christian values fulfilled the function of sanctifying a society's highest ideals and, simultaneously, prevented the state from claiming divine sanctions for its own actions. Contrary to the view of many theorists of secularization, Parsons believed that the process of modernization involved the extension of Christian values to more and more spheres of life. This belief that Christian values were sufficient to motivate individuals to seek new achievements and thereby continue to modernize society led Parsons to conjecture that the chance for non-Christian areas of the world to modernize was probably small. Robert Bellah (1976a) drew a similar conclusion. He argued that the influence of Protestant-type values of discipline, rationality and inner-worldly asceticism (which have their counterparts in the religious values of the samurai and merchant class in early twentieth-century Japan), was conspicuously missing in many underdeveloped parts of the globe.

Nor, as Kokosalakis (1986) has shown in his work on modernization in Greece, do other forms of Christianity necessarily resist modernity. The compatibility of Christianity and modernity is by no means limited to Protestantism. Indeed, in the case of Greece, religion has encouraged the modernizing process. A specific configuration of religious culture surrounding the Greek Orthodox Church, together with the nationalist movement of the nineteenth century, set the political and ideological parameters of the development for modern Greece. Kokosalakis thus shows the complexity of historical transformations in different social settings and adds to the rich evidence for the relationship between religion and modernity.

Religion and political transformation

The link between religion and political change was a theme developed by Karl Marx's co-writer Fredrick Engels (1963). Engels agreed with Marx that religion had the dual function as an ideological prop for the dominance of ruling classes throughout history, as well as a means by which those they oppressed could come to terms with their worldly situation. However, Engels saw a more positive side to religion and identified a link between religion and the demands of oppressed and exploited social strata. He identified in some religious movements the nucleus of a radical challenge to the economic and political powers of the time. Engels believed that this was the case with early Christianity that represented an underdeveloped variant of socialism. However, he argued that these movements, because of their predominantly supernatural worldview, were unlikely to make political revolution their sole aim. Engels believed that they were ultimately doomed to failure and that it would be the working class under capitalism that would adopt for itself the truly revolutionary atheistic creed of Communism.

Despite the pessimism of Marx and Engles regarding the radical potential of religion to bring beneficial change, there is confirmation that it can provide such a function. Evidence suggests that religion can be used as a resource in radical social and political change for oppressed and exploited people. At a broad national level, religion can be part of nation-building, as with Roman

Catholicism in Poland, and similarly in Eastern Europe in the 1970s and 1980s, to aid resistance against the domination of the Soviet Union. In more localized disputes, priests ministering to Hispanic farm workers in California in the 1950s and 1960s could refer to the Catholic church's social teachings (for example, in papal encyclicals) regarding social justice and workers' rights to organize (Mosqueda, 1986). Other examples include that of Jesse Jackson, the Black Presidential candidate, who wove together political and religious images, symbols and modes of expression to support his radical agenda (Wilmore, 1983).

With regard to issues of race, religion can be as much a radical resource as one of conservatism. In many Western societies, Blacks have looked to their preachers for leadership to agitate for far-reaching social and political change and at times it has been forthcoming. Such radical agendas are by no means limited to Christian expressions of Black protest. The Black Muslim movement in the USA, spearheaded by the Nation of Islam, has sought to transform political and economic conditions. Revolutionary, rather than reformist, the movement seeks to construct a separatist Black and distinctly Islamic society in order to address the social ills inflicted on Black people by a materialistic White-dominated society.

The more direct inspiration of Marx can still be seen in accounts of religion in the West today. For example, an approach more pertinent to our understanding of today's advanced capitalist society is that offered by Turner (1983) who argues that religion has lost its primary function of social control in the classical Marxist sense. Turner suggests that modern societies do not exhibit a ruling class ideology, and that this is not even necessary for the continuance of capitalist domination. This function of religion is now redundant. Rather, the ruling class uses its economic power and other forms of coercion to maintain the status quo. The threat of unemployment, poverty and the possibility of legal restraints make the exploited classes conform without religious ideological domination. Turner, however, does identify a form of 'religion' in contemporary capitalist society. This new religion is consumerism which becomes, much like religion, a kind of fetishism and a distraction from the exploitative and oppressive nature of Western societies.

Religion and social class

The enduring influence of Marx's ideas is also discernible in the work of later sociologists of religion, in their exploration of the relationship between religious orientations and social class. With the development of empirical research into the nature of religion from the mid-twentieth century one of the primary concerns was with class and aspects of belief and institutional belonging. In a series of investigations it was found that the lower classes were noticeably absent from church and also that the rich and poor expressed their religious beliefs in different ways. For example, lower-class people were more likely than middle-class people to pray in private, to believe in the doctrines of their faith and to have intense religious experiences. By contrast, the upper class, at least in the USA, appeared to display a greater religious commitment such as church attendance (Demerath, 1965). There also seemed to be a difference in the kind of church attended. For instance, statistics on US church membership has shown that 39 per cent of Episcopalians had annual incomes of $40 000 or more, compared with 14 per cent of Baptists (Gallop and Castelli, 1989, pp. 103, 110).

The work of Max Weber (1965) has also been influential in sociological studies establishing a link between religion and social groups. However, in establishing a link between the material interests and worldviews of distinct social strata, he looked further than social class. Weber was also interested in the connection between religion and what he called 'status groups' – socially constructed strata which may not necessarily be economically defined. Historically, in different social settings, the culture, lifestyles and political interests of particular status groups could be expressed in religious terms, worldviews and, more specifically, distinct theodicies.

While some sociologists have developed the work of Marx and Weber, writers like Schoenfeld (1992) have merged the ideas of both together in order to study social class and religious worldviews in the West. In his survey of the contemporary USA, Schoenfeld suggests that religion is a collective representation and moral viewpoint of particular social classes and, therefore, may be both a force of conservatism and potentially one of change. Religion legitimates either militant or submissive worldviews. In short, it articulates an awareness of the socio-economic status and interest of what are identified as the four main social classes in the USA. This means that in theological terms, the dominant faith – Christianity – is interpreted in different ways (see Table 5.1).

1. *Bourgeois class*
This class prefers a conservative form of Christianity which is submissive to the state and the status quo. Religion reflects the economic interest that is rooted in the free economy. Religion should ideally be free of state interference. This mirrors the preoccupation of this social class with a free market economy. In the USA, this is the 'dominant theology' – shared by the largest majority – but is especially endorsed by affluent white-collar occupations and professional groups. These social constituencies have a vested interest in the existing socio-economic order.

2. *Ascending class*
Here, the form of religion preferred is that of 'inclusive militancy'. There is an emphasis on the values of collectivity, equality and justice. This social class is comprised of groups seeking upward mobility and they project their interests and worldviews in religious terms. It is a religious orientation which is theologically liberal and emphasizes God's justice. This is a rough equivalent to the secular philosophy of equal opportunity. The emphasis is on equality before God since ascending social groups need unity to achieve individual goals, which leads to a kind of collective salvation.

Table 5.1 Interpreting the dominant faith

Ascending class	Retrenching class
Liberal theology	Reactionary theology
Bourgeois class	Alienated class
Conservative religion	Religion as form of escapism

3. *Retrenching class*

For this class religion emphasizes individuality and freedom – an 'exclusive militancy'. Religious views reflect the concern for declining status and the wish to return to earlier social and religious conditions. Religious views come to have a fundamentalist quality with one 'correct' view of God's wishes. Hence, there is a retrenchment of both social and religious conditions. The theology stresses submission, universalism and respectability, and calls for a return to a mythical morality of the past.

4. *Alienated class*

The worldview of the poor, and those with little stake in society, is submissive and anti-class. Religion is a form of escapism – an expression of political and economic powerlessness. It provides a form of compensation and does not relate to any vested interests in this world.

Rural-urban divides

In her study of Britain, Davie reminds us of the enduring variable of urban and rural divides for the significance of social class and religion. She maintains that the discrepancy between believing and belonging is at its sharpest in urban working-class areas – particularly the poorest parts of the major towns and cities. Belief persists, but there is a reluctance to participate and this is partly explained by a sense of alienation from the institution of the Church. Davie (1994, p. 463) suggests that higher social groupings are on average more inclined to outward expressions of religiosity than lower ones. In a middle-class environment, a higher level of education means that people are more likely to make conscious choices about belief and practice.

In contrast, in a working-class environment (where levels of education are lower), there is, apparently, no perceived need to put belief into institutional or liturgical practice. Also, not only is working-class belief largely unrelated to religious practice it is, very often, not articulated at all. Working-class religious views frequently take the form of unexamined assumptions: they exist almost unconsciously and are poorly articulated.

In discussing rural–urban differences, Davie adds another level of complexity to the secularization debate: namely institutional decline which, in terms of church attendance, varies from one area to another within the same society. Davie maintains that in inner-city areas churches operate on a kind of parochial system, where congregations are small and struggle for financial survival. They may, nevertheless, have a practical social function in providing centres for the unemployed and kindergartens for working mothers. In contrast, the suburban churches sometimes flourish and operate on more of a market (as opposed to a parish) principle, attracting worshippers from a wide geographical area. Worshippers are often articulate individuals who choose, very consciously, the type of church to which they wish to belong. Their churches are characterized by high levels of activity and involvement by members, and a much clearer distinction between members and non-members than is found elsewhere. In conclusion, middle-class organizational patterns reflect middle-class ways of believing. The rural context is different again. Churches find it difficult to come to terms with rapidly changing situations. They may provide an anchor in a sea of change although they may increasingly appear, at least in the eyes of outsiders, rather anachronistic. Traditionally, the rural church was the focus of a largely unspoken corporate belief and it can still retain this function as a symbol of community and continuity.

Finally, in terms of encouraging belief and practice generally, geography may be particularly significant. Wade Roof's argument (1976) is that the maintenance of religious commitment in highly differentiated Western societies depends, above all, on a localized traditional perspective shared by persons who interact frequently, thus proving mutual support for belief and practice. However, this theory has sometimes been undermined by subsequent research on Jewish communities in the USA that have found an inverse relationship between community size and formal participation in the Jewish faith. Dispersion is more likely to bring together people in a religion unity and expresses a search for community and ethnic solidarity. Religion is thus vital in strengthening bonds, uniformity of religious practice and a sense of parochial community among Jews (Rabinowitz 1992). This is true of other faiths and in a variety of social settings.

Summary

Today, it could be argued that the speculations of classical sociology as to the link between religion, social change, integration and stability have become irrelevant. In the early twenty-first century it is possible to suggest that, in a largely secular society, religion is so insignificant that it will have few major repercussions on the social environment either as a stabilizing force or otherwise. In short, that religion is so socially marginalized as to be of no great social consequence or relevant to particular social groups such as class. If this is true, it is also possible to contend that the effect of change is uni-directional: that social change brings about transformations in religion rather than the reverse which was commonly the case in the past. In this chapter we have seen that this assumption may nonetheless be a little premature since there is still evidence that religion can be both an integrating mechanism and a divisive force and, at the same time resist and engender social change. This chapter has also suggested the ongoing relationship between religion and social variables such as class and geographical region. The next chapter considers the significance of other factors in shaping the nature of religious belief, practice, and allegiance to religious institutions.

6 Belief, Practice and Belonging

The nature and focus of religious belief and belonging to religious collectives is the subject of this chapter. The core question which it addresses is: If Western society is essentially secular, what are the processes that lead to religious activity and association? The emphasis here is thus upon the crucial social variables that shape religious conviction over the different stages of life, the significance of beliefs in transitional periods of the life-cycle, the link between believing and belonging, religious identity and the nature of conversion to more stringent forms of religiosity.

Religion and the stages of life

The extent of religious belief and the degree of commitment to religious organizations varies over the life-cycle. This is certainly true in pre-modern societies where age-sets are important in ascribing status and role in social terms in general and religious terms in particular and, although they may have declined in Western societies, there is still an important link between religion and age, and the significance of socially created age categories such as 'the young' or 'middle-aged'.

The young

A good index of the decline of religion is the substantial drop in the proportion of children receiving specifically religious training. This is a long-term trend and explains the rise of the Sunday School movement in the nineteenth century with its focus on specialized religious knowledge that was felt by many churches to be necessary in an increasingly secular and differentiated society.

This decline in specifically religious instruction was particularly marked from the middle of the twentieth century. In 1952, in the USA, only 6 per cent had received no religious training as a child. In 1965, this had risen to 9 per cent, and in 1988 to 18 per cent. This does not argue particularly well for the level of belief and belonging in the future. As Reginald Bibby, author of *Fragmented Gods* (1987) argues, the principal reason for the decline in church attendance is the lack of religious socialization. People who attend church as adults are primarily those who attended as children. Active churchgoers seldom come out of nowhere: they are home-grown. However, the proportion of children being exposed to religious instruction outside of Sunday School is estimated by Bibby to have now dropped from three in four to less than one in four.

The *European Values Survey* (Cook, 2000) clearly indicated that belief in God increases up the age scale, as does belonging to religious institutions. This is so for various European countries irrespective of other social variables such as gender and social class, and appears to be the case with most Christian denominations. However, there is indication that the younger cohorts will not, in time, endorse a greater religiosity in old age. The long-term picture then, appears to be one of religious decline. In this respect, Grace Davie notes that opinion poll data over a period of time in Britain indicates that younger generations are less religious than older ones. Moreover, Davie suggests that not only have young people left British churches, they are, it seems, rejecting even the nominal belief that may potentially grow into a greater religiosity in old age (Davie, 1994).

The culture of church life has apparently contributed to the decline of young people belonging to Christian denominations. Philip Richter and Leslie Francis' interviews of those leaving churches in Britain show that they did so because they were found to be dominated by older people and that church displays a culture that was 'old fashioned'. Moreover, those who did not leave the faith entirely tended to gravitate towards those churches which were described as 'more lively', 'exciting', 'creative', 'youth orientated' and 'alternative' (Richter and Francis, 1998, pp. 124–5). At the other end of the age spectrum, older people feel excluded from the very things that made the young feel at home in particular churches.

Middle age and old age

Middle and old age-sets also have links with aspects of believing and belonging. Middle age is generally a period of increasing church involvement for some. In the USA, the overall pattern in adult church attendance shows a steady increase from late teens to a peak in the late 50s to early 60s, followed by a slight decline in later old age (Atchley, 1980, pp. 330–40). These figures do not necessarily reflect greater religious sentiment among middle-aged and old-aged persons, but could be viewed as changing patterns of involvement in voluntary associations. Thus involvement in church life may increase as commitment to work-related, sport-related and school service associations declines over the same period.

Middle age is often regarded as a time of 'identity crisis'. Hence, religious belief and belonging may help establish a new sense of identity and status. Certainly, a prevailing view is that the attraction of religious belonging particularly for women of this age may be linked to the loss of socially ascribed gender roles as well as natural changes in reproductive capacities. This rather common-sense view suggests that the status of 'mother' means little in middle age, while the onset of the menopause can be traumatic because some women consider their reproductive capacity a basic part of their sense of self and personal worth. These assumptions, however, are not easily substantiated and have to be supplemented by the fact that women of all age groups are over-represented in many religious traditions. In explaining the over-representation of women in Christian churches, Walter (1990) believes that much can be accounted for in terms of a search for solutions to a number of negative social and psychological experiences. Feelings of anxiety, a range of emotional difficulties generated by domestic roles and dependency on the male sex, are frequently concerns which need to be psychologically addressed. In addition, compensators might also be sought for such deprivations as poverty, low status and lack of opportunities, again linked to the limitations of female social roles and child-rearing in particular.

There is some empirical evidence to suggest that religion is important in the lives of older people (Gray and Moberg, 1977), while other studies have found that the association is inconclusive (Steinitz, 1980). Christiano's (1987) survey of people of various church backgrounds suggests that older women and older persons in general are involved in church activity, often by force of custom. At the same time, the involvement of the elderly in religious organizations may indicate an increasing social marginalization. Here, there is a stark contrast with traditional societies, where old age may infer a greater social and religious status. Retirement effectively means, for many people, leaving the public sphere. Thus, for the elderly, the bases of identity and self-worth must come from the private sphere – family, leisure, perhaps religion. Increased emphasis on the religious bases of individual identity may represent, for older people, an attempt to transform the previous cultural emphasis on work and parenthood to a new valuation based on spiritual status.

The life-cycle and rites of passage

One of the core themes of anthropological studies of religion in so-called primitive and traditional, non-industrial societies is its relationship to rites of passage – rituals designating the transition of one clearly demarcated stage of life to another, whether biologically defined ones such as birth, puberty, pregnancy and death, or those socially constructed – marriage being the primary example. The exact relationship between religion and rites of passage, however, has been open to interpretation. Turner (1974) suggests that, to a great extent, these 'life crises' are linked to the underlying problem of uncertainty. Childbirth, for instance, has for most of human history been an uncertain and vulnerable time for the mother and close relatives. Rituals surrounding such events may be seen as 'rites of affliction' which deal with vulnerability – a time of possible affliction by evil spirits or the evil intentions of neglected ancestral spirits. Alternatively, such rites may be concerned with negotiating clearly defined social boundaries (Van Gennep, 1908). They typically include ritual action symbolizing detachment, a period of marginality signifying the ambiguity of transition and a final uniting into the new status group. Other interpretations of the function of such rituals include the assertion that they are the means by which natural biological processes are given meaning (Douglas, 1966), or an expression of collective sentiments and structured social relationships in tightly integrated communities (Leach, 1967).

Rites of passage are still observable in contemporary religious groups that have rituals which mark some form of spiritual transition, for example, baptism, while for ethnico-religious groups they may still be important as with the bar mitzvahs among Jews that represent the transition from childhood to adulthood. However, even in the religious sphere such rites appear to have declined. Evidence of this is the near disappearance of 'churching' – a tradition in some Christian churches where women are prohibited to enter church until a month after giving birth.

In wider society, many of the social and psychological underpinnings to rites of passage have undoubtedly been undermined in Western societies. Social and geographical mobility have eroded collective solidarity and sentiment and, subsequently, the need for outward symbolic expressions of social integration. However, perhaps above all, many of the functions of rites of passage have been eaten away by the greater certainty of completing the life-cycle. As never before, the contemporary world, as a result of scientific advances and improved living conditions, enjoys the confidence of fulfilling the life-span and surviving such natural processes as child-birth. At the same time some commentators, particularly of a post-modernist persuasion, suggest that it no longer makes sense to speak of the 'life-cycle'. Social fragmentation and a culture of choice have eroded clearly demarcated stages of life.

Some such social conventions obviously remain. Marriage is one even though the social pressure to marry may now be slight. It is also true that this relatively popular institution indicates levels of secularity since it is frequently stripped of religious significance. Indicative of this is the List of Approved Premises, produced by the Office for National Statistics in Britain, which encompasses a register of legitimate non-religious sites for weddings other than places of worship. They include zoos, soccer grounds, museums, nightclubs, golf clubs and restaurants.

The religious sanctity of marriage is also undermined by increasing divorce rates, which has been interpreted as a symbol of growing rationalism and individualism (Goode, 1963). Just as people rationally choose to enter marriage and select a partner in instrumental terms, divorce, now stripped of its social and religious stigma, is equally pragmatically entered into. This is also reflected in divorce legislation. The philosophy of 'till death do us part' is replaced by a range of rational–secular legitimations for divorce.

If the religious element has been stripped from the rites of passage in industrialized societies, then this may not be for the better. Perhaps this is no more evident than in the case of death. Perceptions of death in Western society profoundly reflect social change – not least of all its increasing individualism and the emerging secularized society. Today, death is not a public event. Rather, it is a private experience and, for the most part, will take place within an institutional setting (Aries, 1974). Western culture is also age- and death-denying. It has an emphasis on prolonging life, of consuming strategies to retain youth, and is unable to tolerate death in a culture orientated towards perpetual happiness (Featherstone, 1982). Moreover, the way that society is organized, its rationalization and emphasis on optimum performance, means that it cannot afford long periods of mourning. Grieving is thus inadequately dealt with, while the standard funeral which generally gives scant reference to the afterlife or religiosity, is often void of meaning and insufficiently deals with the mourning process (Walter, 1999).

Religion, the new voluntarism and identity

If rites of passage and religious commitment throughout the stages of life indicate considerable changes in religiosity, so does the nature of religious belonging. Indeed, in recent years a great deal of sociological attention has been given to the nature of belonging to religious institutions in Western societies. Much has focused upon what has been referred to as the 'new voluntarism'. This term implies that the basis of joining any sphere of social activity is a purely voluntary choice on the part of individuals. This is clearly a consequence of relentless social and geographical mobility which has resulted in the breakdown of communities and primary group association. Free from community obligations and conformity to group norms, the individual is uncompromisingly exposed to the values of an achievement orientated culture and accompanied by the purposeful, instrumental and self-advancement strategies that have come to encompass so many areas of social and economic life (Warner, 1993).

Increasingly, for sociologists of religion, the new voluntarism has overspilled into the religious sphere and marks a profound shift from 'collective–expressive' to 'individual–expressive' religious identity (Roof and McKinney, 1987). This invariably accompanies the general erosion of religious commitment in cosmopolitan, multi-cultural Western societies. Indeed, religious activity can be said to be particularly challenged by contemporary developments since both social and geographical mobility have undermined the 'religious culture' and the community where it has historically been embedded and thrived. The outcome is that there is little or no social pressure on the individual to convert to a faith through the proselytizing efforts of the religious collective since, ultimately, the momentum is derived from the religious 'seeker'. The new voluntarism also suggests that people are more likely to join a group for personal advantage and instrumental reasons, rather than collective concerns since the contemporary world heralds a more profound individualism and utilitarianism that influences the religious domain, whatever the form of religion preferred (Wuthnow, 1993, pp. 39–40).

Hammond (1988) suggests that today there is an increasing link between identity and voluntary religious belonging. This is clear by way of church membership. Previously, people were largely influenced in their religious affiliation by primary group pressure such as the local community or the family. The membership of these primary groups has historically been involuntary. Today however, secondary group membership is becoming more and more important in determining institutional membership. These are voluntary associations which are largely based on age, occupational categories and lifestyle. Allegiance to such associations ise freely chosen and linked with the construction of personal identities.

Wade Roof (1994) similarly argues that religion survives only by accommodating cultural values and if it proves relevant to the experiences of individuals in *this* world. Hence, the advance of achieved, or self-created religious identity is primarily based on personal lifestyles and tastes. This broadly reflects the modern market economy that has increasingly encouraged a culture of consumer choice and accompanies the fragmentation of occupational specialism and the pluralism of life-experiences. Mirroring cultural change, the 'spiritual marketplace' encourages people to pick and choose until they find a religious identity best suited to their individual, rather than collective experience – a freedom to seek a religious faith which reflects, endorses and gives symbolic expressions to one's lifestyle and social experience. The contemporary religious environment therefore permits individuals the freedom to discover their own spiritual 'truths', their own 'reality' and their own 'experience' according to what is relevant to their lives and provides a means by which to create a new self. Religion thus aids the construction of identity and lifestyle preferences as a subjective act of becoming.

Roof is more forward in suggesting that the 'individual-expressive' tendency of contemporary religion is not however necessarily confined to 'privatized', introspective forms. It may still have communal dimensions. Indeed, people (especially through new expressions of religiosity) are now capable of combining individualistic religious exploration with a hunger for community. This conjecture has been supported by fairly recent empirical research in North America. The religious marketplace generates a quest for religious expressions of self-identity. Yet, the search for identity leads to the felt need to be with 'people more like myself' in terms of age, family composition and education.

For many commentators there is now the liberty to seek a religious collective which reflects, endorses and gives symbolic expression to one's lifestyle and social experiences (Lofland and Skonovd, 1981). The contemporary religious milieu permits an individual the freedom to discover their own spiritual 'truth', their own 'reality' and their own religious 'experience' according to what is relevant in their lives (Wuthnow, 1976, pp. 191–2). At the same time, the importance of identity construction can be seen in the locus of religious belonging. Contemporary church congregation are, for example, becoming what Bibby refers to as 'homogeneous clubs' (Bibby, 1993). People are thus increasingly choosing to belong to religious groupings that are constituted by 'people like me' which enforce and sustain identity formation. Such developments are consistent with the market model of religion. Individuals 'buy into' a religious collective where they most feel at home. Successful churches, and other religious institutions for that matter, are therefore those which can establish a sense of belonging to a sub-culture comprised of people of a similar social background, life experience and who embrace corresponding religious aspirations and cultural ethos.

Conversion

Defining conversion

Why and how individuals come to adopt a stringent supernatural worldview has been the subject of considerable sociological speculation – an area of enquiry which has been enhanced by the proliferation of new religious movements (NRMs). The adoption of a distinctive religious view of the world and a new organizational allegiance is frequently seen as the result of some conversion experience; in short, a change in consciousness, a transformation of one's self image and meaning system which engenders a selective perception and interpretation of events or what Snow and Machalek (1983, p. 264) refer to as a change in one's 'universe of discourse'. Whether the conversion experience is rapid or slow, complete or partial, such radical conversion transforms the way that individuals perceive the world, including the social world and their place in it.

The problem, however, is that there appear to be various degrees of conversion. Because of this, several empirical indicators of conversion have been developed which suggest that it ranges in intensity (Newport, 1979). Hence, we may distinguish between:

1. Believing nothing at all to accepting a profoundly supernatural worldview. This is the most intense form of conversion and is followed in descending order by;
2. From being highly committed in one faith to another, say Christian to Islam or from a liberal faith, to a more fundamentalist variety;
3. A 'reaffirmation' of one's religious identity, such as that obtained by confirmation classes;
4. A change in membership status. Studies of both mainstream traditions and NRMs frequently treat shifts in organizational affiliation as indicators of conversion. Usually, these indicators are demonstrated by public displays of status confirmation rituals which affirm a new identity such as baptism, witnessing or proselytizing.

By using such criteria, however, it is not conceptually clear where conversion begins and ends on a continuum and how significant beliefs and levels of belonging are.

The 'causes' of conversion

Most of the research on conversion has been primarily concerned with trying to identify the causes of conversion. The extensive literature in this area can roughly be classified into three historical waves. The first developed during the earliest decades of the twentieth century and was dominated by theological and psychological explanations such as the work of William James (1902) which focused on the personal accounts of those converted and their claims to mystical experiences.

The second wave, inspired largely by the studies of experiences of American prisoners of war (POWs) during the Korean War, featured the development of the 'brain-washing' or 'coercive persuasion' models of conversion and was typified by Sargant's work (1957). Hence, the emphasis tended to be on the activity of the religious group which the individual elected to join. This was inclined to downplay the individual as an autonomous actor searching for a spiritual truth and claiming a special emotional and spiritual experience. Frequently, references to conversion appeared to take place during carefully orchestrated settings, for example, the evangelical revival meeting (Lang and Lang, 1960). Hence, what may be taken as conversion by those who organize such meetings may be no more than group conformity and compliant behaviour.

The actual interaction between the recruit and the religious collective is especially important in bringing about the transformation of worldviews. Perhaps the most obvious factor relates to the proselytizion of potential converts. Some, like Jehovah's Witnesses, put a great deal of emphasis on evangelizing for new converts – a tactic which has the additional function of enhancing the commitment of those already converted (Beckford, 1975). The problem with the emphasis upon the proselytizing efforts of the group, however, is that, as Barker (1983) found to be the case with the Unification Church, only very few of those exposed to such pressures decide to convert.

The publication of the Loftland–Stark conversion model in 1965 signalled the arrival of a third wave of explanatory variables which relied heavily on sociological thinking and in, turn, stimulated a great deal of further research particularly in the area of cults and new forms of religiosity. For Loftland and Stark, conversion was a 'process' involving seven requisites. In turn, empirical research has further explored specific aspects of this process.

1. *Tensions*

Unresolved tensions and contradictions in the individual's life. The stress here is on the individual's personality, biography and personal problems. Some commentators have focused on personality disorders. For example, Levine (1980, pp. 146–51) believed that the appeal of contemporary cults is to offer security and purpose for those who cannot deal with responsibility and the demands of wider society. Others, such as Greil and Rudy (1984), put an emphasis on variables like marital strain, the loss of a family member, loss of job, or the pressures of higher education for the young. Part of this concern is emphasizing the significance of social class, gender, age and level of education.

2. *Religious problem-solving perspective*

The ways open to dealing with problems. The individual may already be predisposed to deal with personal difficulties with reference to religious views of the world.

3. *Seekership*

Actively seeking a way of resolving a personal problem. Here, religious ideas and beliefs may be particularly important. Other research has also emphasized this dimension (Harrison, 1974). The teachings of the group can have significance in the problem-solving exercise. Conversion and recruitment is therefore likely when a recruit's perspective is consistent with that of a religious collective, even when the specific content of the group's beliefs may be unfamiliar. The key point is that a convert's personal experiences are interpreted in terms of the belief system of a religious collective.

4. *Turning point*

The individual comes to a crucial juncture in their life. Many converts appear to describe a crisis that they feel is a turning point. Some crisis may disrupt a person so completely that the individual has difficulty integrating them into the previously held meaning system. Hence, serious illness or unemployment may become turning points. There is, however, nothing predetermined about such a development and diverse individual responses are possible.

Nonetheless, some religious collectives purposely play up the turning point emphasis to reinforce their collective worldviews and to win converts. Beckford (1975, p. 174) has pointed out that Jehovah's Witnesses often approach strangers about common worries such as war, inflation, or crime. The emphasis is upon order-threatening conditions which may magnify the potential convert's feelings of dissatisfaction, fear, or anxiety, and which the person may have previously felt only vaguely.

5. *Affective bonds*
In short, this involves the important emotional networks open to a religious collective. During this resocialization recruits learn to re-define their social world. This process results in a whole new way of experiencing the world and oneself in it. The more extreme view, developed by Snow and Machalek (1983, 1984), is that such networks are of equal, or of greater importance than dispositional susceptibility in determining differential recruitment. What is understood to be of primary importance is the formation and intense interaction with members of the religious group and that this inter-action is generally along pre-existing lines of social relationships which are significant and meaningful to the individual The essential point is that social identity remains unchanged, thereby lessening the anomic impact of a change in transformation of identity experienced by the individual when joining a religious group and enhancing the plausibility of the beliefs. However, not all those with personal links to religious groups are converted. Snow and Machalek deem it necessary to consider 'socio-spatial factors' by which it is vital to consider why some join while others do not when introduced to a religious movement. The key point is that potential converts have more free time, discretion over choice and are less bound up within relationships that inhibit commitment.

The problem with this emphasis however is that, not all of these contributing factors are present or significant for all movements. Jehovah's Witnesses, for example, recruit very little from pre-existing networks of social relationships and more from 'cold' evangelizing (Beckford, 1975).

6. *Neutralization of extra-cult attachments*
This refers to the negation of relationships outside the religious group. At the same time as establishing affective bonds, the recruit

also weakens or severs those relationships that support the old self. Former attachments compete with new commitments since they symbolize a worldview that the recruit wishes to reject, and are based on an identity that the recruit wishes to change. This might be easier if the individuals attracted to the group are already socially isolated. In fact, this is why religion has been interpreted as a form of family surrogate. Glock, Ringer and Babbie's (1967) survey of urban Episcopalian church parishes found that the more deprived of family (spouse, childless and so on), the more likely there is to be involvement in activity in one's congregation. They concluded that the church provides certain functions that some are lacking – that is, emotional and psychological family supports missing in their lives. Glock *et al.*'s 'comfort theory', as it came to be known, triggered controversy and further research which proved inconclusive and even contradicted it (Hobart, 1974).

7. Intensive interaction
The religious group becomes the most important focus of life. The religious seeker is now a fully-fledged member.

While Loftland and Stark never claimed that they had produced a general model of conversion applicable to all religious groups, it has been empirically tested and found to have weaknesses. For example, Greil and Rudy (1984) examined case studies of the conversion process in ten very different religious groups ranging from the Mormons, to Hare Krishna, to evangelical Christian groups. They concluded that several components of the model had to be rejected for conceptual reasons. For example, there is no way of knowing whether 'tensions' distinguish converts from non-converts, since not all those experiencing tensions turn to religious groups to resolve them. On the other hand, other components are to be found in some types of groups but not others. For instance, 'neutralization of attachments', where conversion involves a radical transformation of social roles, could be found more obviously among evangelical Christian groups but not necessarily with those based on Eastern mysticism. Only the 'formation of affective bonds' and 'intensive interaction' with group members seem to be indispensable prerequisites for conversion. Thus, any group, which seeks to successfully convert people, must be structured so as to foster interaction with members.

Learning processes

An alternative account of conversion is the 'role-theory' model. Here, conversion is identified as a kind of learning process. The model developed by Bromley and Shupe (1979) based upon a study of the Children of God, Hare Krishna and the Unification Church, was primarily concerned with the psychological commitment to a religious group. There was no great depth of individual dedication or commitment, feeling of belonging, or intense individual religious experience, while little may be known of the doctrines of the group. Rather, conversion is a 'structured event' arising from relationships with members and roles within the group. Affiliation is an 'exchange process' which involves a link between problem-solving strategies and norms and values of the group whereby the individual's needs become shaped by the group. One becomes a member through five stages:

1. *Predisposing factors*: such as alienation, social availability;
2. *Attraction*: motivation, experience of role models in the group;
3. *Incipient involvement*: the group claims right to compliance, greater depth of individual involvement;
4. *Active involvement*: for instance, witnessing, evangelizing and fund-raising;
5. *Commitment*: which includes opportunity for leadership, a 'master' theology, encapsulation in a sub-culture, a motivational structure which involves the idea of being part of a world-saving elite and a large number of collective experiences and activities.

Other accounts of conversion, which put an emphasis on learning, are typified by Beckford's work on conversion to Jehovah's Witnesses (1978). It includes a study of personal accounts of conversion which, according to Beckford, is 'skillfully accomplished by actors' – the slow acceptance of the movement's version of its own rationale. Conversion is 'achieved' and 'organized'. The individual's conversion account depends on the guidelines of the Witnesses' all-controlling bureaucracy – the Watchtower organization based in New York – and its exclusive ideology. To be a complete member of the Jehovah's Witnesses is to accept a worldview and make use of ascribed rules in certain situations. To be converted is to internalize rules through a 'progressive enlightenment' – an acceptance of the Watchtower as God's visible organization and elect as a kind of theocracy, and publisher of God's intentions. Beckford (1983) observed that, in his research on Jehovah's Witnesses and the Unification Church, it is not uncommon for members to alter their views over time and even pass through distinct phases of commitment that vary in style and strength. Like other commentators (Strauss, 1976), Beckford concludes that conversion entails an interaction during which the recruit constructs or negotiates a new personal identity.

Redressing the balance: the actor's point of view

The preoccupation of the above sociological work with social variables, roles and networks, meant that there has been a neglect of the actor's interpretation of their own conversion experience. However, this subjectivity dimension was emphasized by Snow and Machalek in their later work (1983). Here, the emphasis was more on what individuals *said* about their experiences rather than reductionist explanations focusing on sociological 'causes'. They suggest that what amounts to a personality change is a process which is 'more fundamental than beliefs or identities'. Thus, an analysis of the discourse and reasoning of subjects can provide a fruitful insight to the study of conversion. This approach suggests that while researchers have explored the 'causes and consequences' of conversion, little has been done on the nature of conversion itself. In particular, the characteristics of converts themselves are usually ignored or assumed.

Snow and Machalek speak about the convert as 'a social type' based on an analysis of the talk and reasoning of subjects and supported by their own underlying theory of conversion which stresses certain 'rhetorical indicators'. Based primarily on Snow's (1976) study of the Nichiren Shoshu Buddhist movement, they suggest that converts may be identified by:

1. *The adoption of a master attribution scheme*
Individuals employ causal interpretations to make sense of themselves, others and experience as a common cognitive process. What distinguishes the convert from others, though, is the adoption of a master attribution scheme. When asked to account for the state of the world, self and their actions, converts inevitably resort to one attribution system.

2. *Biographical reconstruction*

This refers to the idea that individuals who undergo the radical change of conversion reconstruct or reinterpret their past life perspective from the present. This does not necessarily entail a wholesale fabrication or distortion of one's previous life, but rather a restructuring in which previous important events may be de-emphasized and less significant ones elevated to greater prominence.

3. *The suspension of analogical reasoning*

This can be seen as a technique for affirming the sacredness of one's beliefs over the profanity of all others, thereby insulating and protecting beliefs and self from the contamination of association with alien worldviews and other people.

4. *The embrace of a master role*

Here, the convert comes to see him/herself in terms of the role of convert and member of a particular group. In contrast, modern life usually imposes role compartmentalization, where individuals are expected to enact a variety of roles depending upon the context in which they find themselves – other roles become subordinate to it.

In turn, Staples and Mauss (1987) present a critique of Snow and Machalek's alternative theory of conversion, and focus specifically on the role of language in the process. They believe that Snow and Machalek fail to distinguish between conversion and commitment. Conversion is, phenomenologically speaking, primarily a change in self-consciousness. It is a way that a person thinks or feels about themselves – a 'self-transformation'.

By using a small sample of evangelical Christians, Staples and Mauss indicate that while some aspects of 1, 3 and 4 of Snow and Machalek's rhetorical indicators were present, the second was often conspicuously missing even to the point of denying a conversion experience. Whereas Snow and Machalek view particular kinds of language and rhetoric to be a reflection of some underlying changes in consciousness, Staples and Mauss see particular types of language and rhetoric as tools individuals use to achieve transformation of self. While Snow and Machalek tend to view conversion as something that 'happens to' a person, Staples and Mauss understand the person to be an active participant in the creation of a 'new self'. The biographical reconstruction does seem to be involved in the process of conversion, but the remaining three (especially the adoption of a master role) may facilitate commitment. Rhetoric is the person's own account of conversion. In contemporary society much focus is put upon individual choice. Hence, rhetoric is often framed in this way and is seen as a personal decision (Tippett, 1973). This decision is said by the convert to be beneficial with an emphasis upon a wonderful new way of life. With sectarian and many NRM groups this is frequently imperative – affirming a worldview which is often in conflict with the world. Converts to more mainline religion may play down this aspect of conflict.

Disengagement from religious organizations

Relatively less attention has been paid to the reasons why people may leave a religious organization and the process by which leaving occurs. To conclude this chapter we may briefly survey a few of the studies which engage with this area by a mention of church leaving and the disengagement from the more sectarian or cultist groups.

In contemporary societies the individual may go through role-exit experiences all the time, for example, changing job or exiting the role as a parent. It tends to be a lengthy period of transition. Ebaugh (1988) suggests that as far as exit from religious collectives is concerned, the pushes and pulls of various social influences are evident. Individuals weigh the advantages and disadvantages of being in or out. Typically, members reach the decision to leave the group only gradually, but just as members' retrospective accounts of their conversion are transformed to fit their new beliefs and image of self, so too are ex-members' accounts of events and decisions to leave. However, accounts of exit frequently include:

1. First doubts;
2. Seeking and weighing role alternatives;
3. A turning point, and;
4. Establishing an ex-role identity.

Alternatively, Wright (1987, p. 176) identifies five factors that contribute to the conditions under which defection is likely to occur. These include:

1. The breakdown in member's insulation from the outside world;
2. Unregulated development of dyadic relationship within the communal context;
3. Perceived lack of success in achieving world transformation;
4. Failure to meet affective needs of a primary group, and;
5. Inconsistencies between the actions of leaders and the ideas they symbolically represent.

Disengagement is often the result of a breakdown or diminished effectiveness of the plausibility structure that supports the group's beliefs and practices. It may include reduced isolation from the outside world, competing commitments especially to family or friends outside the group, lack of the movement's success and apparent discrepancies between leader's words and actions (Wright, 1988). Like the conversion experience, disengagement often entails a turning point although this may be overemphasized by the ex-convert (Richardson, 1980).

Finally, in accounting for disaffection, Jacobs (1989), examines a number of 'authoritarian religious movements' including Christian-, Hindu- and Buddhist-based groups, and stresses the significance of severing socio-emotional bonds to the religious leader. There is a two-stage process of separation in which connections to the group are first severed, followed by emotional disengagement from the charismatic leader. The bond between the leader and follower is shown to be most significant in determining the strength of continued commitment to the movement.

The reasons for, and the processes involved in, leaving the more mainline Christian churches is no less complicated than disengaging from a more unorthodox religious movement. Given the scale of church-leaving in many Western societies, there have been few attempts to systematically gauge what is involved. One of the more recent accounts of church-leaving in Britain is based on the survey by Richter and Francis (1998). The reasons for church leaving are indeed complex and are cut across by variables such as age and gender. However, while not doing justice to the findings, the following are among the explanations for leaving church, even if belief is retained:

- Most churches are unable to help develop members through stages of faith,
- Moving home,
- Work schedules, such as working on Sundays,
- Illness or old age,
- For the young, parental over-enthusiasm in instilling the faith,
- A weighing of personal costs and benefits,
- Worship or inadequate levels of pastoral care,
- Leadership style,
- The church's teachings.

All of these are, of course, complex issues. However, Richter and Francis appear to argue that, in the case of Britain, there is a mismatch of believing and institutional expression of faith; a 'believing without belonging'. In short, the churches are largely failing its members by way of satisfying personal, pastoral and spiritual needs. This gives another twist to the secularization debate in that a high level of belief may be 'out there' but does not find an institutional setting. This is, of course, a highly debatable conjecture.

Summary

The General Social Survey in the USA, from the 1970s until today, indicates a clear link between religious belief and attitudes towards abortion. Those with a strong religious conviction are more likely to state under what conditions abortion is acceptable. Thus, abortion in the case of birth defect or rape might be permissible, but not simply because the woman opted not to have the child as a matter of preference. Similarly, in Presidential elections in the USA, church-goers were found to be more inclined to become politically involved as a result of their attitude towards certain issues including, defence, abortion, welfare services and the feeling that the federal government was generally becoming too powerful (Wuthnow, 1988, p. 318).

Such survey evidence appears to indicate that religion is still important in the lives of at least some sections of the population in Western society. Religious beliefs may aid in shaping a person's experiences, determining choices, enhancing the interpretation of life events, precipitating planning future action and informing orientations towards social and moral issues. However, it is undoubtedly a sign of secularity that religious beliefs are now largely a matter of optional choice and not open to the taken-for-granted truth of previous times. Hence, those with religious conviction find themselves increasingly in a minority and with the constant need of support of their worldview. This is because in the West, as Peter Berger (1973) has cogently explored, religious systems compete with many other worldviews and lose their matter-of-fact status. This may be contrasted with the widespread faith in science whose 'truths' are usually taken as self-evidently true. Moreover, the need to maintain commitment to any religious group is especially difficult in a modern, pluralistic, mobile and individualistic society which has seriously weakened the ability of family and community to offer the individual the stable source of belonging and identity that is the mainstay of religion in pre-industrial societies.

7 Challenges to Western Christianity

The secularization thesis, if interpreted as the alleged decline of religion in the West, is intrinsically linked to the apparent demise of Christianity. Historically, Western societies have been dominated by the Christian faith in terms of belief and practice. In previous centuries, Christianity had important political, educational and social functions to play and claimed, at least nominally, the allegiance of the great mass of people through one or other of its major schisms whether the Orthodox Church, Roman Catholicism, or the numerous strands of Protestantism. Indeed, so dominant has the faith proved to be that the West has historically been referred to as the Christian civilization or 'Christendom'. This is obviously no longer the case in many countries as its declining social and political impact, and the falling level of popular belief in Christianity, indicates. The fortunes of what might be referred to as 'mainstream' Christianity is, however, rather more complex than this simple appraisal suggests. This chapter will address some of these complexities.

Post-Christianity

Don Cupitt (1998) sees the development of the post-Christian West as intrinsically linked to the emergence of the post-modern society. Western culture is no longer dominated by the belief in progress and an optimistic view of history that once characterized modernity. Such ideas provided people with hope for the future and filled the world with significance. In the West, some of these ideas were borrowed partly from Christianity, particularly that of linear eschatological time – one where history had a beginning and an end in the purpose of a benevolent God. Christian hope of the kingdom to come and its secular counterpart displayed in the notion of progress has disintegrated. In the words of Cupitt (1998, p. 218) such beliefs justified present faith, present action, present disciplinary authority and they helped to make tolerable present hardships and incompleteness. But now the 'stories' – whether Catholic, Marxist or liberal – all seem to have lost their strength. They have evaporated, leaving the institutions that depended upon them in crisis.

For Cupitt, this sudden breakdown of the idea of a better future has also meant the disintegration of the idea of a legitimate past. Christian tradition is dying, the past has lost its old authority and the whole idea that social institutions are divinely authorized to establish and maintain a coercive regime of dogmatic 'truth' for the sake of a promised Christian heaven has suffered a rapid demise. What has occurred, then, is that the Christian way of seeing the cosmos, history and reality as an objective 'truth,' has disappeared so that in terms of human meaning there now exists a cavernous vacuum.

Belief in traditional Christianity

There are various ways by which the apparent decline of Christianity can be measured. One is manifest at the level of belief in Christian doctrines. Gill, Hadaway and Marler (1998) have brought together a wide variety of survey findings on religious belief in Britain in order to show the patterns of belief in Christian teachings (Table 7.1). The data from the 1940s up until the late 1990s show a decline in thesistic belief and an increase in disbelief. Overall, the results show an increase in general scepticism about the existence of God, the related erosion of dominant, traditional Christian belief, and the persistence of non-traditional beliefs.

Evidence produced by the European Values Survey over a number of years (Harding, Phillips and Fogarty, 1985; Cook, 2000) show that, in Europe at least, belief in traditional Christianity has been also undermined. Partly, this is because of the rise of competing forms of religiosity such as the new religions and the faiths of ethnic minorities, while levels of disbelief, or at least unconventional interpretations of Christian teachings, have also increased.

Table 7.1 Is religious belief in Britain declining?

Belief	% of British population				
	1940–1950s	1960s	1970s	1980s	1990s
God	–	79	74	72	68
God as Personal	43	39	32	32	31
God as Spirit/ Life Force	38	39	38	39	40
Jesus as Son of God	68	62	–	49	–
Life After Death	49	49	37	43	43
Heaven	–	–	52	55	51
Hell	–	–	21	26	25
Devil	24	28	20	24	26
Disbelief					
God	–	10	15	18	27
Jesus as just a man/story	18	22	–	38	–
Life After Death	21	23	42	40	41
Heaven	–	–	33	35	40
Hell	–	–	68	65	66
Devil	54	52	70	64	67

Source: adapted from Gill, Hadaway and Marler (1998), p. 509.

In interpreting the findings of the surveys, Davies (1999) identifies a clear erosion of the Christian tradition. The afterlife–creation–morality worldview was a coherent one for the best part of 2000 years. However, in the secular Europe of today the tradition has undergone fragmentation. Whereas the past was characterized by one form or another of a strongly integrated system of afterlife, morality and creation in which death was followed by rewards or punishment, for most contemporary European people there is little connection between the afterlife, morality and creation. The most striking figures are those that reveal:

1. The low proportion of the general European population who believe in a personal God (some 30 per cent), particularly in

view of the high proportion of believers in some kind of God, and the low number of convinced atheists;
2. The low proportion who believe in an absolute morality (around 28 per cent);
3. The low proportion of believers in the existence of hell (close to 20 per cent), which is well below the proportions of the same populations who believe in some form of afterlife (around 45 per cent);
4. The surprisingly high proportion of believers in reincarnation (over 20 per cent), given that it is not part of, and indeed repugnant to, the European Christian tradition.

Davies argues that it is now apparent that nearly half the people of Europe believe in some kind of life after death, although they do not know exactly what that constitutes. However, less than a quarter believe in hell, roughly the same proportion as believe in reincarnation. It is also clear that belief in the afterlife and morality have become detached from one another. Likewise, the widespread belief in a non-personal God in a previously Christian culture shows that creation has been split apart from morality and the afterlife. The Western believers, however, are not following Hindu teachings of karma in that they do not see themselves having been or likely to be reincarnated as anything other than human. Neither does reincarnation appear to be attached to any moral code of behaviour.

To conclude, the evidence suggests that some of the doctrines essential to Christianity do not now hold a central place in the belief systems of the European population. Rather, that they have become part of the mix 'n' match of contemporary religiosity. Again, this is not a fresh development and Davies sees the fragmentation of coherent beliefs extending back into the nineteenth century, a characteristic of modernity, not post-modernity. While these figures show a clear change in adherence to Christianity in Europe, the USA is often held to be in many respects different in that its peoples adhere more strongly to Christian beliefs. However, even here there has been an increase in the percentage of the population indicating a faith outside of the three major traditions (Protestantism, Catholicism and Judaism) from 1 to 9 per cent (Roof and McKinney, 1985, p. 28).

Christian churches – institutional decline

The condition of contemporary Christianity is, nonetheless, more complicated than the above evidence might suggest. There are discernible areas of both decline and growth. The segment of decline, in terms of attendance and membership, appears to be in the more established mainline churches and denominations which may be said to constitute the 'respectable' face of Christianity. They may be compared in Stark and Bainbridge's (1985) typology of religious organizations (outlined in Table 7.2) with the more conservative and sectarian forms, since they generally display a low level of tension with the wider social environment. The growth area seems to be those expressions of Christianity more in tension with society, including some forms of sectarianism (a number of which are quasi-Christian sects such as Jehovah's Witnesses).

Table 7.2 Christian organizations and their tension with society

---

Extreme: sects which engender both ridicule and serious antagonism, even to the point of considerable legal intervention in their affairs. There will be socially unacceptable behaviour such as polygamous Mormon communes and/or all groups which are millenarian such as the Jehovah's Witnesses.

Very high: those groups regarded as quite deviant and displaying considerable friction with society, for example, many Pentecostal factions with their emphasis on such religious phenomena as 'gifts' of healing and speaking in tongues.

High: sectarian forms of religion, although there may be some concessions to wider social values.

Somewhat high degree of tension but enjoying some 'respectability', for example, the Southern Baptist Convention in the USA.

Moderate: very little tension with society – most denominations such as the American Baptist Church.

Low: groups which display a low degree of tension with their environment and have been fully transformed into churches.

Source: Adapted from Stark and Bainbridge (1985), p. 135.

The discussion of Christianity here is primarily concerned with expressions of the faith that range from 'Low' to 'Somewhat high' tension with the social environment; those that encompass main-line churches, denominations and conservative expressions of Christianity.

Church

The established Church is a particular type of religious institution. Troeltsch (1931) used the term to refer to a large religious organi-zation where belonging did not need any particular demonstration of faith and where the Church itself frequently attempted to be universal – to embrace all members of society. Individuals, then, are often 'born into' those faiths such as the Roman Catholic or Orthodox churches. In Troeltsch's classical model the Church will jealously guard its monopoly on religious truth and will not toler-ate challenges to its religious authority. To this end the Church, such as the Roman Catholic church, attempts to influence or even become part of the social and political establishment.

Today, perhaps as a sign of secularizing impulses, such tradi-tional churches that are to be found in many Western countries do not conform to a number of these characteristics. For example, in Britain, in 2000, fewer than 2 million of the overall population of 59 million belonged to the Church of England – historically the church of the state and the social establishment. Nor, today, do many traditional churches regard themselves as having exclusive truths, and happily work with other forms of mainline Christianity in ecumenical initiatives.

The fortunes of the established churches are on the wane. Casanova (1994) suggests that this is because they are incompatible with modern differentiated states and that the fusion of the religious and political community is incompatible with the modern princi-ple of democracy. This differentiation ensures the freedom of the state, of religion and the conscience of the individual. This invari-ably means a decline of centuries of power and privilege. It is for this reason that some churches still concern themselves with keep-ing hold of their historical monopoly of allegiance and religious truths. Certainly, in countries such as Spain, Italy and the Republic of Ireland, Roman Catholicism still attempts, with varying degrees of success, to be the universal religious authority over the nation as a whole. It is in these environments that Catholicism has often found itself in tension with society over such contentious issues as abortion. Political resistance to some of these changes has been expressed in Christian Democratic parties in countries of Western Europe with strong Catholic cultural roots (Buchanan and Conway, 1996).

Denominations

An early account by Niebuhr (1929) also typified denominations in terms of their membership. Thus, the denomination draws its membership from a fairly wide social spread although it is less likely to be derived from the upper class. Neither does the denomination identify with the state in the same way as the Church, or claim a monopoly of the truth. In addition, the denomination is fairly world-accommodating in terms of accepting prevailing social values. There is, then, little 'tension' with society.

A rather different definition of the denomination is offered by Roof and McKinney (1987). Here the key characteristics are the following:

1. The free, uncoerced consent of the individual and a type of religiosity emphasizing a practical, everyday faith;
2. The children of members are not automatically recruited and individuals have more control over their own faith than in churches;
3. The emphasis is more on living a moral life than accepting strict theological doctrines, while members are freer to make choices over issues of conscience;
4. Authority is more democratic than the centralized hierarchy of the Church typified by the Roman Catholic church, and tends to allow a high degree of autonomy for the local congregation.

The denomination, in contrast to the Church, is a common but relatively recent form of religious organization. In some countries, notably the USA, in the absence of an officially state-sanctioned Church, the denomination is the primary form of religious organization and may explain higher rates of church attendance. Here, the development of denominational pluralism is a qualitatively different phenomenon from the European historical dichotomy of Church and sect and is a logical response to the secular style of the

American constitution and the diversity of faiths. In an increasingly secular context, as Wilson (1968) suggests, denominational pluralism is an appropriate religious pattern of organization that has been diffused to most other English-speaking countries. Wilson argues that many of these denominational American churches display the minimum of ideological differences (being generally liberal in orientation) and function as voluntary associations, and this explains their resilience. The denominations are therefore primarily social and charitable institutions orientated to many of the needs of people in this world.

Liberalization

Generally speaking, there appears to have been an increasing liberalization of mainstream churches and denominations on both sides of the Atlantic, in theological terms and by way of social and moral outlooks. This is because certain developments have placed considerable pressures on these expressions of Christianity to become increasingly world-accommodating. Some of the pressures are exerted from the wider social environment, while others have built up within the Christian organizations themselves.

Institutional differentiation

Theories of the development of modernity would suggest that, at a very broad level, mainline Christianity has undergone the process of institutional differentiation and specialization evident in the rest of society (Wilson, 1976). In short, Christian churches have been forced to experience change as a result of wider social transformations. This has meant the standardization of a worldview in terms of well-defined doctrines, religious roles performed by specialists and an organization to control doctrinal and ritual conformity and promote organizational programmes.

Differentiation has been accompanied by rationalization and bureaucratization. For instance, the ministerial role has become increasingly professionalized, embracing achievement orientation and social mobility in line with wider society. Moreover, traditional church organization in the denominations, particularly in urban areas, has undergone modification. Typical is the USA, where churches have moved towards more stringent organizational structures, and have grown to embrace this-worldly theology which includes the acceptance of an ecumenical philosophy (Wilson, 1968, p. 74).

Many of these tendencies have proved to have implications even for some expressions of Christianity that initially set out to resist bureaucratization and rationalization and establish themselves aside from the world. Pentecostalism is a case in point. In its early days the movement turned its back on the world, shunned the institutional arrangements of other churches and wished to put the emphasis on unmediated spiritual experiences and loosely organized church structures. However, the pressures of the outside world, as much as the rapid growth of the movement, challenged its principal ideals. In rapid time, many of its major strands had established institutional structures (Poloma, 1989).

Even Christian, so-called 'intentional communities' cut off from the outside world, seem to be adapting themselves to the wider social environment. Typical are the Roman Catholic Jesuit orders, which hitherto may have approximated Goffman's model (1961) of the total institution – a completely encapsulated and totalitarian way of life. However, as Weigert (1971) discovered, the Jesuit orders are beginning to put a greater emphasis on individual development and lifestyles, and the more instrumental and pluralist values of the dominant society. Such a development is, according to Weigert, facilitated within the orders by their increasing rationalistic emphasis of means-ends and prevailing intellectualism. This is accompanied by the concern with non-coercive and potentially universalistic norms of enlightened obedience rather than any particularistic sacred behaviour and deference to traditional religious authorities.

'Relevance to modern man'

Although the Christian churches had long been racked by doctrinal and ecclesiastical divergence, a new source of division became significant in the nineteenth and early twentieth centuries, namely, a fundamentalist–modernist split that was often articulated through conservative–liberal theological debates. The debate is essentially stimulated by changes in the modern world and the challenges they offer to the faith. In the nineteenth century, theologically liberal churchmen foresaw the difficulties for the survival of Christianity posed especially by the separation of Church and state. To retain cultural power and influence, Christian intellectuals embarked on a process of accommodation, engaging with newly emergent scientific and philosophical traditions. The conservative-minded, by contrast, were concerned with how to resist such changes and hold on to what was perceived as the fundamentals of the faith.

Central to the liberal agenda, at least within Protestantism, was the felt need to be 'relevant to modern man'. Much of the inspiration here could be traced back to the theologian Schleiermacher who established a variant of Christianity that he saw making sense in the modern context. In many respects this marked what can be referred to as 'internal secularization' – an attempt to adapt to a rapidly changing and increasingly sceptical world. The imperative was to retain the basics of the faith whilst reducing the supernaturalist element that was to be judged in the light of human reason so that, typically, Biblical miracles were restricted to metaphors or said to have some 'deeper' moral significance.

A more cynical interpretation of the growth of a radical liberal theology, however, has been offered by Hofstadter (1955, pp. 151–2). The carriers of liberal reform were often clergymen. Liberalism became an ideology which they could use in their own interest. The profession had lost social status and was generally undermined by the decline in Christian observance and the advance of rationalism and science. The clergy were no longer the moral and intellectual leaders they once were. Embracing secular ideas restored some of their credibility, while they also came to have sympathy with other marginalized groups and thus embraced the call for reform and social criticism.

While Modernism, as the pre-1914 liberal theology was called, foundered under the impact of the First World War along with other forms of optimistic humanist theology, in the mid-twentieth century it arose with a new vigour. In Britain, in the 1960s, John Robinson's *Honest to God* created controversy by providing a critique of Christianity from within. It amounted to a search for the relevance of the faith in the face of an increasing secular society. Some were prepared to go further even if it meant considerably diluting and even abandoning many core aspects of faith. These included beliefs in the virgin birth, heaven and hell, Christ's bodily resurrection and His second advent. In Britain, two decades later, controversy was stirred in church circles when David Jenkins, the then Bishop of Durham, called the resurrection a 'conjuring trick with a bag of bones', hence denying its traditional supernaturalist interpretation.

In recent decades the liberals have embraced a range of touch-stone issues such as race, poverty, anti-capital punishment, anti-capitalism and toleration of homosexuality, which they sought to advance. In terms of relationship with other traditions of Christianity and even other faiths, the core agenda was ecumenism. The latter was not only partly a result of the decline of institutional religion but was ideologically seen by many as a progressive stage in the development of the Church. In short, that the Church's divisions and long-standing disputes could be overcome, and a new unity established.

The problem generated by this apparent progressive stance was that, in some respects, it was counter-productive. At the very least, the liberal defence of Christianity weakened its own cause. In attempting to be relevant to modern man, in directing itself to social issues and the ills of this world, liberal Protestantism lacked a clear theological mooring and eroded its own distinctively 'religious' base. The problem appears to be that liberal Christianity can deal with social issues, but that it is now so close to culture that it cannot retain a clear identity. In the USA, Johnson (1985) believes that trends suggest that liberal denominations will continue to decline. They have survived by championing social causes and advancing popular secular psychotherapeutic techniques that appealed to their congregations. However, they are now virtually devoid of new and stimulating ideas by which to influence society and bring membership growth.

There is evidence that it is the liberal mainline churches which have declined the fastest since the 1960s. Nevertheless, this should not mask the continuing influence of liberal Protestantism in American as a potent part of cultural life and a political force of some reckoning (Roof and McKinney, 1987, pp. 86–7). Likewise, in Britain, Peter Gee (1992) argues that liberalism should not be underestimated. He cites the number of liberal bishops in the House of Lords, numerous high-profile liberal churches, the number of broad-based inter-denominational liberal organizations such as the Christian Education Movement, and many 'single-issue' groups including Christian CND, the Lesbian and Gay Christian Movement and the various loosely knit Christian feminist networks. Moreover, if liberal Christianity has no clearly defined programme, argues Gee, it does have an implicit church agenda; pro-ecumenism, pro-women's ministry, pro-liturgical reform and pro-critical theology, while more liberal views of moral issues, such as the acceptability of divorce, is increasingly discernible among church members.

Gender issues: an index of liberalization?

Issues related to gender in contemporary Christian churches are very much tied up with the broader topic of liberalization, although they are by no means limited to the Christian faith. Indeed, the apparent increasing involvement of women in areas of authority would appear to provide a good index of liberalization in many forms of religiosity in the West. Hence, the philosophy of being 'relevant to modern man' has also been extended to women who, when in positions of ecclesiastical power, seemed to perpetuate the liberal cause. Women who do have the opportunity to serve in pastoral capacities frequently redefine these roles with a style which is often more relational, less authoritarian and more democratic – involving their laity in decisions and advancing a feminist theology (Carrol, Hargrove and Lummis, 1983).

In the public rituals of several major religions women's traditional roles have been clearly subordinate. Men have historically held all important leadership and symbolic functions, while women have been given lesser roles and excluded from positions of authority. Today, in many religious groups, women are pressing for changes in ritual symbols in order to reflect their experiences in the outside world and broader changing social attitudes. Much of the focus of some women's dissatisfaction has been seen in the pressure to permit greater participation in ritual and symbolic roles, such as the Roman Catholic Mass, because they are important expressions of male power and status.

It is the issue of the ordination of women that is the most controversial because of its great symbolic importance and because the role of the clergy is more powerful than the lay role and clearly presents an alternative image of women. The call for female ordination in the mainline Protestant denominations started in the

1880s at about the same time as the Women's Suffrage Movement began. Although some women were ordained in a few denominations in the early part of the twentieth century, it was only after the 1950s that a notable number were granted ordination. The Methodists and Presbyterian churches allowed women ministers beginning in the 1950s, and in the 1970s the Lutheran and Episcopalian churches followed but only after much controversy and some defection. The attitude of Christian denominations also varied. Studies in the USA and Europe show lay church members in mainline Protestant and Catholic churches to be generally positive about women in the ministry, although resistance may still be discerned from the laity sometimes afraid of controversy over the issue (Lehman, 1985).

Has anything like a true parity with men been achieved? Despite increasing numbers of women in seminaries, they are still greatly underappreciated in the clerical profession. Evidence of this is that the proportion of women in the ministry (4.2 per cent in 1980) was half that of women in medicine and law in the USA (cited in Carrol *et al.*, 1983). Moreover, despite ordination women are often underemployed, paid lower salaries and less likely to be considered for promotion or placated with some lesser role such as 'assistant minister' (Umansky, 1985).

There is also another way of interpreting women's increasing involvement in the church and that is what Wilson identifies as one overlooked aspect of secularization – the long-term decline of the clerical profession (Wilson, 1992, p. 198). Clerical salaries are now sub-professional and falling. The profession struggles to recruit well-qualified people, as indicated by the declining educational levels of the clergy (Towler and Coxon, 1979). It is also an ageing profession and as congregations decline so does the pool of people who might come forward into ministry. Crisis is temporarily averted by drawing on the unpaid services of lay volunteers, while women are allowed into the full-time profession. From this perspective, the liberal concession to women's participation in church life appears to result from other, more pragmatic considerations.

The conservative response

From the nineteenth century, as many Christian traditions attempted to accommodate the advances of science and respond positively to the modern world, there was a conservative reaction often articulated, at least within Protestantism, by sectarian schisms and fundamentalist expressions of Christianity. This was, for Berger (1979), an inevitable process that tended to polarize the faith between accommodation and reaction. The latter condemned the modernist tendencies in Protestant denominations and seminaries and resisted attempts to refine the faith by incorporating contemporary scientific beliefs, such as evolutionary theory. After the First World War the conservative defence of the faith came with the 'neo-orthodoxy' expressed in the theology of Karl Barth and others. Barth's view of the world was one which focused upon a literal interpretation of the Bible and which saw the social gospel as secondary to what the gospel message was really all about; saving man from sin, evil and suffering. The world was thus under God's wrath and judgement. Far from attempting to accommodate the world, conservative theology was more concerned with who was inside and who was outside the Christian community, and brought a heightened awareness of the so-called evils of the modern age.

The varying fortunes of conservative Christianity

The fortunes of conservative strands of Christianity have varied over time and from place to place in the Western context. In Europe there is mixed evidence. The attempt of liberal Christianity to be relevant and practical may have had the unintended effect of alienating people. Alternatively, in other cases, it is conservatism which has solicited this response. Sihvo (1988) suggests that in Finland people feel that the Lutheran Church has become too secularized; that it has nothing to say in terms of real personal faith. As a result, those leaving the churches may embrace more conservative forms of religion or abandon their religious faith altogether. In the Netherlands, however, Goddijn (1983) maintains that both the Dutch Reformed Church and the Roman Catholic Church have been conservative in social and cultural matters and have taken an authoritarian approach – one which has resulted in diminished church attendance. As these churches have reacted strongly to secularizing forces, 'progressively minded' people have left these churches because they are irrelevant to their lives. Conservative Christianity, then, appears to be marginalized and at odds with the world.

It is in the USA where the Protestant conservative constituency seems to be growing significantly, to the extent of undermining the secularization thesis. Roof and McKinney (1987) categorized the following churches in the USA as 'conservative': Southern Baptists, Church of Christ, Evangelical/fundamentalists, Nazarenes, Pentecostal/Holiness, Assemblies of God, Churches of God and Adventists. Using survey data they estimated that conservative Protestants made up nearly 19 per cent of the American population in 1984. The evidence indicates that these groups have been growing since the 1920s. In 1967, the Southern Baptist Convention overtook Methodists as the largest Protestant denomination. Other data suggests that up to one-third of Americans claim to be 'born-again' Christians – usually a badge of conservative evangelical Christianity (Stark and Bainbridge, 1980, p. 1). In terms of social impact, conservative Protestants have, according to James Hunter (1987), succeeded in widely publicizing and promoting their views in the USA. By the early 1980s they had set up 450 colleges and 18 000 schools, and established 275 periodicals, 70 evangelical publishing houses and 3300 Christian bookshops. Hunter does not claim, however, that the growth of conservative Protestantism disproves the secularization thesis, but does suggest that the process is complicated by cycles of secularity and religious upsurge.

Developments within Roman Catholicism

The liberal–conservative dichotomy is a complex one. As Gee (1992, p. 141) points out, it is sometimes misleading to differentiate between individual 'liberal' and 'conservative' churches and congregations. A survey of many supposedly liberal congregations would reveal a wide diversity of perspectives from extremely conservative to incoherently radical. At the same time it is important to realize that within different Christian traditions, there have been both movements of reform and reaction. This is abundantly clear in the Roman Catholic church.

Dobbelaere (1992, p. 122) argues that the Catholic church now has two theological options open to it in the contemporary world:

the 'Augustinian heritage' and the 'pagano-Christian heritage'. The former sees the contemporary Catholic church as facing a crisis of marginalization (similar to the period following the end of the Roman Empire and during the French Revolution). Under such conditions it may opt to confront aggressively the contemporary culture that ignores or undermines spiritual values, alongside the pluralism that leads to extreme individualism and social fragmentation. The second response could endorse a positive vision of the evolution of Western society towards democracy, and the secularity of civil institutions and culture. It is one which promotes dialogue with the world and is prepared to learn the point of view of others, and even admit past errors.

The hierarchy of the Catholic church, in recent decades, has wavered between these two responses. Up until the 1960s, the church practised a policy of 'cultural defence' and generated a 'collective–expressive' form of religious identity (Hornsby-Smith, 1992, p. 134). A strong religious socialization was an essential part of this strategy. Thus there still remains an emphasis on Catholic schools especially where these are strongly supported by close parochial links. Yet, from the mid-1960s, and exemplified by the reforming council Vatican II, Catholicism seemed to be setting out on the road that Protestantism had taken earlier in its search for accommodation with secular culture and other faiths. The church has thus increasingly engaged with the modern world. For instance, in the 1990s a top priority was given to the pursuit of peace – shown in the establishment of diplomatic relations between Israel and the Vatican, and the latter's support of peace accords in Northern Ireland and between Spain and the Basque separatists.

Even before Vatican II, a number of Pope Paul XXIII's encyclicals suggested reform. This included *Princeps Pastorum* (1959) which stressed lay participation; *Mater et Magistra* (1961) on social progress; and *Pacem in Terris* (1963) on peace. Also indicative of this new spirit was that, during the 1960s, there was the rapid translation of Latin Mass to the vernacular throughout numerous nations of the world. Nonetheless, membership reduction, loss of authority, the declining involvement of church members and the dissolution of the distinctive Catholic sub-culture brought about more reactionary tendencies by the mid-1970s. In many countries, even those with a Catholic minority, the Roman Catholic church stood firm against the temptation to compromise with the emerging post-Christian culture and held a hard line against theological and moral compromise. More than other Christian traditions, Catholicism's responses were dictated by the global strategies of the Church. However, it was a resistance strongest in those contexts far less affected by modernization and industrialization than the pluralist cultures of North West Europe and North America.

In this period of reaction, a familiar pattern emerged. In age-old tradition, claims Dobbelaere (1992), the Catholic church, when faced with crisis, has turned to its three policies of centralization, the charismatic authority of the Pope and the accentuation of the special position of priests. This has proved to have mixed success. The first strategy involves the appointment and dismissal of bishops, as well as professors of theology and editors of periodicals, and the authoritarian imposition of matters related to faith and morals. This included frequent pronouncements by Papal nuncios that bishops should conform to policies preferred by Rome; in recent years, the Vatican has also increasingly been dominated by conservative bishops. Secondly, the emphasis on the charisma of the Pope has meant that Pope John Paul has been presented to the world as having extraordinary capacities and in the role of world leader.

The third strategy, the enhanced status of the priesthood, has not been forthcoming. Indeed, there has been a loss of status, which has come to have considerable implications. The priesthood appears to have lost prestige in the eyes of lay people. Partly, this results from the marked decline of private confession even in such countries as the Irish Republic where the faith has remained very much alive. This is partly because Catholics are increasingly less inclined to believe in an intermediary between the individual and God. Also, the Eucharist, administered by priests, is seen as more of a commemorative ritual rather than the traditional magical re-enactment of the 'primary' salvation by Christ. The priesthood and its function have thus been 'demystified' and put on a par with the Protestant ministry. Consequently, claims Dobbelaere (1992, p. 118), many Catholics have become endeared to the idea of abolishing clerical celibacy and opening the priesthood to women. Moreover, while some 50 per cent of parishes across the world are without a priest, around a quarter of priests leave the church very often to get married and at a time when the ban on women clergy is retained.

Such developments, however, should not suggest that Roman Catholicism is in a wholesale state of reaction. The responses by the Catholic Church, both its ecclesiastical hierarchy and laity, to the modern world indicate a complexity perhaps greater than that found in other Christian traditions. There are thus movements of reform alongside those of conservatism. Moreover, there is evidence of considerable variability of both belief and practice of belonging, and of customary forms of religion. Certainly, far from being a tightly structured belief system, Catholic doctrines and attitudes have become highly differentiated. Hence, in terms of belief and belonging, Dobbelaere (1992, p. 119) refers to a 'pick and choose Catholicism' – an individualistic form of faith where people can decide on the merits of ethical and doctrinal problems.

To some extent, as Hornsby-Smith suggests (1987, pp. 89–115), there has been dissolution of the defensive walls around the previously distinctive Catholic sub-culture. Indeed, there have been strong indications of a substantial convergence, at least in the case of Catholics in England, towards the norms of the general population on matters such as contraception and divorce and to a lesser degree, abortion. In addition, today, a liberal or 'progressive' wing has developed in the Catholic church and, according to Hornsby-Smith, can be identified in the following ways. First, in having a 'post-Vatican II theology': a critical orientation to the Church and its authority, advocating liturgical change, and a community emphasis. Secondly, a this-worldly religious stance including a socio-political commitment and anti-nuclear weapons preference. Thirdly, a call for the liberation from 'sinful' social structures and a rejection of traditional, sexual and marital proscriptions.

Today, then, there is evidence of considerable variability of both belief and practice in the Catholic church, and the decline of customary forms of religion reflecting the breakdown of processes of religious socialization. On the other hand, a more traditionalist wing still exists which holds tight to Catholic dogma and praxis. Indeed, Archer (1986) has gone so far as to argue that there have developed two 'churches' in the West – one comprised of traditional working-class Catholics and one that is more progressive and middle-class.

What, then, of the future of the Catholic church? Although church attendance and membership has declined rapidly in many Western countries, they have been noticeably slower than for mainline Protestant churches. Two decades ago David Martin (1978) pointed out that in such countries as France, Spain, Italy, the Irish Republic and Portugal, the Roman Catholic church retained an important, if declining social role. It still influenced government policy in areas such as education and laws relating to marriage, divorce, contraception and abortion. In these countries church attendance was relatively high since there was little religious pluralism and divisions were inclined to be within the Catholic church rather than between different religious organizations. Other countries, like West Germany and Switzerland, were split between a Protestant majority and a large Catholic minority. In these countries Roman Catholicism tended to have an allegiance among the less affluent. This effectively broke the connection between social and political elites as found elsewhere. By contrast, where there was a dominance of Protestant churches but with a large Catholic majority, secularization was likely to be more rapid than where Roman Catholicism inclined towards a monopoly.

Martin's version of what amounts to his rendering of the secularization thesis is a sophisticated one. However, Catholic church attendance in recent years is rapidly approaching that of the Protestant churches. Yet, it is not all gloom and doom. Crippen (1988) argues that the future of traditional churches such as the Roman Catholic may be quite rosy. As Western societies grow in size and structural complexity, the elements of traditional religious consciousness do not simply disappear; instead they, too, transform in conjunction with changing economic and political circumstances. For instance, the Roman Catholic strongholds of southern Europe appear to be relinquishing their social and political significance. However, they may, like other expressions of Christianity, embrace certain aspects of Western culture which are compatible with the belief system. This might be referred to as a kind of 'selective de-traditionalization' whereby traditional Christianity becomes more democratic in structure and closer to grass-roots sensitivities. It may also attempt to relate to contemporary issues as did Pope John Paul II, in 1989, when he proclaimed the first papal statement devoted exclusively to ecological issues.

Charismatic renewal

Perhaps the most noteworthy movement within Roman Catholicism in recent decades has proved to be the charismatic renewal movement. However, it is by no means limited to Catholicism and it is probably correct to say that it has been *the* significant strand of Christianity in the West in recent decades. The movement cut across the Roman Catholic–Protestant divide and came to have global implications (Martin, 1990). It also proved to be, at least in the West, an alternative Christian reaction to the challenges of the secular world.

In his work *The Heretical Imperative* (1979), Peter Berger outlines the three possible responses of Christianity to the challenges of the modern world. First, as we have seen, an accommodation to the world and a demystification of Biblical myths evident in liberal theorizing. Secondly, to defend the faith through a Biblical literalism. This response is displayed in conservative and fundamentalist interpretations of the Bible. Thirdly, by attempting to rediscover the spirit that started the faith and to live out the experience of early Christianity. Such was the self-assigned aim of charismatic renewal.

Renewal movements, of this type, inside and outside the established churches, litter the history of Christianity in the West. For example, by the end of the eighteenth century practically all Christian denominations, including Orthodox, Catholic and Protestant churches had experienced revitalization alongside the emergence of new movements ranging from the Wesleyan revival in Britain, to the New England 'Great Awakenings' in the USA. In the mid-twentieth century the charismatic renewal movement rapidly spread across the USA, to Europe and beyond – permeating various Christian traditions. Otherwise known as neo-Pentecostalism, it began as a fresh version of an older religious manifestation. The earlier Pentecostal movement, with its own legendary origin at the Azusa Street mission in San Francisco in 1906, and its counterpart in Britain during the Welsh Revival, is now typically referred to as 'classical' Pentecostalism. In time-honoured tradition it was, in essence, a sectarian movement which set its face against the established denominations of the time and eschewed institutionalized ecclesiastical arrangements. Its distinctive features were the doctrine of 'baptism in the Spirit' and an emphasis upon the charismata including speaking in tongues, prophecy and healing.

Pentecostalism emerged in the 1960s in the form of a renewal movement inside the historical denominations, although it also inspired the creation of numerous independent evangelical congregations. It advocated the return to the pristine condition of the first-century Church in order to reverse decline. For those involved in the movement this meant a spiritual renewal where the terms 'revival', 'awakening', or the 'outpouring of the Holy Spirit' were frequently used to designate a return to the Pentecostal experiences of early Christianity in an attempt to counter the growing routinization and general demise of the Church.

Like its predecessors, the renewal movement confronted increasing secularization, rationalism, disbelief and pluralism. For many church leaders it appeared to be a force capable of arresting the long-term decline of Christianity in the West. It was able both to attract people indifferent to mainstream denominations and to infuse elements within almost every denominational community with a spiritualism capable of transcending established ecclesiastical loyalties. Roman Catholics and Protestants came together in a kind of ecumenical movement to discover what united rather than separated them 'in the Spirit'. On the other hand, it was often divisive and some church leaders frequently feared the threat of entire local congregations going over to Pentecostalism and losing respect for traditional authority and liturgy.

The renewal movement impacted in varying degrees in Western countries. In the USA it became rather lost in the general rising tide of Christian conservatism. In many parts of Europe it was inclined to be a short-lived growth area in Christianity across the denominational divide. While many conservative and liberal churches fell into decline, the charismatic movement brought new life to many others. Within twenty years however, it had run out of steam. As it began to flounder, it fairly rapidly diluted some of its principal elements. The supernaturalist component was one which began to fade as the movement impacted on churches hitherto untouched by renewal. While this can be attributed to the relentless process of the routinization of charisma in the sense that a spiritual revolution was becoming more ritualized, its watering down was also in order to widen its appeal and increase its 'marketability'. By the 1990s, the growth area in the movement was the churches that had adapted themselves to a distinct Christian sub-culture. They have come to constitute what Harvey Cox calls 'designer churches' that wished to be judged by the speed of growth of their congregations, funds available, attractive buildings and other hallmarks of success which reflected the wider enterprise culture (Cox, 1994, p. 272).

The market model and the churches

Neo-Pentecostalism has come to exemplify the tendency for many forms of Christianity adapting to the spiritual marketplace. Hammond (1986) suggests that the decline of religion in the West as indicated by the loss of the 'established' status for the Christian churches, the separation of Church from state and the voluntary organizational status of religious participation, has meant that religious groups are now forced to see themselves as units in a market, competing for the time, loyalty and money of a limited clientele. In this situation, churches now largely behave in the same way as secular, commercial units operate in their markets; with an eye to mass appeal, advertising and sensitivity to competition, 'profit' innovation and so forth. For Hammond a significant implication is that pressures towards ecumenism are partly a result of pressures to gain some measure of control over the ecclesiastical cost/benefit ratio. Whatever its theological rationale, the ecumenical movement among the mainline Protestant denominations, at least, is also an effort to 'rationalize' a very competitive market.

Church-switching

That contemporary Christianity has adapted itself to the contemporary religious marketplace is also discernible through church-switching – a relatively common phenomenon, especially in the USA. Several studies have shown that some 40 per cent of the US population have switched denominations at least once (Roof and McKinney, 1987, p. 165). Trends towards changing are most common in liberal Protestantism because of the long tradition of encouraging freedom of choice (Roof and McKinney, 1985, p. 34). However, it is increasingly the case that church-switching also explains, rather ironically, the growth of conservative churches. The steady growth of conservative churches since the 1950s was linked to the declining membership of the liberal churches and the marked de-mobilization of denominational constituencies (Bibby and Brinkeroff, 1983). Although the evidence was sometimes questioned, the widespread belief among some American academics was that people were steadily leaving the liberal churches for the attractions offered by the more conservative variety.

An alternative explanation, which was outlined by Bibby (1978), suggested that it was only some conservative churches that were expanding. He argued that conservative churches were largely 'circulating saints' among themselves. In other words, people were moving between one conservative church and another because of what individual churches had to offer. A variation of this, as exemplified by Mauss and Perrin's survey (1989) of the highly successful Association of Vineyard Churches, is that there is evidence of members of successful conservative churches having conducted a period of 'shopping' in the conservative segment of the religious marketplace after becoming disenchanted with the mainstream churches.

The thrust of Mauss and Perrin's account emerges from the debate with the highly influential work of Kelley (1978) on successful religious movements. They argued that Kelley was essentially correct in that 'seekers' in the religious marketplace are looking for 'the essential functions of religion', that is, 'making life meaningful in ultimate terms' (Kelley, 1978, p. 166), but that he was largely incorrect in that successful churches do not demand personal commitment and self-sacrifice through a change in lifestyle. Kelley emphasized that conservative religion makes demands on members in terms of belief and lifestyle. By contrast, liberal denominations have been less successful because they do not offer a comparable religious certainty. They are pluralistic and open-minded, and do not demand great conformity. On many issues their theology cannot easily be distinguished from alternative secular ideas.

Mauss and Perrin, however, argue that successful conservative churches strive to accommodate lifestyles at the same time that they are able to provide a belief system of great meaning. The key point is that this accommodation of lifestyles by market orientated conservative forms of Christianity might be more evidence of the relentless process of secularization in the sense that religion generally adapts to the prevailing cultural environment, and finds it difficult to sustain itself in its more sectarian forms. What might be referred to as 'New Paradigm churches' – the large independent and post-denominational churches – combine a biblical literalism with a more self-centred spirituality. The attraction of those such as Calvary Chapel, Vineyard Christian Fellowship and Hope Chapel is the emphasis on personal conviction and experience, alongside attractive lifestyles and an emphasis on the development of self.

Wuthnow (1993) maintains that this increasingly user-friendly nature of contemporary Christianity is also linked to the problem in identifying where the spiritual life begins and identifying where secular culture ends. In short, there is an increasing difficulty faced by the Christian churches in channelling the individual into a single religious worldview against the backdrop of cultural and functional pluralism. Wade Roof (1994, pp. 104–5) makes a similar point. He suggests that in the Western world there has always existed a contradiction between Christianity and wider cultural norms. However, this is a gulf which invariably widens in the contemporary setting. The essential disharmony is that traditional Christianity has always advanced the values of altruism, self-sacrifice and community concern, whereas Western culture is increasingly self-centred, individualistic and egoistic. Accommodating cultural values and giving scope to secular life experiences helps overcome some of these discrepancies and aids the survival of the faith into the next millennium.

Summary

It is evident from the broad discussion of contemporary Christianity in this chapter that the various strands of the tradition have undergone many challenges and changes. Indeed, so varied have the developments been that it is difficult to draw conclusions about the future. The key element may be that of choice. This is a theme explored by Hervieu-Leger (1998), who maintains that the increasing significance of choice in religious life means that people can legitimately choose between a variety of orientations and commitment to the Christian faith. Hervieu-Leger distinguishes four basic dimensions in what is largely a post-modernist account of religion today and the choices which it presents:

1. *The communal dimension*: this refers to the social and symbolic expressions of belonging to a community including undergoing initiation and submitting to the foundation of the faith;
2. *The ethical dimension*: this involves accepting the values of a particular tradition such as the morality of Catholicism;
3. *The cultural dimension*, which encompasses the heritage of doctrines, texts, rituals, history, legends, art and folkways;
4. *The emotional dimension*: intense experience generated by religious assemblies, as emphasized in Durkheim's work.

These four dimensions interact with one another and engender six different types of religious identification which are evident within the context of Christianity:

1. *Emotional Christianity*, combining the emotional and communal dimension as in Catholic pilgrimages;
2. *Patrimonial Christianity*, combining the cultural and communal. People identify with the religious tradition as a cultural heritage marking 'us' from 'them'; for instance, a particular form of Christianity may be linked to national identification;
3. *Humanitarian Christianity*, combining the emotional and ethical, in an orientation that attempts to overcome deprivation and justice through social action;
4. *Political Christianity*, which combines the communal and ethical. Compared to the humanitarian expression, political Christianity adopts a militant conception of the role of the church in bringing about socio-political change;
5. *Humanist Christianity*, which combines the cultural and ethical. It appeals to particular forms of intellectualism associated with cultural capital which enables a selection of certain aspects of Christianity as a value system;
6. *Aesthetic Christianity*, which combines the cultural and the emotional. This involves extolling the virtues of the aesthetic inheritance of Christianity such as its art and literature – a form of sophisticated self-indulgent tourism.

The relationship between these six modes of identification with Christianity and the mainstream churches is fluid and changeable. The important aspect is that the post-modern condition allows the increasing ability of believers to assert their right to a version of Christianity most to their choosing.

8 Sectarianism and Fundamentalism

Fundamentalism and sectarianism are frequently regarded as extreme, bizarre, or even dangerous forms of religion, at odds with mainstream society and outside established faiths. Certainly, a fair amount of public ignorance exists regarding the motivations, aims and beliefs of these expressions of religiosity. At the same time, a great deal of sociological ink has been spilt discussing sectarianism and, more lately, the related area of fundamentalism. This preoccupation is understandable given the proliferation of sects throughout the nineteenth and early twentieth centuries, and their apparent increase in recent years. Sects are of interest at least because they provide opportunities to examine the membership, processes of conversion, 'deviant' beliefs and practices and the social and ecclesiastical dynamics which generate distinct forms of religious organization. The interconnected area of fundamentalism is of no less interest to sociology. Indeed, it is one of the most noteworthy developments in contemporary religion, having a widespread significance within the context of globalization, and an increasingly high profile within Western secular societies.

Sectarianism – early typologies

Many of the early sociological accounts of sects were concerned not so much with classifying them as unique forms of religious organization, but specifically as distinct types of collectives within the Christian tradition. This not only reflected the rather ethnocentric view of the world employed by early theorists, but the fact that there is something intrinsic about Christianity that makes it

121

more likely to develop a wide range of organizational types than other faiths such as Hinduism which do not exhibit the same kind of tension with the world (Martin, 1965, pp. 10, 22). It is debatable, therefore, whether the Church-sect typologies can be applied in any meaningful sense outside the Christian context.

The usual starting point in a discussion of sects is the work of Troeltsch (1931). Troeltsch differentiated sects from churches on several grounds and, like other models of religious collectives, included the degree of organizational differentiation, specialization and complexity, as well as orientation towards the outside world. His typology is illustrated and critiqued here with contemporary examples. Troeltsch identified the principal characteristics as follows:

Sects are fairly small and well integrated in terms of membership

Sects, like cults, have generally tended to be smaller, less complex organizations than churches and denominations. However, in the nineteenth and early twentieth centuries (the period with which Troeltsch was familiar), there occurred the proliferation of numerous very small sects, some of which have grown extremely large, particularly in recent decades. For instance, the Jehovah's Witnesses, at least according to the organization's own statistics, appear to be have expanded in Britain from nearly 98 000 in 1980 to nearer 115 000 in 2000.

Rather than drawing members from all sections of society and being closely connected with the state, sects are associated with the lowest social strata

According to Troeltsch, this was especially so with those opposed to the social and economic status quo. However, the identification of the sect with the lower class and the Church with middle or dominant classes is harder to sustain today. Since the 1960s, as part of the wider picture of profound religious transformation, sects appear to be multiplying. In the USA, at least, the growth seems to be more obviously linked to the recruitment of marginal and disadvantaged groups. For instance, the Black Muslim movement provides for the needs of many poor Blacks. Although, beginning in the 1930s among Afro-Americans, the movement grew at a time of pressure for civil rights in the 1960s and began to attract middle-class members.

Sects reject the world and the values of mainstream society

There are many forms of sectarianism that illustrate this. Albeit a small Protestant denomination with straightforward evangelical Christian beliefs, the Exclusive Brethren, which originated in Dublin in 1872, today rejects many of the values and developments of the wider social environment and imposes its own values including a prohibition on watching television and using computers.

Sect members are expected to withdraw from the outside world

In the case of the Exclusive Brethren, socializing with anyone outside the fellowship is prohibited. The children of the sect are educated in normal state schools, but are not allowed to take part in competitive sports or any extra-curricular activity, and are strongly discouraged from making any friends outside the sect. University education is not sanctioned since it is believed that student life is full of wickedness and temptation.

The problem with this appraisal of the sect and its apparent tension with the world however, is that as we have seen, some more recent forms of sectarianism, such as the 1970s Jesus movement (Fox and Adams, 1972), appear to reintegrate social outcasts back into society and inculcate at least some mainstream values.

Sect members are expected to be deeply committed to beliefs and demonstrate that commitment

The Exclusive Brethren, for instance, will exclude from their fellowship anyone who does not share their beliefs and does not adhere to absolute standards of purity. This creates a kind of mutual surveillance.

Sect members join voluntarily as adults rather than being socialized into the sect

While children of the sect are brought up to accept its teachings, as adults they are expected to make the decision to opt for membership or leave.

Sects believe that they have a monopoly of the truth

Sects are likely to claim they have superior beliefs. This may even extend to a claimed monopoly of 'correct' doctrines. Hence, the

Jehovah's Witnesses prefer to describe themselves not as a religion, but as *the* 'Truth'. In many cases some particular beliefs are often stressed and held to be a badge of a self-assigned elite status and help constitute the boundaries with other religious groups. At the beginning of the twentieth century the emerging Pentecostal movement insisted that its members spoke in 'tongues' and in so doing drew boundaries with what was regarded as nominal Christianity.

There is also the tendency for sects to denounce other churches and refuse fellowship with them. Exclusive Brethren keep apart from every other Christian collective. They hold their exclusivity as a primary virtue by refusing to share the Eucharist with those outside the sect 'in view of maintaining suitable conditions for partaking of the Lord's Supper' (Barrett, 1998, p. 70).

Sects have no hierarchy of paid officials or priesthood

The development of a specialized ministry, bureaucracy and formal organization, according to Troeltsch, seems to accompany Church-like forms, but not sects. However, this is not always the case. Both Jehovah's Witnesses and Scientology are highly differentiated and complex organizations, while also retaining their negative view of society. To allow for this variable, the terms 'established sect' and 'established cult' (Nelson, 1968) have been reserved for highly organized groups that retain their sectarian or cultist stance.

Sect transformation

In his discussion of the processes that lead to the development of sects, Troeltsch (1931) built upon some of the earlier insights of Max Weber. Weber (1965) had argued that the routinization of charisma meant that many religions would begin in sectarian form (as had Christianity in developing as a sect out of Judaism). Here, a more bureaucratic form of organization emerges and eventually, over time, the sect loses its initial impetus. The authority based on charismatic leadership becomes routinized through the traditional or legal–rational authority of official and priestly office. In this situation, the sect becomes a break-away group of believers who seek to take the religion back to its perceived 'true' origins by way of beliefs, practices and lifestyles. As schismatic groups, sects like to present themselves to the world as something older, seceding from a tradition which has drifted into apostasy, not as an entirely new phenomenon. In Christianity, this has often been accompanied with claims to restoring the first-century Church. This is the philosophy of the Exclusive Brethren and Jehovah's Witnesses both of whom embrace the idea of restoring the 'true' Church after 2000 years of apostasy and heresy. Such sects tend to emphasize simplicity of worship, with no ritual or set form of service, since it is envisaged as a return to first-century practice.

Troeltsch starts with the assumption that different religious outlooks will be expressed in different types of religious organization. Working largely within the framework of Christianity, he distinguished two broad tendencies in early Christianity which led to rather different types of religious organization. One emphasized the egalitarian community outside of mainstream society. This orientation tended to play down organization and hierarchy. The other tendency stressed the independently organized community, which attempted to make use of the surrounding social institutions for its own ends. The former displayed a radical inclination and the latter a more conservative one. While the conservative tendency associated with the Church came to dominate, the radical variation expressed itself in discrete ways including monasticism and sectarianism. The Church comes to largely accept the secular order and 'desires to cover the whole life of humanity' (Troeltsch, 1931, p. 331), while utilizing the state and appealing to the ruling classes in becoming an integral part of the social order. In contrast the sect, which throughout the history of Christianity has typically broken away from the Church and condemned its worldliness, has attracted the lower classes who feel oppressed by the state and are opposed to the status quo.

Troeltsch's model has proved a constructive one in understanding developments within the history of Christianity. His two typologies obviously still have some validity, as does his third type of religious expression which he calls 'mysticism'. Here doctrine and worship give way to purely personal and inward spiritual experience and conviction. Historically, it was rather unique in that it was linked to the growth of individualism in medieval towns. It is characterized by a free fellowship of believers with little by way of organization, and appears to be particularly attractive to the prosperous middle classes. This typology has nonetheless been exploited in understanding contemporary expressions of faith. For instance, Thompson considers the Roman Catholic charismatic renewal movement as close to Troeltsch's mysticism. He sees it as a loosely organized movement operating within church structures, and based on a form of mysticism that is particularly attractive to middle-class people (Thompson, 1974).

By developing some of Weber's ideas, Niebuhr's work (1929) also marked an important milestone in the discussion of sect transformation. His focus was upon what he identified as an endless cycle of Church-sect development. Niebuhr argued that sects tended to attract marginalized members of society. For such individuals, the sect brought a new status and, often through millenarian themes, stressed a new set of values in conflict with the world, attacking injustices and embracing the hope for the imminent return of Christ. In turn, the sect is denounced by the established churches as heretical, extremist and unrepresentative.

For Niebuhr, the sect was not capable of surviving long. It would either adapt itself to prevailing circumstances or die. Moreover, there was the 'problem' of the second generation. In short, the second generation of adherents to the sect would generally fail to have the zeal and commitment of the first. At the same time, the years of this-worldly asceticism would bring prosperity to later generations which would lift them out of poverty and help integrate them into the wider social environment. As the sect developed into a more worldly orientated Church, a new sect might emerge as part of an endless cycle. The history of Christianity is littered with instances of such developments. A recent example is within the Seventh-Day Adventist movement. Although itself beginning as a sect, numerous small factions have broken away from it. Since the 1980s, various organizations have sprung up which are often referred to as 'independent ministries'. These ministries have the avowed aim of bringing Adventists back to the 'pillars of the faith'. One, known as 'Hope for Today', calls for members to come out of 'apostasy' back into the 'truth' because the official Adventist church is perceived to be in danger of becoming part of 'Babylon' – the evil world order (Porter, 1992, p. 199).

In turn, other sociologists have attempted to develop some of these earlier theories of sectarianism or have offered critiques. One of the most significant contributions has come from Bryan Wilson

(1970) who rejects Niebuhr's view that sects are inevitably short-lived. He points out that some sects do survive for a long time without becoming denominations or churches. For Wilson, the crucial factor as to whether they do or do not is the way a sect answers the question 'What shall we do to be saved?'. One type, the 'conversionist sect', is likely to evolve into a denomination and this is typically the pattern in the USA. The aim of this type of sect is to convert as many people as possible by means of revivalist preaching. Becoming a denomination, and developing the organizational structure necessary for proselytization, does not necessarily compromise its position. The other type of sect is the 'adventist sect'. Seventh-Day Adventists and Jehovah's Witnesses, like many others that arose in the nineteenth century, await the Second Coming of Christ that will establish a new order in which sect members are guaranteed a place. These sects preach a separation from the world. To become a denomination they would have to compromise this position. In discussing transformations within contemporary Western societies, Wilson recognizes that the process of sect transformation to denomination was speeding up and that this was an indication of the influence of an increasingly secular society.

In turn, Wilson's work on sects has inspired others – particularly his emphasis on the separateness and distinctiveness of the sect and its claim to possess the 'truth'. Perhaps the most significant contribution in this respect has been Robertson's four-fold classification of religious organizations showing the difference between sects and other organizations and likely sect developments.

Robertson's classification uses two sets of distinction to create four categories (Figure 8.1). First, there is 'Inclusive membership' – membership open to anyone, as opposed to 'Exclusive membership' where some test or qualification of eligibility is required. Then, there is what he calls the self-conceived basis of legitimacy which the sect takes as either a claim to sole possession of truth or an acknowledgement that other religious groups also possess at least elements of truth.

Sectarianism – variations on a theme

The infinite complexity of sect–denomination–church transformation has informed more recent sociological and historical accounts

Self-conceived basis of legitimacy

		Pluralist legitimate	Uniquely legitimate
	Exclusive	Institutionalized Sect	Sect
Membership principle			
	Inclusive	Denomination	Church

Figure 8.1 Robertson's classification of religious organizations (from Robertson, 1970)

of religious organizations. While using some of the earlier key typologies it is clear that an infinite variation of organizations exists.

Sectarian communal collectives

The intentional community is where members choose to live together communally and are generally separated from the outside world. In the Christian tradition this has largely been in the form of monastic communities which date back to the sixth century. One alternative is when a religious community withdraws from society in order to preserve its distinctiveness including the Jewish Hassidim and a variety of Anabaptist groups including the Brüderhof. In the case of the Hassidim, an ultra-orthodox group of Jews, their withdrawal is not to a rural refuge, but retreat into distinct urban areas in order to retain a religious identity. Today intentional communities are also represented by Pentecostal groups and new religious movements (NRMs) such as Krishna Consciousness. Monastic orders, using Wilson's definition, can be seen to be forms of sects within established churches (Hill, 1971). While such collectives tend to last longer than the non-religious so-called 'intentional communities' which became so popular in the 1960s, they have proved increasingly harder to sustain economically.

Church transformations

Churches also may experience sectarian orientations as a result of changes in the wider social environment. If a Church is unable to maintain its monolithic status, it may not continue as a church-type collectivity. Churches that retain their claims to unique legitimacy are likely to take on sect-like characteristics. This was so with the Roman Catholic church of early twentieth-century immigrants to the USA which maintained a highly sectarian stance to protect its members from the beliefs and practices of the predominantly Protestant culture.

Sects within churches

In his study of charismatic Roman Catholics, Harper (1974) outlines commitment to a 'sect' type of organization within an established Church, in that it has a small, unbureaucratic, voluntary membership which nonetheless is subject to strict social control. It includes a focus on religious socialization, an ambivalence towards the institutional Church and its teachings, an emphasis on the 'Pentecostal' conversion experience and a stress on constant membership interaction ranging from loosely related prayer cells to large-scale renewal conferences.

Denominational transformations

History provides several examples of groups arising out of churches in the form of a denomination rather than a sect. For instance, the Reform movement among the Jews was, from the start, more tolerant towards society than Orthodox Judaism and established denominational structures. Alternatively, a religious group may move from a denominational basis and develop more sect-like elements. The Salvation Army became a sect after its more pluralistic beginnings. Similarly, some Southern Baptist denominations, through their increasing fundamentalism, have resorted to a greater degree of sectarianization (Ammerman, 1987).

New religious movements

Some NRMs may take sectarian form along the lines outlined by

Troeltsch. This means that new types of religion do not conform to established patterns of growth since many are not break-aways from established churches, even though others are. Unique features including the age and background of participants (see Chapter 10), the combining of elements of the counter-culture, and in some cases a fairly democratic internal structure, mark them out as distinctly different from the classical model of the sect (Davies and Richardson, 1976, p. 339).

Sects and deprivation

The link between sectarian membership and deprivation has been an important and enduring dimension of the study of sects. In the earlier sociological work, deprivation usually meant poverty and social marginalization. However, in accounting for the rise of sectarian-type groups, Glock (1958) stretched the notion of deprivation to understand how sects in various ways provide a channel through which their members are able to transcend their feelings of deprivation by replacing them with feelings of religious privilege. Sect members no longer compare themselves in terms of their relatively lower economic position but by way of their superior religious status. The principal forms of perceived deprivation are:

- *Economic deprivation* – a subjective criterion by which people feel themselves underprivileged in terms of the distribution of incomes;
- *Social deprivation* – underprivilege in whatever society regards as important such as prestige or power, often in modern society youthfulness, male superiority, or reward by merit;
- *Organismic deprivation* – levels of mental or physical health not matching up to society's standards;
- *Ethical deprivation* – when the individual feels that the dominant values of society no longer provide a meaningful way by which to conduct life and a desire to find another set of values;
- *Psychic deprivation* – which results from a consequence of severe and unresolved social deprivation. The individual is not missing the material advantages of life but has been denied its psychic rewards.

Where these conditions exist, according to Glock, the organizational structure to overcome deprivation may be religious or secular. Religious resolutions are more likely to occur where the nature of the deprivation is inaccurately perceived or where those experiencing the deprivation are not in a position to work directly at eliminating the causes. The resolution is likely to be secular under conditions where deprivation is correctly assessed by those experiencing it and they have the power to deal with it directly. Religious resolutions, then, are likely to compensate for feelings of deprivation rather than to eliminate its causes. However, sects may bring resolutions as effectively as secular ones in the case of ethical and psychic deprivation. Different sects appear to cluster around distinct deprivations. For example, organismic deprivation may attract ideas about new forms of healing. Some sects are also longer-lived than others. Those dealing with merely ethical deprivation tend to be rather short-lived.

Social dislocation

Another interpretation of the emergence of sects (and cults) suggests that they arise and respond to the problems of social dislocation. The Holiness movement, an off-spring of Pentecostalism, spread rapidly in the 1930s among rural people who had migrated to urban environments (Holt, 1940). Similarly, the continued emergence of sects in New York State over a long period of time may have correlated with the anomic conditions caused by dramatic economic fluctuation which produced periods of alternating rising expectation and disappointment (Barkun, 1986). Sects bring certainty in a time of uncertainty and ambiguity.

The significance of sects is that they allow members to protest against the environment in which they find themselves, whilst simultaneously overcoming some of the difficulties of dislocation by finding a new community in small, close-knit networks that operate as a kind of surrogate family. A present example would be the British-based Jesus Fellowship – a community-orientated fundamentalist group which claims a membership of some 2500 (Hunt, 1998). At the core are leaders who are well-educated, middle-class committed Christians that have sought a deeper expression of spiritual life. Beyond this core group is the rank and file drawn from the 'underclass' of young homeless people often with a background of alcoholism, drug abuse or family breakup. The Jesus Fellowship offers shelter, rehabilitation, a puritan lifestyle and moral support to what it calls 'generation X'. A slogan of the fellowship is one borrowed from the Salvation Army in the nineteenth century: 'Those who do not belong to anyone else belong to us.'

Sectarian organizations

Recruitment

Some sectarian forms of religion are clearly more successful than others. Hence, a measure of sociological work has been geared towards finding out how the apparently successful recruit, consolidate and deploy members, and how they maintain their organization and arrange leadership. Gerlach and Hine (1970) have shown that there were various organizational factors which allowed Pentecostalism to spread and consolidate (these were also found to exist within political Black Power movements as well). They included:

1. The relationship among networks of local groups of the movement which provided a flexibility that promoted the movement's spread;
2. The recruitment along the lines of pre-existing social relationships, including social class, family and friends;
3. An emphasis on a clearly defined commitment, act, or experience;
4. An ideology offering a simple, easily communicated interpretive sense of sharing, control and promised rewards, and a feeling or personal worth and power;
5. The emphasis on the perception of real or imagined opposition.

Repairing cognitive dissonance

A classical study by Festinger, Riecken and Schachter (1956), *When Prophecy Fails*, has often been read as demonstrating another reason why some sects endure. The argument is that, paradoxically, sectarian movements are strengthened by the failure of prophecy. The argument draws on the social–psychological theory of cognitive dissonance. Festinger *et al.* used cognitive dissonance theory to explain the behaviour of members of a flying saucer cult. The crucial point was that far from abandoning their beliefs, the cult members increased their efforts at proselytizing in order to bring more people into the movement and thus reduced the dissonance between the leader's prophecy and the failure of either the cataclysm or the spaceships to appear as predicted. Failure led to a stepping up of the proselytizing effort since if more and more people were encouraged to join the group, the belief-system would become psychologically more plausible to the existing membership.

There are many reasons to doubt that this account necessarily stands up. For example, Bainbridge (1997, pp. 134–8) points out that in the context of a small group, the researcher's involvement would have enhanced the sect's own sense of purpose and possibly have been a spur to evangelizing endeavour. However, despite the weaknesses with the Festinger *et al.* thesis, there is further historical evidence of how the failure of prophecy can lead to the growth of a sectarian organization. A good example would be that of the Seventh-Day Adventists (SDA). The movement grew out of the Adventist movement of the early nineteenth century when William Miller, an American Baptist minister, attracted thousands of followers with his message, based on prophecies in the Biblical books of Daniel and Revelation, that Christ would return in 1843. When it did not happen, he calculated it to be the next year. Believers sold their properties and possessions in readiness. Once again, nothing occurred and the event became known as the Great Disappointment.

The movement has, however, flourished, despite the Millerites, as they were often known, later sub-dividing into different churches. In addition, there were other ways of dealing with the failure of prophecy. One was the claimed divine insight provided by Hiram Edson the day after the Great Disappointment. Edson maintained that Christ had not returned to earth in 1844, but had entered his heavenly sanctuary to cleanse it and divide out the sheep from the goats in preparation for the Judgement of God. Another response, based on a teaching put forward by Joseph Bates in 1846, was that Christians must obey the Jewish Sabbath – hence the present core doctrine which separates the SDA from other Christian groups.

The problem, however, is that such date-fixing in predicting the end of the world may ultimately be self-defeating. This is a problem that has confronted Jehovah's Witnesses. Its official mouthpiece, the Watchtower organization, predicted the second coming of Christ on various dates at the end of the nineteenth century, before moving the date to 1914. Christ was to return openly, and then, when the advent failed to materialize at that time, the leaders of the movement insisted that it was an 'invisible' return. This date was also said to mark the beginning of the End and that those who witnessed 1914 would not die out before the arrival of God's kingdom. With the generation alive in that year now dying out, the Watchtower organization is presently confronting a doctrinal dilemma and is forced to admit that 'Not all that was expected to happen in 1914 did happen, but it did mark the end of the Gentile Times and was a year of special significance' (*Jehovah's Witnesses in the Twentieth Century*, 1989, p. 7).

Fundamentalism defined

The apparent opposition of fundamentalism to the modern world has led some commentators to prefer the term 'neo-traditionalism' to describe movements that self-consciously attempt to represent or reassert an authentic religious tradition against what is perceived as the threat of modern developments (Sharot,1992, p. 25). With regard to Christianity, fundamentalism is associated with religious and social conservatism and is linked to divisions within the faith. It appears to be primarily concerned with the reclaiming of traditional moral and religious values and a protest against changes that have taken place and those who support such changes. Very often it is linked to the attempts of certain strands of Protestantism, particularly of evangelicals, to come to terms with social change (Bebbington, 1989). Perhaps even more than confronting social change, the emphasis here is on defending the inerrancy of scripture or articles of faith and opposing liberalism and modernism within the Protestant tradition (Barr, 1978). As a religious phenomenon, fundamentalism is frequently linked to sectarian aspects of religion, although it may develop into full-scale social movements which attempt to alter state policy and to change the moral attitudes and behaviour of society.

Evidence suggests, however, that Christian fundamentalism displays a selective rejection of modernity. This is clear when Church historian Martin Marty (1987) characterizes fundamentalism as 'a world-wide reaction against many of the mixed offerings of modernity'. Christian fundamentalism criticizes secular humanism, liberal theology and moral permissiveness, but not necessarily the technology which it may use for its own purposes such as evangelizing campaigns (Sharot, 1992, pp. 32–6). For instance, while fundamentalist evangelicals have opposed some modern advances including those that developing in the mass media such as the cinema, television and radio, they have long grasped the significance communication technology has for successful evangelism.

Fundamentalists may also disagree among themselves. Marty (1978) notes that differing groups are often deeply hostile to each other, even if there is a measure of broad agreement on the nature and location of fundamental articles of faith. The source of this division is usually that of Biblical interpretation. This fact, along with the apparent ambivalence towards the modern world, means that fundamentalism is not a unified phenomenon. This has led Martyn Percy (1995) to suggest that it is best understood as a particular worldview which displays some key elements. For Percy, fundamentalism is not to be understood as a tightly integrated dogmatic system, nor necessarily derived from a Biblical literalism, rather it constitutes a self-enforcing view of the universe which feeds back and shapes subjective experiences and provides a complete 'world' in which individuals and communities exist, magnify their identity and process their 'cosmic experience'. This includes a backward-looking interpretation for present practice. Very often, fundamentalists will embrace the claim to an exclusive validity of selected Biblical references which then establish their absolute legitimacy as the 'elect'. Fundamentalists also perceive God working through them. They regard themselves as his people and the means by which he is believed to mediate his past, present and future designs. All other religious traditions, even within the same faith, are outside this self-designated elite.

The New Christian Right and political activism

Fundamentalist Christians in Western countries have never constituted an entire movement united in a common cause. Rather, they are to be found in numerous churches of a conservative disposition. Some have turned their backs on the world, including many conservative evangelicals and Pentecostals. They have left humanity to its own destruction. Thus for them, political campaigns to change what is perceived as a God-forsaken world are seen as irrelevant. Some may choose not even to evangelize. Others however, often driven by their own expression of fundamentalist conviction, have attempted political and moral campaigns in order to bring salvation to the human race. They have frequently worked together, throughout the nineteenth and early twentieth centuries, in an attempt to influence social agendas concerning the family and the alleged corrupting effects of popular culture through a series of moral crusades: against alcohol, ballet, brothels, contraception, gambling, erotic literature and even ice-rinks (Bristow, 1977).

As a result of the so-called 1925 'monkey trial' controversy concerning the theory of evolution and the repeal of prohibition in the USA, the credibility of fundamentalism was undermined. The subsequent demands of the Second World War and the social effects of the expanding capitalist market and urbanization made fundamentalism appear anachronistic on both sides of the Atlantic (Simpson, 1983). However, since the 1960s, the fundamentalist constituency has become more active and more vociferous. This rise of conservative Protestantism, particularly in the USA, with its strong commitment to doctrine and refusal to compromise, took many sociologists by surprise. Moreover, its increasing political activity in the form of the New Christian Right (NCR) in the 1980s appeared to fly in the face of theories of secularization.

What was new about the so-called 'New Fundamentalism' of the 1980s was its ability to transcend the continuing disputes regarding political activism in some churches (Ammerman, 1987). In other words, it was establishing an unprecedented unity and support. In the USA, the NCR has attempted to mobilize sectarian dissent into political action. Ministries such as that of Jerry Falwell targeted the Baptist and independent evangelical constituency and gained 4 million members including 70 000 church ministers (Leibman, 1983). The aim, as Falwell's book *Listen America* makes clear, was at a time when there appeared a lack of faith in political institutions. Hence, his style of fundamentalism constituted a call to America's so-called 'Moral Majority' to come 'back to God, back to the Bible, back to morality' (quoted in Willoughby, 1981). In the USA, this has been epitomized by conflict between educational authorities and conservative Christians over prayer in public schools that resulted from the state's accommodation to non-Christian or non-religious minorities.

Although highly vociferous and attracting a good deal of media attention, Bruce (1988) argues that the NCR has had relatively little impact. Very few of its members who stood for national office won their elections. No more than five senators supported the NCR and they failed to get any notable new Federal legislation enacted. Opinion polls showed no significant public shift towards their views on moral issues. In Bruce's assessment the NCR achieved no more than to 'remind cosmopolitan America that fundamentalists were not extinct and still had some rights'. This relatively insignificant impact seems difficult to appreciate since around 34.1 million households frequently tune into the 'electronic church' – Christian television shows with popular, usually fundamentalist preachers. Studies, however, indicated that those who watch are almost always already converted conservative or fundamentalist Christians and that the programmes perhaps do little other that simply affirm their beliefs (Stacey and Shupe, 1982). Indeed, this tendency shows the need of Christian fundamentalism to constantly reaffirm the worldview of their members and, as Ammerman suggests (1987), this is done by immersion into the 'appropriate' religious audio recordings, reading matter, even to the point of cooking with a Christian cookbook.

At the same time, paradoxically, an indication that conservative Christians have become increasingly accommodating of secularity is their acceptance, if somewhat grudgingly, of the principles of liberal democracy. They are quite unlike Islamic fundamentalists in that they are not, for the most part, advocating theocracy. Increasingly they are contending their opposition to moral issues such as abortion not so much because it is unbiblical but because it infringes human rights. They do not argue that school children should be taught Creationism because the Bible says so; they maintain that Creation Science is as compatible with the evidence as evolution. More often than not, they confine their moral campaigns to the courts and elections. Bruce (1999) suggests that these developments indicate constraints on the NCR and that modern societies confine religion to the private sphere and encourage the spirit of individual liberty to which even the most ardent fundamentalists succumb.

The moral and political campaigning of the NCR should not be underestimated. In Britain, in the 1960s and 1970s, the equivalent movement to the Moral Majority in the USA established the Festival of Light and the National Viewers and Listeners Association. From this base groups including CARE (Christian Action Research and Education) used magazines, campaign posters and all-things-modern for their moral campaigning, and to good effect. Such groups were sufficiently influential as to convince local councils to refuse certificates for controversial films including *Caligula* and *The Life of Brian* in the 1970s and to close 500 sex shops, while influencing the 1982 and 1985 Cinematographic Acts which severely limited the growing sex cinema industry. In legislative terms, the British groups were more successful than the NCR in the USA.

On occasions campaigning by fundamentalists has deteriorated into 'moral panics' – an overexaggerated fear of the decline of moral values. This sometimes has serious repercussions. Thompson (1997) draws our attention to the example of 'satanic panics'. False signs of satanic ritual abuse identified by Christian social workers in Britain enhanced the belief that abuse was rampant in the early 1990s. The accusation (sometimes directed towards parents) was never proved. A prophecy that 50 satanic cults in Scotland would be exposed by Christians had catastrophic consequences. In 1995, eight children were returned to their families in Ayrshire, Scotland, after being taken into care by social workers. Other similar cases followed throughout the country. The parents where cleared of any guilt. Many families were left emotionally scarred and their children traumatized after being body searched for signs of sexual abuse. Similar occurrences have also been documented in the USA where considerable money and power was gained by groups combating imaginary satanist activities (Victor, 1992).

Status discontent theories

Explaining why particular individuals embrace fundamentalist expressions of Christianity, and why they might become involved in moral campaigns, brings us back to the significance of deprivation. In his work on Christian fundamentalism, Marty (1987) argues that those who advocate fundamentalism do so as a smoke-screen since they are not really motivated by religious beliefs but by psychological dispositions and are a product of social forces and historical events. In short, they have some motivation other than their stated conviction to change the world in religious terms. Further studies have come to similar conclusions. Those conducted in the USA have tended to focus on the declining middle classes who are motivated by status discontent. Much work was infused by Gusfield's (1963) suggestion that those involved in the USA temperance movement in the 1920s were suffering a loss of social group status which they sought to retain through a symbolic crusade to gain public acceptance of their group's values over those of their opponents (Tracey and Morrison, 1979). To put it succinctly, those whose status is threatened by changing cultural norms assert their values politically in order to re-establish the ideological basis of their status. This kind of theorizing has also been more recently used to explain the activities of anti-abortion and anti-pornography campaigners (Zurcher and Kirkpatrick, 1976).

There is an alternative approach, however. The differences between supporters and non-supporters of the NCR are perhaps less matters of economic class than of cultural (Christian) lifestyle differences (Johnson and Tamney, 1989). In other words, it is the belief system and values that are most significant. One study of US Protestants found that people who were dissatisfied with the amount of social respect given to groups representing traditional values (for example, people who were involved in churches, people who worked hard and obeyed the law – people like themselves) were especially likely to support the agenda and organization of the Christian Right wing (Wald, Owen and Hill, 1989). Hence, the New Religious Right may be primarily a political defence of a set of lifestyle criteria.

This latter interpretation of fundamentalist activism comes closer to Percy's understanding of fundamentalism. Thus moral campaigns are a way in which a cognitive minority engage with the secular world and whose motivation is no more than what it says it is, religious. In other words, religious beliefs can run parallel to secular motives and the symbolic use of targets, and they can provide motivations outside and beyond economic and status considerations. There are no other 'real' sociological factors, then, other than the actor's explicit meaning. While socio-economic circumstances may produce a susceptibility towards taking social action, an individual's motives invariably come from within that person's own belief system.

Summary

Fundamentalism is often on the receiving end of a 'bad press'. This is particularly so with its more extremist or even violent wing. In response to the perceived threat to the American way of life, a plethora of quasi-military organizations have sprung up in the USA since the late 1980s. Their literature often offers doomsday warnings that are anti-Catholic, anti-Semitic and anti-media. One of many extremist Right-wing sects is that which calls itself The Militia. In May 1998, one of its members reduced the Federal Building in Oklahoma City to rubble in a kind of retribution against the federal government. The Militia's belief is that the government, the gun control lobby, genetic mutations, UFOs and certain military bases throughout North America are all part of a grand conspiracy to overthrow the USA and turn it into a communist-style state. Some such groups take the form of 'survivalist cults' – storing food, guns and resources for use after what is predicted to be the total breakdown of Western civilization. This is often within the framework of an apocalyptic scenario which prophesizes the world as falling into the hands of the anti-Christ.

Such fundamentalist groups may appear bizarre and offer a real threat to Western society or merely be perceived as a lunatic fringe. They are, however, only one face of fundamentalism. All in all, fundamentalism is a broad movement and does not necessarily have to be viewed as a social threat. While it may be an intrusive phenomenon motivated by its own distinct worldview, it has also been created as much by contemporary Western society as anything else and is evidence of the increasing penetration of the outside world into the sphere of religion. Secular and permissive society sets the agenda and demands that certain issues are addressed whether individualism, children's education, or feminism or pluralism. It is frequently wider society which initially engages religion, rather than the other way around and in doing so engenders fundamentalism and, to some degree, helps establish sectarian divisions.

9 Cults and the New Religiosity

Much of the discussion in previous chapters has focused on the fortunes of Christianity in its different forms in Western societies. The decline or growth of the mainstream churches, sects and fundamentalist movements, their organizational frameworks and the challenges that they have faced, have all been considered. Non-Christian forms of religiosity have so far been rather marginal to our analysis. The chapters to come will consider some of these alternative expressions of belief and practice. This chapter and chapter 10 will consider new forms of religiosity, in particular cults, new religious movements (NRMs), and the New Age.

Cults

In the media and in public discourse the terms 'cult' and 'sect' are often used interchangeably. To some extent this is understandable since there may be discernible overlaps. For instance, both are perceived as deviant forms of religiosity and frequently appear to be in conflict with their social environment. Nonetheless, they are precise sociological typologies and, conceptually at least, are worth separating.

According to Stark and Bainbridge (1980) cults, unlike sects, are not schisms arising from established religions. Instead, they constitute forms of 'cultural innovation' and may be completely new by way of core beliefs and practices. Alternatively, others may constitute cultural importation derived from an entirely different social and religious context. Since the 1960s, the most noteworthy types of cult have probably been the range of Eastern mystical religions introduced into the West, but they are by no means restricted to

142

this type. Both forms of cult are likely to express a fairly high degree of tension with their social environment.

When such cults grow beyond a certain size of membership and organization it is legitimate to refer to them as a 'movement'. Hence, many NRMs often begin as cults but develop to embrace tens of thousands of members, are frequently highly organized and have a global significance with representation in many different countries. To complicate matters, however, the terms 'cult' and 'new religious movement' are often used interchangeably and some, moreover, will display sectarian characteristics. It is obvious then, that we are contemplating a complex, often wide-ranging expression of religious life. This is one of the reasons why several classifications of cults have been attempted.

Cult typologies

Stark and Bainbridge (1985) have identified three types of cult according to their degree of organization and, secondly, by way of the 'rewards' and 'compensators' they offer their adherents:

1. *Audience cults* are the least organized and involve little interaction between members and leaders. While wishing to adhere to a cult representing their interest, a member's commitment may amount to no more than mail-ordering and attending the occasional specially organized event.
2. *Client cults* are rather more organized – offering services to their followers which, in the past, tended to focus on healing miracles, astrological predictions, or forms of spiritualism. Today, however, they generally specialize in the area of 'personal adjustments'. The emphasis is not so much on enhancing the spiritual as the worldly opportunities of the membership. Scientology may be cited as an example. Dianetics, as it is otherwise known, aims to establish 'a civilization without insanity, without criminals and without war, where the able can prosper and honest beings have rights, and where man is free to rise to greater heights' (*The Church of Scientology: 40th Anniversary*, 1994, p. 56). Developing what he regarded as a science, L. Ron Hubbard, Scientology's late founder, believed that the 'reactive' (unconscious) mind hoards the trauma of all

past unpleasant experiences in a kind of pictorial form called 'engrams'. Scientology thus offers its 'clients' courses aimed at eradicating 'engrams' and thereby allowing personal development in practically every aspect of life.

3. *Cult movements* involve their followers to a greater extent. At the same time, they attempt to satisfy all the spiritual needs of their patrons and forbid their members to adhere to other faiths. While some demand little more than a commitment to a set of beliefs and the occasional attendance at meetings, others may endeavour to completely dominate the individual's life. Not infrequently, client cults develop into cult movements for their most devoted followers. For instance, the Siddi programme offers advanced techniques in Transcendental Meditation. The techniques may come to dominate a person's lifestyle and there may be a demand for strict adherence to the movement's practices and doctrines which includes a belief in occultist powers.

Stark and Bainbridge (1987) argue that different types of cults offer different kinds of 'rewards' and 'compensators' for their followers. To appreciate this distinction it is necessary to refer to their general theory of religion. They argue that the recent proliferation of cults in the West must be viewed as an integral part of a religious revival. The human need for religion even in the face of rationalism and science continues. Since it deals with ultimate questions of human existence, religion will still be formulated in transcendental or supernaturalist forms. However, its expressions have changed. Cults proliferate to deal with the very different needs of individuals in today's society. While older forms of religion cannot provide for such needs, neither, generally speaking, can sects (although they may provide for the needs of some).

Cults, as innovating forms of religiosity, are concerned with particular contemporary requirements and this is evident in the different ways that they deal with 'rewards' and 'compensators'. 'Rewards' are defined as those things which humans desire and are willing to incur some cost to obtain. These may be specific or more general needs including solutions to questions of ultimate meaning. 'Compensators', by contrast, are explanations of why rewards are not obtained and may offer the hope for future rewards, sometimes in non-verifiable contexts. Different types of cults offer different types of compensators:

1. *Audience cults* offer very weak compensators which may provide no more than a mild vicarious thrill. This suggests a certain degree of superficiality and is in line with a culture that puts emphasis on transitory experience.
2. *Client cults* offer more valuable specific compensators as does, for example, astrology in predicting the future and answering queries relevant to the life of the individual. Yet, these cults do not offer general compensators such as an explanation of the meaning of life or the guarantee of life after death.
3. *Cult movements* insist on greater commitment and offer general compensators and address the great questions of life and death.

At the same time, Stark and Bainbridge (1987) have attempted to provide a model describing the process by which cults emerge.

The psychopathology model
This suggests that mentally ill individuals concoct novel compensators and accept them as rewards. The relevance of mental illness is that it liberates the individual from conventional ways of comprehending the world and thus allows considerable creativity. Stark and Bainbridge (1987, p. 159) argue that mental illness can primarily be interpreted as a mode of behaviour which fails to conform to whatever a society regards as normal or acceptable. As their behaviour is not limited by social norms, cult leaders are relatively free to devise patterns of behaviour and establish wholly new compensators and religious ideas which they are subsequently able to convince others to accept and which, in turn, become incorporated into a new religious cult.

The entrepreneurial model
This suggests that cults are rather like businesses established by individuals with flair and talent. These cult leaders profit, often financially, by offering innovating compensators in return for rewards from their followers. In many cases these are financial, but they may also include personal admiration, status, or power. Cult leaders are not always cynical and manipulative individuals. Indeed, Stark and Bainbridge distinguish between honest cult founders who offer only those compensators which they person-

ally accept and more unscrupulous ones who would not themselves countenance what they offer to others. Often, the cult leader may have had previous involvement in one or more cult. This provides him/her with the skills and knowledge needed to establish and continue a successful cult to which they may add elements of the beliefs of their earlier cults. They may even tag on fresh teachings and thus create a totally new synthesis of doctrine.

The sub-culture/evolution model

This draws on the sociological work on deviant sub-cultures. Some cults are likely to be relatively isolated from mainstream society by way of interaction and exchanges, novel explanations and, therefore, novel compensators, which are at odds with mainstream culture. The cult grows through a process by which new compensators are collectively invented and membership acquired through a series of small steps consisting of exchanges. If the process goes on for some time a new cult may emerge which amounts to a marginalized sub-culture relatively insular from society and with a highly integrated membership. Stark and Bainbridge argue that such a group will tend to generate compensators of an increasingly general kind and thus qualify as a full-blown religious cultist movement.

New religious movements

There is nothing particularly new about new religious movements (NRMs). Especially in the form of cults and not infrequently expressed through types of Eastern mysticism, new religions have, since the nineteenth century, permeated Western cultures. However, from the end of the Second World War, and especially from the late 1960s, they have expanded rapidly in many Western societies. While it is hard to estimate numbers, the records of INFORM (the data bank of NRMs at the London School of Economics) estimates that there are now nearly 2600 new religions (Barker, 1999, p. 16).

Contemporary NRMs are noteworthy for their wide variety. They range from those such as the Unification Church, the Children of God, the Divine Light Mission, Krishna Consciousness, Scientology, Rastafarianism, Transcendental

Meditation and the Rajneeshes. Many of these appear to have very little in common. Some NRMs mark a continuation with other older religions (the charismatic renewal movement could be placed under this rubric).

Other NRMs, however, are more syncretic in terms of their belief and seem to be genuinely new forms of religion. Indeed, it is this syncretic aspect which is so distinctive about NRMs. A prime example is the Unification Church. Its founder, Sun Myung Moon, teaches the unification of world Christianity which he believes has gone astray. Moon, claiming himself as the new messiah in 1992, sees his historical role in restoring its 'correct' teachings. In *Discourse on the Principle*, he outlines his key teachings and the 'fuller revelation'. God's original plan was for men and women to have a flawless relationship with him. When Satan tempted man and Adam fell, the perfect 'family' of God, man and woman was destroyed. Moon re-established this bond in his perfect marriage and offspring that restored man's true relationship with God. While these teachings have a strong Christian orientation, Moon also integrates Taoist and Confucian elements and, as we have seen, the desire to be morally and culturally appealing, particularly in the USA, has also meant that the movement has adopted a politically Right-wing platform.

Categorization of new religious movements

The variety of teachings advanced by NRMs has led Eileen Barker (1985) to propose that they may be classified according to the religious tradition from which they originate. For instance, Hare Krishna and the disciples of Bhagwan Rajneeshi were originally rooted in Hinduism, while Zen groups are derived from Buddhism. Some NRMs are more syncretic and merge together different religious traditions. Others have an occult, pagan, or witchcraft source. Alternatively, a number display little connection with previous religions but are part of what Barker calls the human potential movement. However, she points out that some groups are so idiosyncratic that they defy any classification. At the same time, she suggests that another way of classifying NRMs is according to the degree of commitment shown by their members. Hence, at one pole would be those with sectarian forms of organization, and at the other, those which are closer to Stark and Bainbridge's concept of an Audience cult.

An alternative means of distinguishing NRMs has been provided by Roy Wallis (1984). Like Troeltsch, Wallis categorizes NRMs in terms of their relationship to the outside world. He identifies three principal forms:

1. *World-rejecting movements* can be identified by a clearly defined concept of God, a morally ascribed set of often puritanical beliefs, a theology which is critical of and in conflict with the world that it actively seeks to change, millenarian outlooks, strict separation of members from the world, strong charismatic leadership, and sometimes a communal lifestyle.

2. *World-accommodating movements*, according to Wallis, neither totally embrace nor reject the world. They might display some elitist attitudes and seek to restore the purity of a religious tradition. For instance, Sudbud has origins within Islam although it makes significant departures from it. Broadly translated Sudbud means 'to follow the will of God'. Beginning in Indonesia, in the 1920s, it has several thousand members in the USA and Europe. Like Sufism, it is a more mystical expression of Islam that claims that God's 'spiritual energy' can be experienced through 'spiritual exercise' ('latihan').

   Sudbud has now so departed from Islam as to encourage members to stay in the religion to which they originally belonged. In this way world-accommodating movements are frequently tolerant of other expressions of their faith. Hence, they can often be seen as denominational forms and identified as religious types that are keen to present a 'respectable' set of religious beliefs which often mirror the respectable lives of their adherents. The key aspect is that such NRMs separate the spiritual and worldly in a distinctive way which serves the needs of the membership.

3. *World-affirming movements*, by some criteria, hardly constitute religions at all. Very often they have no organizational basis or 'church'; no collective acts of worship or clearly articulated doctrinal framework. Nonetheless, they do claim to provide access to superhuman or supernatural powers, hence they must be regarded as religions. By definition, world-affirming NRMs tend to affirm the world as it is, are inclined to be congruent

with the dominant values of Western society and are extremely liberal in their attitudes towards other faiths. Notions of salvation or spiritual perfection are frequently conceived in terms of personal advancement, while the emphasis is on members to fulfil their abilities.

More often than not, adherents to world-affirming movements do not constitute a membership at all, but are customers who are buying a 'service' such as healing or realizing personal potential. It is largely for these reasons that there is little attempt by the organization to regulate beliefs and practices, and it rarely seeks to convert people in the traditional sense. Some, arguably including Scientology, may be totally new and innovative in terms of beliefs. Alternatively, others may be derived from traditional forms or offer syncretic variations and sometimes attempt to improve the nature of society as well as the lives of individuals. For instance, Nichiren Shoshu, an innovating form of Buddhism, offers a faith which affects every part of the individual's life and, so it is argued, wider society.

Wallis realizes that no religious group will conform exactly to these categories. Many combine elements of each type and more particularly, aspects of the conventional society and the counter-culture. Indeed, he points to a number of groups that occupy an intermediate position such as the Healthy, Happy, Holy, Organization (3HO). 3HO is a spin-off of an established religion, namely Sikhism. Like world-accommodating movements it employs techniques which, it is claimed, will bring benefits such as happiness and good health, while appealing to those who otherwise lead conventional lives. On the other hand, it has some characteristics in common with world-rejecting movements: the organization has a clear concept of God, while members dress in unconventional white clothes and turbans. However, while members live in communes (ashrams), they do not embrace the total sharing of belongings. Some restrictions are placed on behaviour including vegetarianism and abstinence from alcohol and tobacco. Occupying the middle ground allows the followers of 3HO to combine elements of an alternative lifestyle with conventional marriage and employment.

Explaining the rise of new religious movements

'Crisis' theories

Several explanations have been advanced to account for the rise of the new religions. At least some of these are interwoven in wider debates about the legitimacy and desirability of such religions. In the USA, the original home of numerous NRMs, a whole range of theoretical frameworks has been put forward that are located within a broader reference to some 'crisis' of modernity which precipitates social and/or individual psychological malfunctioning.

Experimentation and social critiques

Many NRMs sought an alternative lifestyle to an increasingly materialistic and atomized society, as well as offering a critique of technical rationality, the scientifically dominated culture and established social institutions and forms of morality. Growing at the end of the 'hippie' decade of the 1960s they advanced a more effective criticism, while also marking an attempt to restore a supernatural worldview (Wuthnow, 1976).

Moral ambiguity

Anthony and Robbins (1982) see the emergence of NRMs located in the moral ambiguity of contemporary culture that arises from pluralism, social differentiation and the subsequent decline of civil religions. They identify two means by which NRMs contribute to the overcoming of this moral hiatus. The first, typified by the Unification Church, seeks to revitalize political and religious values and has been referred to as a 'civic religion sect'. The other, more mystical expression, encompasses the therapeutically orientated and human potential types which resist the intrusion of political and civic concerns and values into spiritual life. Hence, these movements emphasize individual self-transformation and realization in an essentially narcissistic way. Both types create a form of social integration and overcome dysfunctional social aspects. A similar conjecture is also advanced by Bromley and Shupe (1981). For them, NRMs embody fresh sources of meaning which reflect emergent needs and aspirations among significant sections of society. In that respect they may be seen as part of a normal cycle of religious movements in the USA, in which periods of stability are followed by a time of religious revitalization.

The decline of community

Another alleged 'crisis' of modernity is identified as the so-called 'decline of community'. Marx and Ellison (1975) focus on the emphasis that many NRMs have in restoring community by offering bonding, fellowship and a sense of belonging lacking in wider society. This is achieved through an emotional and ecstatic religious experience in movements which combine all the attributes of a surrogate family with a set of universalistic values and beliefs that are often expressed as a spiritual force operating in the lives of all members.

The search for identity

Pre-dating more stringent theories of post-modernity, earlier commentators identified a link between the new religions and a search for self-identity that is precipitated by the contemporary world dominated by bureaucratic structures and fragmented social roles. NRMs are said to address this need by promoting a holistic conception of self especially through therapeutic movements and mystical cults (Westley, 1978). Cult-like groups offer the ability to control and change one's social identity and self. In contrast, the more sect-like groups address the search for self-identity by consolidating all of the individual's fragmented social identities into a single, central, religiously defined self which is strengthened by the strict control of the more fundamentalist type group.

These 'crisis' theories have their limitations. While the NRMs which proliferated from the 1960s may deal with some of the problems created by contemporary society, whether of moral flux, the breakdown of social bonds, or alienation, there is much about some of the religions which is clearly in line with Western society and fulfils culturally specific needs. This kind of explanation of the rise of new cult movements is closer to that offered by Stark and Bainbridge (1980, 1985). They see the new religions as generally free of the deficiencies of the older religious faiths, dealing with the needs of individuals in Western societies. The new religions thus fill the 'gaps' left by more traditional forms. The growth of the new religions is also enhanced by the breakdown of religious 'monopolies' and the proliferation of a 'spiritual marketplace'. This is, however, by no means limited to the West. In modern Japan, as Finke (1997) points out, thousands of new religions such as Soka Gakkai have emerged with the decline of state-subsidized Shintoism.

There are other, totally different criticisms of the emphasis on some contemporary 'crisis'. First, since innovating forms of religiosity in the West are far from new they cannot be accounted for by the unique developments arising in the second half of the twentieth century. Secondly, they are unable to explain the relative decline of NRMs since the 1980s, despite the continuity of technological and cultural change. Thirdly, while the social developments highlighted by many studies are to be found in most Western societies, the origins and popularity of NRMs in the USA point to specific circumstances to be found there. Stark and Bainbridge (1980) maintain that there are proportionately more NRMs in some European countries. For example, they claim that in the late 1970s in the USA there were only 2.3 cult movements per million inhabitants, compared to 3.2 in England and Wales. However, Wallis (1986) shows that the methods used (that is, counting headquarters rather than membership rates) makes this misleading. The reality is that the USA is more receptive to religious innovation than any other country. Indicative of this is that a Gallup opinion poll in 1998 displayed marked levels of awareness of the newer religions with around 5 per cent of the population of the USA actually involved to one degree or another.

Why has the USA proved to be fertile ground for the new religions? Glock and Bellah (1976) argue that the pressure for profound religious changes had been building up, especially in the USA, since long before the 1960s. However, the trigger for NRMs, and the counter-culture that created them, was the Vietnam war which effectively brought challenges to the dominant culture more to the fore.

An alternative, and rather more simple approach to explaining the growth of NRMs is taken by Melton (1987). Many NRMs are based on occult mysticism and Eastern thought. In the 1960s and early 1970s, there was a vast expansion in the missionary endeavour on the part of many Eastern religions that seemed to dovetail with the popularity of experimentation in such areas as psychedelic drugs and humanistic therapy. Magnifying and hastening the effect was the rescinding in the USA of the Oriental Exclusion Act which allowed many Eastern religious teachers and leaders to enter the country. While undoubtedly valid, this explanation does not, in turn, account for the receptivity which existed, nor explain the growth of the more 'home-grown' movements such as the Californian-based Jesus People.

Recent developments in the new religious movements

For some individuals the world-rejecting movements still undoubtedly offer an appeal. David Martin (1982) maintains that those such as the Unification Church, in much the same way as Christian fundamentalism, have an attraction for idealists who seek a profound meaning to life and wish to be embraced by a totalitarian form of religion. Yet, because of the extreme demands they make on their members, the world-rejecting movements are, he argues, likely to be reduced to a small constituency.

It may indeed be the case that many of the world-rejecting movements have had their day. Increasingly it appears that those such as the Unification Church or the Jesus Movement which emerged in the 1960s and 1970s were a product of a time and place, whether resulting from the counter-culture, rapid social change, or some moral malaise. Today, the membership of some of the largest movements which came out of the period are dwindling and it is unlikely that they will stand the test of time. Eileen Barker, a long-time student of NRMs, suggests that despite the large number of NRMs and the present sizeable membership of a few, there is no indication that any one movement is likely to become a major religious tradition in the future (Barker, 1999, p. 15).

Martin (1991) notes other developments within the NRMs. The speed of the transitions within the movements ever quicken in pace. In this way they provide a marker of the speed of social change in the outside world. Movements rapidly rise, grow and disintegrate. This is because they cater for particular needs and demands of particular people in Western Europe and the USA but, in line with cultural developments, these requirements are constantly altering. Martin also contends that there are discernible today various categories of commitment to these movements, perhaps expressed in different levels of membership. Many now permit sojourn pathways between the religious universe and the wider secular world. Such movements, then, find it difficult to survive in pure world-rejecting form and must allow compromise with the world in order to survive. It is a recognition that few

people seek a full commitment and immersion in a radically different and totally religious way of life.

NRMs are sufficiently flexible not only to reflect life experiences but also to satisfy the needs of some individuals more
dynamically to create a change in their self-image and self-
perception. In short, to transform their life experience through
religious symbols and beliefs in dealing with felt deprivations and
in fulfilling aspirations (Strauss, 1976). Today, many NRMs allow
aspects of the self to be chosen, shaped and transformed, especially
through healing and therapeutic techniques. In doing so they
reflect wider social developments and the growing notion that the
emotions and the body are not given, but are reflexively malleable
parts of one's identity.

There are good grounds for arguing that in performing these
functions it is the world-affirming form of NRM that is increasing
in popularity at the expense of the more world-rejecting and
world-accommodating types. It is the former that is more compatible with the conditions of contemporary society and cultural
values. It is also this type of movement that demands a much lower
level of commitment than the other forms and is less stigmatized.
In addition, they may offer, as Marx and Ellison (1975) point out
of human potential groups, a sense of community and fellowship
on a part-time basis without the less attractive full-time, more
utopian and demanding aspects of the more sectarian orientated
movements.

Wallis (1984) also recognized such a tendency. What he
referred to as 'epistemological individualism' is increasingly
expressing itself in religious terms in a consumer society where
there are ever-changing tastes and fashions. It follows that world-
affirming groups become more popular since they offer immediate
gratification for those who take part. Some, world-rejecting
groups however, as Heelas (1996) points out, may still resist this
tendency towards weak commitment and marketable strategies.

Evidence to support the increasing domination of world-
affirming groups has been presented by Khasala's (1986) survey of
the 3HO Foundation and Vajradhatu (a Tibetan Buddhist church
whose members are mostly well-educated, middle-class, white
Americans). These groups have become less world-rejecting and
have developed an ideological orientation that supports worldly
success as a religiously significant venture and thereby they see no

contradiction between the spiritual and the earthly realm. This development did not result from the transformation of sect ideal-type to a church ideal-type, nor did it follow from increasing institutionalization. Rather, the evidence suggests that the transition was initiated by a rational leadership decision in response to changing social and economic conditions in an attempt to promote group maintenance and survival. The turn to worldly success provides a solid foundation on which the religion can grow. At the same time, it provides otherwise deviant groups with a strong image of legitimacy and as Khasala suggests:

> What better way to become an accepted part of American society than by embracing some of the values that this country holds most dear: utilitarian individualism, capitalistic enterprize, and most definitely, financial success. (Khasala, 1986, p. 245)

The New Age movement

The more recent developments in the new religiosity have thrown existing categories of the new religions into question. This is no more so than in the growth of the so-called New Age movement. The various interrelated strands which constitute this movement display a profoundly eclectic and syncretic system of beliefs and practices which weave together ancient faiths with contemporary cultural themes. This frequent mix 'n' match form of religion has proved to be highly attractive to some people as an alternative to mainline religion, while some of its key ideas have permeated various aspects of social life.

So diverse is the nature of the New Age that it is extremely difficult to characterize its distinctive features. Woodhead and Heelas (2000, p. 113), however, have suggested that it could be described as incorporating a number of 'expressive spiritualities'. Such spiritualities are the central cultural current of the New Age in that they seek an inner quest for freedom and self-expression; to express what one truly is, to live life as the expression of one's authentic nature, and to affirm oneself as bound up with the natural or authentic order as a whole. The emphasis then, is on the self and self-discovery within a holistic frame of reference which embraces the universe and this world through an essential 'truth' and unity. At the same time, the New Age is a highly optimistic, celebratory, utopian and spiritual form of humanism. As Heelas (1996) puts it:

> Ultimacy – God, the Goddess, the Higher Self – lies within, serving as the source of vitality, creativity, love, tranquility, wisdom, responsibility, power and all those other qualities which are held to comprise the perfect inner life.

The New Age movement should not, however, be seen as something completely 'new'. Although many of its strands claim to be totally innovating, even the more exotic have their roots in identifiable clusters of prior beliefs and practices (Albanese, 1993). In this respect, the movement appears to be taking some of the developments observable in the new religions from the 1960s to their furthest conclusions. This includes the adoption of the older Eastern religions, Celtic forms, Mediterranean and Polynesian native religions and shamanism. Indeed, McGuire (1992, p. 282) refers to the New Age movement as involved in a kind of pseudo-anthropological legitimization of a cluster of beliefs to justify and give meaning to present practices. The emphasis is on the earlier 'simple' societies' truths about healing power, gender and the environment, which modern societies are deemed to have lost. Hence, the New Age borrows myths, legends, rituals and symbols. These restored 'truths', however, are not always historically accurate and, as Bowman (1993) suggests in the New Age's depiction of Celtic religion, there is a certain amount of idealization and reinvention of past religious forms.

Another distinctive dimension of most strands of the New Age is their pluralistic outlook. This means that they tend to display syncretic characteristics. Largely middle-class adherents may participate in a variety of groups and there is a great deal of toleration of the beliefs of other religions. To some extent this displays the movement's strong root in Theosophy and the idea that all religions have some essential common truth. New Age therefore tends to plunder other religions for a religious core. To this is added holistic philosophies which see human beings as mind, body and spirit – hence, alternative healing is a popular theme and is indicative of how the movement is in line with the syncretic nature of the contemporary religious marketplace.

The New Age may be said, however, to display cult-like

characteristics in the sense that it often embraces a range of counter-cultural values. It rejects rationalism as the only way of interpreting the world and it seeks to show the legitimacy of other bodies of knowledge such as alchemy and astrology. It also opposes that which is believed to threaten the organic unity of mind, body and spirit. Hence, there is a strong overlap with the 'Green' revolution. This emphasis on environmentalism is seen as bound up with personal problems in that an essential harmony is sought that links the individual with the cosmic order. Thus the earth is revered as Gaia, an animate organism upon which all life depends. The emphasis on environmentalism perhaps gives the New Age its most radical edge, witnessed by the protest of its 'Ecowarriors' against the erosion of the countryside and the exploitation of nature and natural resources.

In endorsing these older forms of religiosity, the New Age asserts that it draws on the wisdom of ancient civilizations and native peoples untouched and unspoiled by Christianity. Of major importance here is that strand of the New Age embracing what has come to be known as neo-Paganism. However, it has to be noted that those who subscribe exclusively to these forms of alternative religion are likely to object to being placed under the rubric of the New Age. This is not so much because they are not 'new' but because these ancient expressions of religiosity tend to dismiss the central concern with what the New Ager frequently refers to as the 'higher self' in preference for a veneration of gods, goddesses and other supernatural forces, or at least hidden spiritual powers.

Today, the term neo-Paganism denotes a revival and reconstruction of ancient Nature religions adapted for the contemporary world. Although as a movement, neo-Paganism can be traced back to the nineteenth century, it was the counter-culture of the mid-twentieth century which increased its popularity, particularly in the USA where a rediscovery of the ancient cultural traditions of the native American Indians became popular. Beyond that, neo-Paganism displays a remarkable diversity. Indeed, practically everything that can be termed neo-Pagan is eclectic since it is derived from various sources. Hence, shamans, witches and druids all have different aspects. They are often based on diverse national traditions, and within each broad group there are many different emphases. Nonetheless, there are discernible overlaps between the principal strands. There are, for example, links between some forms of Wicca and Druidism, and between both of these and shamanism.

Generally, because of its vast diversity, neo-Paganism has a lack of any central organization: adherents tend to be based in non-hierarchical small groups. This prevents the movement becoming dogmatic and authoritarian but it also makes it impossible to estimate how many people are involved. Nonetheless, umbrella organizations have emerged over the years. In the USA there are several different nationwide federations of neo-Pagans. This includes the Universal Federation of Pagans and the Covenant of the Goddess which is a legally recognized Wiccan Church, but in the attitude towards associated congregations it appears to function more like a federation and operates in the same way as some Christian denominations. Federations and other umbrella groups serve a number of goals: to exchange views, mutual support, publications and central information for the media and official bodies. In Britain, the Pagan Federation and PaganLink work towards establishing the same rights for neo-Paganism as for members of other religions including hospital and prison chaplains, and weddings and funerals. Once dominated by the Wiccan movement, it now puts more emphasis on non-Wiccan neo-Pagans.

One variation of neo-Paganism is the restoration of the ancient Norse and Germanic religions or what can be referred to as the 'Northern Tradition'. In fact, those who follow such traditions frequently opt for the term 'heathen' (meaning 'the beliefs of the people of the hearth') rather than pagan. For instance, many who follow the Norse religion prefer the term to distinguish themselves from the more Goddess-based Wicca movement. In turn, heathenism constitutes perhaps the most diverse of faiths within the range of neo-Paganism. Many gods and goddesses may be evoked from very different polytheistic systems. Thus there are various movements within the broader constituency of heathenism. These include the Ring of Troth, the Odinic Rite and Odinshof, each of which has its own accentuation. Many of these movements embrace a number of beliefs which appear to be at odds with modern society and are primarily concerned with re-establishing an ancient morality in a alienating world increasingly void of clear moral systems. Hence, it is argued, there must be an emphasis on community bonds, family values and responsibility and respect for elders. This seems to amount to a form of tribalism which frequently displays conservative and patriarchal overtones.

Typical of the multi-dimensional nature of the movement, New Age has a wing that is derived from Christianity, or at least a modification of traditional Christian beliefs, which frequently converges Biblical text with esoteric sources. For instance, a key teaching is that the advent of the New Age will be apocalyptic and characterized by terrestrial and social upheaval in what is typically a pre-millenarian form of Christianity. Christ's physical return is predicted to follow a period of catastrophes which will inaugurate the New Age millennium. One such expression, the Church Universal and Triumphant (originating in the late 1950s), sees Jesus as a great 'Ascended Master' in his time on earth but that his teachings were corrupted by the New Testament writers. The task of the movement, therefore, is to discover and fulfil these original truths (York, 1995).

While the New Age opposes much of contemporary society there is still a great deal which it also appears to endorse. The most obvious is the emphasis on human potential. Heelas therefore refers to the 'humanistic expressivism' of the New Age – meaning a focus on the interior life, self-exploration and self-development. Heelas subtitles his book on the New Age *The Celebration of Self and the Sacrilization of Modernity* (1996). This emphasis on the self in many respects differentiates the New Age from earlier NRMs, although many NRMs are increasingly stressing ideas of the development of 'self' for materialistic and psychological ends. The New Age takes this to its logical conclusion by merging physiological, emotional and spiritual powers. There is an attempt to find the 'true' self and to be liberated from socialized identities.

Heelas (1996) speaks of the increasing popularity of the New Age movement to empower a person's life, rather than to transcend it. The emphasis is on a spirituality through the notion of a process of self-development or what he calls 'self-spirituality'. Thus, self-development, in terms of the development of 'higher self', takes on a spiritual quest. There is an attempt to find the 'true' self and to be liberated from socialized identities. It is a development of mental, physical and spiritual perfection through quasi-religious therapeutic cults. Here the self is regarded as potentially perfect and divine but this potential is restricted by social arrangements and psychological blockages.

The New Age apparently provides a radicalized version of humanistic expressivism, resting on spiritual rather than psychological foundations. This brings the New Age close to Stark and Bainbridge's classification of Client and Audience cults – a loosely structured set of organizations with little personal commitment expected and which provide services for individuals to improve their lives in many different ways. In this sense, the New Age does not constitute a unified, coherent, or highly mobilized movement. Yet, even this is an overgeneralization, since the New Age allows various levels of commitment which Heelas (1996, pp. 117–19) distinguishes as three levels:

1. *The fully engaged* – those who are deeply committed and have given up conventional lifestyles for a spiritual quest and are often practitioners providing services to others;
2. *Serious part-timers* – their spirituality is compartmentalized as part of their life, albeit a serious one. However, this does not prevent them from living conventional lives and following conventional careers;
3. *Casual part-timers* – this includes people who are interested in exotic and esoteric things as consumers, but fail to get seriously involved. This group is the smallest but, as Heelas laments, is expanding and threatens the movement with its superficiality.

It is this variation in commitment which enhances the consumer choice, as well as the range of ideas it incorporates, which makes the New Age so typical of contemporary forms of religiosity.

While the New Age appears to have profoundly private dimensions, it impinges, in many discernible ways, into the public arena with a distinct social and political agenda. While Beckford (1992) admits that the number of activists and true believers deliberately pursuing or cultivating the principal ideas of the New Age may be relatively small, he contends that the movement's holistic consciousness has already made inroads deep into public thinking about such issues as ecology, peace, gender and health. It has made its way into organized religion and other social spheres; medicine, sport, leisure, education, dying and grieving, self-help, animal welfare and social work. Success can be measured by the growth of green politics and green products – taking the movement from the alienated fringes of public life to its centre.

The New Age also increasingly appears to have practical application including the employment of its techniques in management
training – advancing those which are mood-altering, induce
behavioural change and bring the alleged spiritual development of
human resources (Roberts, 1994). All this suggests a growing
recognition, in each of these spheres, of the strength that can be
derived from emphasizing the whole person, the interconnectedness of the human and non-human environment and the essential
global nature of social and natural processes. The thrust, then, is
towards a transcendent, but not necessary supernatural, point of
reference.

Summary

The years since 1960 have seen a remarkable change in the religious scene in the West. The growth of alternative religions, albeit
far from new, has brought a variety of diverse practice and belief.
Sociological focus has turned accordingly to explaining and
analyzing these new forms of religiosity. A great deal has been
written on the new religious movements which emerged from the
1960s. More recently, attention has turned to the New Age movement. One conclusion is that it marks a transformation away from
a counter-culture religiosity that was once world-rejecting, all-
embracing and community-based, to one which exemplifies the
spirit and even the inherent contradictions of post-modernity.
From one viewpoint it is the definitive religion of the 'gaps'.
Heelas (1998), for instance, believes that the disintegration of the
certainties of modernity has left a situation in which post-modern
religion flourishes. In this sense mystical or New Age spiritualities,
or what Heelas terms 'self-religions', have emerged to fill a spiritual vacuum and satisfy the need for meaning which traditional
religions can no longer provide and which give way to those
congruent to the culture of the twenty-first century.

10 The New Religions – Issues and Controversies

The new religions, ranging from the new religious movements (NRMs) to the New Age, have obviously attracted a great deal of academic interest. Among the themes that have been explored in depth are; who is attracted to the new religions, why are some more successful than others and why do a very small number control their members in an abusive way to the extent of bringing the self-destruction of the group? This chapter considers these issues and also looks at how state authorities and the public at large have responded to these new movements and examines what the wider implications are.

Who joins the new religions?

Another way of accounting for the rise of the new religions is through analyzing what kind of people constitute their membership. A popular conception is that converts are derived from deprived groups. However, these do not necessarily have to be the poorer sections of society. They may also be relatively deprived younger middle-class people. The latter are individuals who do not necessarily lack material wealth, but feel spiritually deprived in a world which they see as too materialistic, lonely and impersonal. While usually not appealing to the needs of the more economically deprived which are, more frequently, provided by world-rejecting groups, world-accommodating varieties offer a kind of spiritual substitute for those who otherwise lead fairly mundane respectable lives. Wallis (1984) touches upon this in his account of recruitment to world-accommodating religions. He claims that members are generally those who have some stake in the world;

162

however, such movements help members cope with their social roles, sometimes by offering the safe haven of a sub-culture to which they can retire. Often unconcerned with trying to alter the world or furthering the worldly opportunities of members, numerous movements seem orientated to dealing with the negative effects of modern society.

Other studies have found that members of world-affirming types tend to be rather older than those from other NRMs. The average age of participants in human potential groups was found to be 35, while Ellwood (1973) discovered that 43 per cent of members of Nichiren Shoshu were over the age of 36. These recruits were inclined to be even more predominantly middle-class and affluent than those of other movements. Many of them seemed professionally qualified and had started promising careers. Wallis argues that, in contrast, although open to all types of people, the attraction of world-affirming movements is often to wealthier social groups who have a significant interest in the world as it is. Members seek no compensation, only religious expressions which enhance their lives by offering a religious path to guilt-free, spontaneous self-advancement largely though human potential therapies.

Studying what might be interpreted as a world-rejecting movement, Judah (1974) found that 85 per cent of Krishna Consciousness members in the USA were under 26 years old, while only 3 per cent were over 30. In terms of social background, many were upper-middle-class in origin. Also in the USA, Ellwood (1973) discovered that participants in the Jesus Movement were mostly aged between 14 and 24 and largely of middle- and upper-class background. Similarly, in Britain, Barker (1984) found that the average age at which recruits joined the Unification Church was 23, while that of first-generation converts was around 27. About 80 per cent of members were between 19 and 30 and appeared to be mostly of middle-class origin. However, Barker refuted the suggestion that those who might be thought to be most vulnerable – the young, socially isolated, deprived, or those not succeeding in their lives – were particularly attracted.

These findings raise the obvious question of why often affluent and well-educated middle-class young people, with so many worldly opportunities before them, should be particularly attracted to NRMs of a world-rejecting nature. The question is particularly pertinent since such people would presumably be the most resilient to NRMs that are supposed to be coercive and manipulating. A simple answer would be that these individuals are those more fully involved in counter-culture experimentation. Indeed, there is evidence of the link with middle-class youth who were more involved with the 'hippie', drop-out, drug counter-culture of this time. The longer period of higher education and an unparalleled growth in affluence and job security encouraged a spirit of experimentation (Ellwood 1973).

In later years NRMs such as the Divine Light Mission, the Children of God and ISKCON (see below) were interpreted as partly embodying a retention of certain counter-culture values but translated into a new idiom that rejected its anarchic, ill-disciplined and often destructive lifestyle. Typical was Tipton's work suitably entitled *Getting Saved from the Sixties* (1982), where he considers three very different groups in California including one derived from the Jesus Movement, a Zen meditation group, and a human potential therapeutic group. Largely middle-class in composition, Tipton sees members as 'survivors' from the 1960s and a counter-culture that was an inadequate basis for a new lifestyle which these new religions could provide.

This kind of theorizing however, has its limitations. If a number of the movements did recruit heavily among ex-participants in the counter-culture this was not true of all (Barker 1984). Moreover, Rochford (1985) found that while early recruits to ISKCON, better known as the Hare Krishna movement, had been involved in the counter-culture, the later members were not. Nor do the doctrines of all these NRMs largely embody counter-cultural values (Wallis 1984).

Women and the new religions

Another finding of several studies on NRMs is their apparent appeal to women. It is, however, easy to read too much into such findings since women are over-represented generally in most religious groups – new or well established. Much appears to be linked to the potential of NRMs to shape identity in relation to gender. One observation is that what many NRMs offer

to women is a feminist spiritual path and an emphasis on receptivity, love and devotion in a discipleship to a god and guru
(Puttick, 1999, p. 146).

All these forms of religiosity frequently provide women with
more liberating roles, pathways to self-transformation and image
construction, and provide an alternative source of authority and
power through distinctive beliefs, rituals and symbols. For the
most part, they are consciously articulating alternative spiritual
beliefs and practices which envisage and celebrate positive views
of womanhood, such as female images of a deity, rituals of female
empowerment and moral norms which do not promote female
submissiveness. Most appear to advance positive images for
women by focusing on non-hierarchical relationships; a few,
however, go so far as to invert male–female and status relationships.

Historical evidence suggests that traditional forms of religion,
above all through the established churches, have only advanced
roles which reflect those ascribed by wider society. In the nineteenth century, however, new religions emerged which reinter-
preted women's roles – often giving women significant
leadership positions and ritually expressing women's needs and
experiences. For example, Scientology, Theosophy, Christian
Science and Spiritualism have long offered women opportunities
denied to them in the Christian churches. Today, less orthodox
forms of religiosity, such as the Mormon church, have developed
alternative gendered spiritualities. This is also true of new forms
of alternative religions including witchcraft, neo-Paganism and
spiritual eco-feminism, but it is also apparent in the liberal wings
of established religions such as Christianity or Judaism. In all of
these expressions of religion, teachings and practices are
frequently loosely defined and display an aversion to hierarchy
and the regulations of male-dominated institutions.

Susan Palmer's (1994) work on the roles of women in seven
unorthodox religious movements in Western culture is one of
the few comprehensive treatments of the link between NRMs
and gender identity. Palmer explores the innovative roles that
many NRMs supply. They allow women to experiment with
new concepts of gender and sexuality. In Krishna Consciousness,
for example, women are defined solely as 'mothers'. Unmarried
or childless women hold the same status within the organization.

A number of the more mystical NRMs believe that a woman transfers her spiritual qualities not only to her male partner but to the whole community. Through this transfer, the woman may earn respect and offer authority within the organization. While the developments of such roles may be seen as part of the construction of female identities, they may also permit women to take the position of power and leadership denied by more orthodox forms of religiosity.

Men, too, have developed their own spiritual groups and these very often seem to be linked with identity construction. Some of those organized more on a voluntary basis are often derived from New Age philosophy, and among their attractions may offer to men mutual support in developing the more sensitive 'feminine side' of their natures. Others however, do not appear to have any grass-root basis and operate more like client cults. Many of the more enduring ones work rather like support groups that reject the approach of the newer movement towards articulating a spiritual/ritual expression of a new masculinity. In contrast, they seem to be posited on the belief that individual men are not functioning well psychologically – indeed, may be emotionally and socially harmed because they have been inadequately socialized into a 'natural' masculine role.

Who are the New Agers?

The concept of membership is very difficult to apply to the New Age and its popularity cannot be measured by estimating the number of adherents of particular organizations. There is little by way of well-developed research literature nor sound statistics on who joins the New Age. It is probable that different elements of the New Age attract particular types of people. However, a fairly wide assumption is that, rather like the earlier NRMs, most of the adherents are derived from the middle classes.

For the most part, the New Age is open to those who have sufficient means to embark on voyages of self-discovery. Empirical evidence is presented by York (1995, pp. 187–8) who quotes the New Age Spirituality Survey and other findings which shows 73 per cent of New Agers to be female and 23 per cent between 18 and 34 years old, 42 per cent between 35 and 49 and 35 per cent over 50. In terms of education, 18 per cent have attended high school, 18 per cent have a degree, 12 per cent a higher degree. By way of occupation 25 per cent have a professional/technical background, 19 per cent are retired or unemployed, 13 per cent are clerical employees, 12 per cent are to be found in the service industries, 11 per cent are managerial and 6 per cent are involved in sales work.

The New Age, much like the NRMs, offers much to women. It rejects organized religion, typically the Judaeo–Christian tradition, which is seen as destructive. This attempt to return to some pre-Christian spiritual state is exemplified in the New Age's approach to gender issues. Many of the strands of the movement attempt to link biology or anthropology to gender issues with reference to men's or women's 'nature' – a common core nature that has allegedly been distorted in modern society. Hence, those components of the New Age which embrace the teaching and practices of Wicca (witchcraft) claim to bring liberation for women from the constraints of Christian gender roles and sexuality (Crowley, 1994, p. 116).

Very different from the middle-class adherents is the more experimental constituency of New Age travellers. In England they are constituted by the impoverished and urban young who have sought a simpler and more mobile life very much in contrast to the material culture of mainstream society. They have been attracted to different aspects of the New Age than those offered by the client cults of human potential or the witchcraft or magic as practiced by more organized New Age groups. Rather, the focus of this younger movement has been on neo-Paganism. One centre of attention was the Druid movement at Stonehenge and Glastonbury ('the lap of the Mother') in the West of England which long had a mystical significance. The 1984 gathering at Stonehenge attracted an estimated 30 000 people. They were by no means all New Age travellers but a good contingent were and many were initially linked to the wider Peace movement of the 1980s. If any deity was worshipped it was the Earth Mother, along with a desire to recapture a Celtic past. Ritual tended to develop spontaneously with circle-dancing, chanting, drumming and the use of mantras. The movement has been described as not so much an alternative lifestyle but as a new form of tribalism (Kemp, 1993, pp. 49–51).

Accounting for success

It is broadly accepted that cults and the new religions are highly precarious forms of religious organizations. Some become particularly successful and endure, while others quite rapidly decline and die. Their characteristic pluralist doctrines, their members' general individualistic mode of adherence, alongside problems of authority, frequently render many of them fairly unstable. Although some new forms of religion can stabilize as established cults, as has Spiritualism for nearly 150 years (Nelson, 1968), most which do endure typically undergo transformation from cult to sect as evidenced by the Jesus Movement, Scientology and the Unification Church.

Accounting for the success of NRMs has often led to the utilization of so-called resource mobilization theory derived from the pioneering work of Tilly, Tilly and Tilly (1975) on social movements. Here, issues of power, conflict and the distribution of political resources come to centre stage. The more successful social movements are those pursuing political goals by mobilizing 'resources' appropriate to their situation.

In regard to religion, resource mobilization theory is interested in considering the restraints within which religious organizations work and the causes of success. This includes examining how they mobilize resources including the charisma of the leader, money, publicity and media in establishing a religious movement or organization and pursuing their goals or, alternatively, how more established religions utilize the resources at their disposal in furthering aims, whether in order to win converts or increase their social power. Loftland (1979) has shown how even apparently small, marginalized and fairly insignificant movements can attract members by manufacturing favourable images of themselves. This includes portraying their movement as a growing force, as an instrument of divine will, and the teaching of warfare with evil powers within the framework of a wider cosmology. This kind of theorizing has even been applied to explaining the failure of anti-cultist groups to undermine the growth of some new religions. The lack of resources included the shortage of money, members and political lobbying (Shupe and Bromley, 1980). The possibilities of applying the theoretical framework thus seem endless and now preoccupy a great deal of work in the sociology of religion, at least in the USA.

It is clear that a belief system, particularly when it constitutes an entire worldview, is undoubtedly significant. Belief systems can have various functions, not least of all in unifying individuals within the collective by articulating core beliefs and embodying goals and the appropriate means by which they are meant to be realized. However, several commentators have suggested that stringent worldviews have also become a commodity in the 'theological marketplace' in winning over converts. In short, people are attracted by dynamic religious teachings particularly when they have relevance to their lives (Greely, 1981).

In exploring a number of other important 'resources' we may cite the Children of God (COG) which originated in Los Angeles in 1968 with a membership of twelve, and was merely one of several new religions to have worked with 'hippies' in the region. By the mid-1970s, the movement could claim to have 4500 adult members and a representation in over 70 countries. Davies and Richardson (1976, p. 338) attributed the growth, compared to other strands of the Jesus movement, to 'the rational approach to governance that has been developed over a period of years'. The year 1972 marked a considerable transfer of members of the COG to Latin America and Europe – becoming well established in England and Holland. Until 1973, the evangelistic style that the COG embraced was mostly street witnessing through a vibrant music ministry which set Psalms to rock music. Rapid growth continued and can be explained by way of a number of variables. They include financial resources derived from possessions of members, gifts from parents and above all by selling evangelizing literature that is printed today in 28 languages. Secondly, there was a conscious calculation to be less vigorously 'American' and assimilate other cultural patterns. Thirdly, the deliberate attempt to gain greater respectability by associating with other Christian churches.

Another important resource is the image of respectability. The position of an NRM may be strengthened if it can demonstrate its ties to an ethnic community and/or a major world religion. To improve its image ISKCON has emphasized its relationship to the wider Hindu community (Carey, 1987). It claims to have a priestly function derived from its roots in the ancient tradition of Vausnava Hinduism, which cultivates worship of the god Vishnu and his avatars (incarnations), Krishna and Rama. This had the effect of moving the cult towards the structure of a denomination

– hence the attempt to seek a greater respectability in the eyes of the outside world (Rochford, 1985). Scientology, by way of another example, seeks respectability in combating drug abuse through an organization known as Narcanon. Also attempting to generate a good image has been the Soka Gakkai movement. An offspring from the Nichiren Shoshu movement, it has founded a university campus in California and regularly awards honorary degrees to royalty and politicians. Finally by way of example, the Unification Church owns numerous businesses including those producing pharmaceuticals and the *Washington Post* newspaper which sponsors its activities, while it has a number of 'front' organizations including the International Conference on the Unity of Sciences and the World Peace Academy.

Dangerous cults

Some NRMs draw public attention for all the wrong reasons and the very small minority which have been destroyed in outbursts of violence make front-page news. The People's Temple was perhaps the most notorious. In 1978, an estimated 917 members (including children) of the cult's commune were found dead in a jungle clearing in Guyana. A crisis occurred when a US Congressman visited the site, accompanied by pressmen, to investigate complaints of brutality. When attempting to leave, the party was killed. The mass suicides and executions of cult members were found the next day. When the cult's financial affairs were investigated it was discovered that its founder, the self-styled Reverend Jim Jones, had amassed a personal fortune of over $5 million dollars. The events which led up to the horrific climax began three months earlier when Jones, a man of compelling personal attraction, took his faithful flock to the proclaimed paradise in Guyana to start a new life and to prepare for Armageddon (the end of the world). Jones had founded his movement in California, attracting mainly poor people from ethnic minorities with a promise of a world in which all would live as equals in an egalitarian Christian community. At its height the People's Temple claimed congregations numbering some 3500 members.

There were other examples of more hazardous cults in the 1990s: the Temple of the Sun (Europe), Heaven's Gate (USA) and the Aum Shinri Kyo movement either self-destructed or, in the case of the latter, launched a gas attack on innocent members of the public in protest at the materialistic society of Japan. However, while the ill-fated end of these cults can be blamed on the unscrupulous designs of leaders and seemingly bizarre beliefs, too much condemnation is frequently heaped upon the movement itself, and rarely on the repercussion of the way that the group responds to the real or perceived threats of the outside world. This was clear with the events surrounding the Branch Davidians. This movement began as a splinter from the Seventh-Day Adventists (SDA) when the leadership felt that the 500 000-strong membership had become too worldly and that what was needed was the whittling down to the biblical 144 000 Servants of God mentioned in the book of Revelation.

Although the Davidians can be traced back to 1929, the cult after 1986, fell under the leadership of David Koresh and was centred on a commune in Waco, Texas. Koresh, in the minds of his followers, was the new messiah who preached an apocalyptic message. By 1993 the federal authorities were looking for justification to penetrate the heavily armed camp at Mount Carmel after tip-offs that the cult possessed illegal firearms. The storming of the commune ended in the death of four federal officers, as well as six Branch Davidians. The assault was repelled and a stand-off ensued that lasted for fifty days. It created abundant and often lurid media coverage and compulsive viewing for millions world-wide. Waco became as much a byword for how not to deal with a marginalized cult as for any intrinsic danger that could be provided by a cult with a powerful charismatic leadership and apparently idiosyncratic teachings (Tabor and Gallagher, 1995).

Cult controversies

Few cults deteriorate into the violent confrontations as witnessed with the previous examples. Nonetheless, other NRMs have fallen foul of the authorities for various reasons. One which has found itself in continued difficulties is the Unification Church. In the USA, the Attorney General spent four years investigating the movement before eventually concluding in 1988 that it should be allowed to continue as a registered charity. Court cases in the USA against the church have been frequent and tended to be brought by individuals, usually ex-members with a personal grievance. In 1982, Moon was prosecuted for non-payment of taxes on interest on his personal bank account: he was fined $13 000 and imprisoned for 13 months. Another cult, the Rajneesh movement (now Oshu International), was also dogged with controversies throughout the 1970s and 1980s. Much centred on the late leader and guru Bhagwan Shree Rajneesh – not least because of all his ostentatious wealth, accusations of exploiting money from his followers, slave labour in his commune, claims that he rigged local elections in the USA, non-payment of taxes and sexual exploitation.

Cult controversies and debates surrounding the attempt at recruitment are not new since they were also evident in the nineteenth and early twentieth centuries. The charges then, as they are very often now, were of control, deprivation and systematic brainwashing, of sexual abuse, deluded charismatic personalities (often with the felt need to overcome their own personal crisis), dangerous conspiracy theories and dualistic worldviews and exploitation of vulnerable and emotionally unstable people; the homeless and those with alcohol or drug problems.

One of the more controversial cults has been the Children of God (COG), although it has more recently reformed its practices. Possibly the first anti-cultist group, FREECOG was established as early as 1972 specifically for parents to 'rescue' their teenagers from what constituted one of the largest strands of the Californian Jesus Movement. The most serious accusations against the group was that of sexual abuse. The leader David ('Mo') Berg shared the wives of some members of the movement and, from 1976, encouraged members to practice sexual exploration. Some ex-members allege that he advocated group sex, and the sexual involvement of children, alongside the notorious policy of 'flirty fishing' – a kind of prostitution in order to win converts.

Such control and abuse is not easy to account for. However, in the case of Berg it may have emerged from an ultimate need to control the membership as a result of the process of routinization within the movement. Wallis (1982) explains that the organizational growth of the COG undermined his charismatic authority. Berg criticized leaders for building institutional structures which challenged the purpose of the movement but which, in reality, presented alternative centres of power to his own. To counteract this he attempted to reinstate his charismatic authority. Appealing to the rank and file membership over the heads of the leaders, Berg proclaimed new prophetic insights, removed members with declining commitment and insisted on a firmer control over remaining members using forms of regulation which, arguably, led to excessive abuse.

There is increasing evidence that some NRMs are particularly abusive to women. As we have seen, many new religions are particularly attractive to women. However, there is a darker aspect. Puttick (1999, p. 147) identifies corruption, particularly sexual abuse, in the 'shadow side of the master—discipleship relationship'. She points out that in the past such abuse has often been perceived as a problem for Asian gurus encountering more permissive Western lifestyles. However, situations of sexual abuse are largely the result of harem-style structures where women are encouraged to compete for the gurus' favours. Puttick also sees it as increasingly part of the more Christian-based groups and results from patriarchal control. Harder (1974) comes to a similar conclusion concerning such patriarchal dominance in what she calls 'a youthful fundamentalist sect' of the Jesus Movement. It was seen to constrain females into the traditional, rigid and submissive roles which contrasted so sharply with the women's liberation movement that had permeated more traditional churches.

Cults and religious liberty

Despite the more menacing side of a small minority of NRMs, it is not appropriate to tar them all with the same brush. The problem is that the debate as to the merits or otherwise of NRMs is often clouded by cultural and ideological considerations. To question why anyone would wish to abandon all the attractions of secular society and join an NRM is clearly a reflection of public opinion (Snow and Machalek, 1984). At the same time, the freedom to express religious beliefs, no matter how seemingly bizarre to mainstream society, is a matter of civil liberties (Robbins, Anthony and McCarthy, 1983). Again, there is nothing particularly new here. In the early 1940s, Jehovah's Witnesses were involved in the so-called 'saluting the flag controversy' in the USA. This involved the movement's refusal to observe the Pledge of Allegiance to the flag which, after a long legal campaign, was upheld by the Supreme Court in 1943.

As far as coercive tactics or brain-washing by NRMs is concerned, sociologists who have studied NRMs have found no widespread evidence to substantiate claims (Bromley and Shupe, 1981). Particularly impressive is Barker's work (1984) on the Unification Church. The church's 'workshops' are often cited as a means of coercing people to join. They appear to include constant attention or 'love bombing' followed by the withdrawal of affection, endless rounds of activities and seclusion from the outside word. Barker studied those who failed to be converted to the Unification Church as well as those who were. Nine out of ten of those who attended two-day workshops did not join and there appeared to be no difference in their social background when compared to those who did. Recruitment techniques seemed persuasive and even manipulative, but not coercive. Neither did Barker find any attempt to coerce members to remain, should they wish to leave, by physical restraint or isolation.

More evidence against the 'brain-washing' thesis is how rapidly new members of many religious groups decide, of their own accord, to disengage (Bird and Reimer, 1982). Mounting evidence from studies of many of the NRMs over four decades indicates that far from being the malleable, passive, gullible dupes portrayed in the media, recruits are active, meaning-seeking individuals who exercise considerable volition in deciding to convert to a new religion. Furthermore, a striking fact concerning membership of NRMs is its transitory nature. Sensationalized media stories convey the impression that converts are trapped, indeed, 'lost' indefinitely. In fact, much conversion to NRMs is temporary (Wright, 1988). Barker (1985) found that, as far as the Unification Church was concerned, after two years of involvement with the membership only about 5 per cent of those initially attracted were still members.

The anti-cult movement

Bromley and Shupe (1981) believe that anti-cultist groups have largely shaped the public perception of NRMs and constitute more of a threat to civil liberties than the religions themselves. Negative propaganda includes overstating the numerical significance and social impact of NRMs. This is frequently accompanied by 'atrocity tales' of kidnapping, brain-washing and mind control which can provide a justification for the use of drastic methods by families of converts to remove their relatives from NRMs.

De-programming, or what has been scathingly referred to as 'the New Exorcism' (Shupe, Spiermann and Stigall, 1977), can be seen as a contemporary way of dealing with socially unacceptable beliefs and practices. There have been found to be significant implications. Ex-members' recollections of their experiences with various contemporary movements are reconstructed differently, depending on whether they left the group voluntarily and on their degree of contact with de-programmers and anti-cult counsellors (Solomon, 1981). Persons who had voluntarily left are inclined to remember their affiliation with the group as a positive experience, even though they had later changed direction. By contrast, people who are de-programmed are more likely to recall their experiences as one of deception and brain-washing. If they subsequently became involved in the anti-cult movement, their new allegiance includes telling 'atrocity tales' about their former groups (Lewis, 1989).

There can also be psychological effects on leaving the cult. A Dutch study of former members of NRMs found that around half of the respondents in a survey had psychological problems when joining. Moreover, many successfully dealt with their problems in their time with the cult, only to have them resurface again after being forcefully removed (Derks, 1983). A similar correlation appears in studies of the so-called 'cult withdrawal syndrome'. Psychologists affiliated with the anti-cultist movement hypothesized that NRMs use 'mind-control' techniques that produce negative psychological and emotional difficulties including nightmares, hallucinations, altered states of reality and violent outbursts. Other studies found that persons who were forcibly deprogrammed were significantly more likely to experience troubling psychological symptoms than were persons who left the groups voluntarily and were not subject to any 'exit counselling' (Lewis and Bromley, 1987).

Societal reaction to new religious movements

In his study of societal response to Scientology in Britain, Wallis (1993) shows how the construction of deviant labelling of NRMs is frequently undertaken by the mass media and representatives of the British state in a process of 'deviance amplification'. It is this kind of reaction by which claims of cultist abuse must be at least partly considered. Wallis argued that the initial deviation from social norms by Scientology led to a hostile societal reaction which encouraged the movement to adopt strategies of defence, looking inwards and, in turn, to launch an attack on its detractors. This was construed by the press and the state as the confirmation of their initial diagnosis. A set of generalized beliefs and a stereotypical characterization of the movement were formulated and disseminated by the mass media and moral crusades, leading to a panic reaction resulting in changes in the law. This kind of persecution from outside also has consequences for the internal dynamics of the movement. In the case of the Unification Church (Barker, 1983), criticisms from outside tended to generate a greater solidarity within the movement and bound members of the organization more closely together.

Societal reaction against cults are also shaped by a number of other factors. One is the policy of the state. Even among Western societies, wide differences in the response is evident – from extensive, if at times reluctant, toleration in the USA and Britain to a systematic hostility manifest so vigorously in France. In the Federal Republic of Germany, religious organizations with public law status enjoy the benefit that the state will collect taxes on their behalf from their members. To achieve public law status, a movement must prove its durability. It is required to show that it is well organized, with a sizeable membership and sound finances. It must also have been in existence for at least thirty years. The law is designed to exclude short-lived 'volatile cults'. In 1984, a resolution was passed by the European Parliament – the Cottrell Report – which focused attention on practices associated with certain religious beliefs and which proposed a voluntary code of conduct for each movement. However, in the late 1990s more draconian methods for dealing with cults and general hostile attitudes by the state had surfaced in such countries as France and Sweden.

Summary

The controversies related to the new religions are often out of proportion to their size and membership. The state, the media and the public at large have all shaped the perceptions of a number of movements. While some of the new religions, for good or for bad, are capable of pulling attention to themselves, the perception of what such religions amount to in terms of beliefs, practices and tactics of conversion have frequently been constructed by wider society. Moral panics are often the result – leading to an amplification of the alleged deviance of particular groups. This is not because these movements are generally non-Christian, but because they exist in a highly secular environment that engages the new religiosity, at least in the form of world-rejecting movements, in an atmosphere of suspicion and very often hostility. A similar observation may be made of the religions of the ethnic minorities and it is these faiths which constitute the subject matter of the next chapter.

11 The Religions of Ethnic Minorities in the West

No discussion of religion in Western societies would be complete without a survey of the faiths of ethnic minority groups. In the 1980s such an overview would not have warranted a separate chapter of a book on contemporary religion. Today, the extraordinary ethnic diversity which has developed in the West now makes this imperative. The significance of these faiths is that their proliferation influences a number of the principal debates already addressed in earlier chapters, most notably those related to secularization, religious pluralism and the nature of religious belief and belonging. At the same time the religion of ethnic groups provides new issues and challenges to the major world religions as well as the largely secular principles of the societies of Europe and North America.

Perceptions of ethnic religion

In political terms there are good grounds for arguing that liberal democratic societies, with their traditions of tolerance and respect for the cultural beliefs and practices of minority groups, should be able to represent the wishes and interests of such groups to the full. The reality, however, is that sometimes stark differences exist between Western democracies both in terms of the structures regulating relationships between religion on the one hand and state attitudes towards ethnic minorities on the other. As regards ethnic religion specifically, policies range from state neutrality in religious affairs, as in Belgium and Holland, a state religion in Denmark, to the overt secularism of Sweden.

More broadly, most Western nations at least pay lip service to the idea of a multi-cultural society, although others, such as France, have strong assimilation policies. Additionally, there are varying attitudes regarding citizenship which may encourage different levels of political activity by the religio-ethnic group. For instance, it seems that political activity by Moslems has tended to emerge more quickly in those countries where immigrants could acquire citizenship relatively easily, notably Britain and France.

Liberal democratic societies also tend to divide private and public life and involvement in the latter means ascribing to an essentially secular ideology. This can create problems for some religious groups in terms of both politics and cultural practices. Islam is a prime example. Moslems generally do not separate the two spheres of secular and religious life since their religion provides a comprehensive rule of conduct for the believer. This suggests that for them the reality of life in a non-Islamic country presents particular problems. Many Moslems view, with considerable antipathy, the combination of a diffuse Christianity and the outright secularity of the contemporary Western world. This points to the fact that the question of ethnic minority rights in liberal democratic societies is far from resolved and raises all sorts of paradoxes.

In Britain much was epitomized, in 1989, by the so-called 'Salman Rushdie Affair'. Rushdie, a liberal intellectual with an Islamic background, antagonized Moslems across the world with his novel *The Satanic Verses*, since it was interpreted by many as both insulting and blasphemous. The stark issue was between the liberty of literary expression on the one hand and, on the other, the rights and sensibilities of non-Christian religions and cultural minorities in the context of secular hegemony. More broadly, it had profound implications for the relationship between Western societies and Moslem countries since Rushdie found himself the subject of death threats from the more fanatical wing of Islam.

Another source of destabilization as far as relationships with the religions of ethnic minorities in the West is the global context. The post-Cold War period no longer means the potential world nuclear confrontations of the superpowers which dominate political issues but the conflicts of nationalities, ethnic groups and divided communities typified by the former Yugoslavia and other nations in central and eastern Europe. Today, a particular form of nationalism tends to be linked with religious tradition such as Polish or Croatian Catholicism, or Timorese Buddhism.

For many of the ethnic minorities in the West political developments in these regions remain of great significance. Sikhism is a prime example since it is very much concerned with nationalist aspirations, that is, the independence movement in the Punjab. Religious and nationalist sentiment was raised in 1984 when the Indian army invaded the Golden Temple in Amritsa – the Sikhs' most holy site. There have been implications for the West. The more militant pro-Khalistani groups regard countries with large Sikh communities, such as Britain and Canada, as bases from which the nationalist struggle can be pursued. Moreover, in Britain the contest for control of the Sikh temples has at times been a rivalry between 'moderates' and 'militants' with different attitudes to an independent state of Khalistan (Tatla, 1993).

As a result of such global conflicts minority religions may be labelled as 'deviant' and perceived as challenging dominant cultural values and political institutions and, therefore, engendering social divisions and instability. However, it is unlikely today that, in a secular society, they are perceived as being very different in as much as they are not within the remit of 'official' historical religion, that is, Christianity. Nonetheless, their status is very much tied up with the culture of ethnic minorities who may be designated as social 'outgroups'. Furthermore, in a largely secular society the visibility of ethnic faiths is obviously enhanced and they may, therefore, become even more the object of curiosity.

Research indicates high levels of prejudice against ethnic religious minorities, although across Western societies this picture is relatively mixed and is dependent on a number of localized circumstances. Whatever the precise context, discrimination or even what may merely appear to be a clash of cultures, frequently becomes a contentious political issue. There are numerous examples. Eade (1993) has shown how discourse by white locals in a dispute over the utilization by Moslems of public buildings in London made reference to an 'alien Islamic invasion', while Kuusela (1993) has explained how anti-immigration lobbies in Sweden used the issue of the construction of a mosque by Turkish immigrants as a symbolic confrontation with what was perceived as an 'outgroup'. Similarly, Bloul (1996) has explored how local conflict in France over the right of Moslem schoolgirls to wear hair covering in class was blown out of all proportion. The issue was utilized by native French to arouse fears of the Moslem population as an 'internal Islamic threat' while, in response, the migrants used the controversy as part of the construct of a contrary worldview or what Bloul terms an 'alternative universalism'.

Such discrimination against ethnic minorities has to be seen in wider perspective. The historical evidence suggests that prejudice changes in intensity over time and has, at its base, various levels of political and economic insecurity. Conflict perspectives within sociology can provide insights into this prejudice. Castles and Kosack's Marxist approach (1973) identifies powerful economic and political interests at the heart of the process of discrimination. Migrants are identified as a 'reserve army of labour' who are in competition with indigenous white workers for employment, housing and status. The basic insecurities of the manual classes render them particularly prey to racism as a result of perceiving the migrants as a threat rather than social class allies.

On a more general level it can be seen that the all too familiar pattern of social upheaval and the link to high levels of prejudice has emerged more recently against a background of economic problems in the West since the 1980s (Hunt, 1993). In its most visual expression it has been observable with extreme-Right violence against Turkish Moslems in Germany, and in France and Italy towards North African immigrants. It was also evident in Scandinavia against Vietnamese refugees.

Religion and ethnic communities

Another assumption that is frequently made is that the arrival of non-Christian religions in the West is a relatively new development and, therefore, indicates a source of recent social instability. Judaism, and to a lesser extent other major religions such as Islam, have had representation in Europe for many hundreds of years. Indeed, for some Western countries religious diversity in the form of ethnic faiths *is* closely woven into their historical evolution. In the case of the USA, the nation's history is primarily that of the migration of ethnic and religious minorities. The mass migrations from Europe, Asia and Latin America in the nineteenth and early twentieth centuries, in providing labour for the nation's burgeoning industries, constituted the largest movement of people in the history of the human race. Having acknowledged that while the arrival of ethnic minorities in the West is far from new, it is nonetheless clear that in the last fifty years a very considerable migration has taken place to the West from more diverse regions of the globe than ever before.

Sometimes migrants have been refugees from political upheaval, or have sought asylum from political and sometimes religious persecution. Whether it be Asian Kenyans fleeing to Britain in the 1970s, Vietnamese to the USA and Europe in the 1980s, or a variety of peoples from eastern Europe in the 1990s seeking release from ethnic persecution, the West has been regarded by many as a haven. The great majority of migrants, however, originate from Third World countries and are responding in a large part to the demands of the modern global economy. Since the mid-twentieth century the Western nations have called upon labour migrants from various regions of the globe for their economic expansion.

As a result of such migration the populations of Western societies have become, ethnically heterogeneous and pluralist. There are over 3 million Moslems in the USA, with lesser constituencies of Hindus, Buddhists, Sikhs and Jains. Part of Britain's 55 million population comprises approximately 1.1 million practising Moslems and 400 000 Hindus located in London and other major cities. Almost 50 per cent of Moslems have been born in Britain and many others are growing up in a country in which they have elected to live permanently (Anwar, 1995, p. 48).

The integral part religion plays for many ethnic minorities may be realized with reference to Durkheim's (1915) understanding of the social source of its expression. The significance of religion to an ethnic group is its collective nature and function in that it symbolizes the core values of the collective and is bound up with a profound sense of belonging. There are, nonetheless, a number of complexities in discussing the relationship between ethnicity and religion which deserve to be briefly explored.

First, an ethnic group might be divided, as much as united, by religion. In the former Yugoslav state of Bosnia in the 1990s, conflicts between major religious communities included Moslem, Orthodox and Catholic Christians, yet none of these factions are particularly different in ethnic composition. In the West, as much as in their country of origin, Pakistani Moslems are divided into various Islamic sects. People from the Indian subcontinent may be Hindus, Sikhs, Moslems or Buddhists, while individuals from the

Caribbean may be separated by their allegiances to different Christian denominations. Conversely, Black Caribbean Christians may identify more with fellow believers from the white population of Western societies, while Islam may unite individuals with different ethnic and national origins.

Secondly, few of the major world faiths are 'internally' united. Just as Christianity has its Roman Catholic, Orthodox and Protestant wings, most global religions display major divisions which complicate their link to ethnicity and nationality. This is why it is difficult to make generalizations regarding the Islamic community in the West. The history of Islam has resulted in the formation of numerous different strands and ways of believing. The major division today is between the Sunnis, who now constitute approximately 90 per cent of all Moslems in the Middle East and the Indian sub-continent, and the Shi'a who constitute 10 per cent of Moslems. Some countries such as Britain do have sizeable Shi'a populations worshipping in the many, often impressive mosques funded by the wealthy Ismali 'Sevener' community. This group migrated from the ex-colonial East African countries. However the Sunni, particularly those subscribing to the Hanafi school of Islamic law, predominate among Moslem communities in most Western societies.

Another example of how religion can be disunited by belief and practice is Buddhism. The Buddhist faith is divided into various strands which have impacted in different ways in Western countries. The Theravada tradition of Sri Lanka, once part of the British empire, became the predominant orientation of the Buddhist Society (founded 1907) and Buddhism generally throughout Britain. Nonetheless, Zen Buddhism and the Tibetan Vajrayana are two other alternatives. The latter has grown since 1959 following the Chinese invasion of Tibet, when many leading lamas succeeded in fleeing to the West. The historical development in the USA took a different route. The predominant tradition there has always been Zen, which continues to have a strong influence today. This resulted from Chinese immigration into California in the nineteenth century, followed after by immigration from Japan.

Despite these complexities in the relationship between religion and ethnicity it is clear that religious faith remains a central aspect of life for ethnic minorities. This is particularly so for those from the Third World where religious belief and practice are an integral part of social existence. It is also the case that the importance of religion for ethnic minorities may actually be enhanced in what is frequently the anomic situation generated by the process of migration and the transition from one cultural environment to another.

Part of the link between ethnicity and religion is the matter of boundary maintenance. Such maintenance is aimed at confirming the integrity and solidarity of the ethnic group by firmly demarcating the cultural differences with wider society. Its role for the early generations of migrants is imperative. The strengthening of boundaries is frequently why ethnic groups survive in the face of even the most overwhelming adversity. The importance of religion is that it brings a clearer delineation of the culture of a community and promotes internal solidarity even where it was not especially strong beforehand. Indeed, Sarna (1978) argues that when individuals from particular ethnic minorities first arrive in the West they are often highly fragmented, have little in common and frequently display no great sense of shared unity or purpose. This changes largely as a result of the 'outside agency' (the host society) in designating them as 'different' and 'alien' ('ascription') and as a consequence of hostility and exploitation ('adversity'). Discrimination, persecution, or even perceived persecution, can increase solidarity and internal cohesion and enhance religious faith, as part of the process of what Sarna refers to as 'ethnicization'.

Islamic communities have often provided a good example of the processes of boundary maintenance. For Moslems, the institution of purdah, the rules of behaviour and dress which reinforce the separation of male and female spheres, has not only often been retained but strengthened in response to the insecurities and threats in the new surroundings of the West. Mandel's (1996) study of the Turkish Moslems in Berlin shows how they perceive themselves in the land of the 'infidel', surrounded by things profane and haram (forbidden). In this situation they manage to create a world for themselves – establishing frontiers of distinctiveness ranging from dietary habits to language, from dress to domestic arrangements, which provide meaningful expressions of Turkish Moslem identity abroad. Such markers of cultural identity may be internally imposed, yet they are frequently fostered by experiences of discrimination. This can be illustrated by the experiences of the Islamic community in Britain. Here, the government's tightening of immigration controls, especially since the 1960s, precipitated the creation of Asian community support groups and enhanced cultural bonds which encouraged the dedication to the Islamic faith and the stepping up of the construction of mosques as centres of community life (Barton, 1986).

Assimilation or pluralism?

Although the relationship between religious belief, cultural maintenance and ethnic groups is important for the first generations of migrants, a wider issue has to be addressed regarding what is likely to be the long-term developments for ethnic religious minorities. Can it be predicted with any certainty that they will be assimilated into Western ways of life or will they remain distinct cultures in their own right? As we have seen, much may depend on the attitudes of the host nations. Western states vary in their policies towards the assimilation of religio-ethnic groups. Those policies encouraging assimilation in many respects seem to be at odds with the alleged virtues of pluralism and of a democratic society in that the vitality of democracy rests upon the diversity and fragmentation of social as well as political power. Moreover, the built-in assumption that assimilation is the natural or desirable goal may be criticized because it suggests adjustment should derive primarily from ethnic minorities and, in turn, belittles their culture and religious values. It also tends to exclude any possible benefits of 'cultural exchange', that is, that ethnic minorities can, through their culture, offer something beneficial to wider society.

The sociological issue, however, is not whether assimilation is desirable, but whether it is inevitable. Here, the key issues tend to polarize around theories of assimilation on the one hand, and on the other arguments supporting the view that ethnic pluralism can be maintained. The latter emphasizes the indefinite persistence of cultural heritage as the basis of the continued vitality of ethnic minorities and argues that assimilation is by no means a foregone conclusion. In fact, Theodore Hanf (1994) maintains that the classification of people by their 'analogous sociocultural status', that is their 'origin, language and religion', is of increasing importance in

Western societies especially with the processes of modernization and urbanization. Diverse cultural groups collecting within urban areas tend to compete in a kind of 'marketplace'. Those united by religion, even more than by ethnicity and language, are better established and more resilient against assimilation, and hence particularly effective in advancing their interests, since religion encapsulates the core values of any sizeable community.

In contrast to pluralist accounts, assimilation theories argue that, all things being equal, the tendency is for minority groups based upon distinct cultures to be swallowed up by mainstream society. Thus, with each generation the minority community adapts itself to the external social environment and adopts the culture of mainstream society. In order to give coherence to this assumption numerous models have been drawn up regarding the general pattern of assimilation. Typical is that utilized in Gordon's study of immigrants in the USA (1964) which gives evidence of the important distinction between cultural and structural integration. He agrees that social or structural assimilation occurs before cultural assimilation and can proceed only in this order. Hence, although migrants may be integrated into employment structures, ethnically segregated worlds of neighbourhood, friendship and family still remain as does the legacy of culture, including principal religious values, which take longer to dissolve and assimilate. It is not until such communities disperse and integration with the host society at a primary level takes place, exemplified by inter-marriage, that the sharing of a common culture emerges.

A rather different approach to assimilation is advanced by Hammond and Warner (1995) who stress the transformation of religion into more private expressions. They argue that the evidence suggests, at least in the USA, that the relationship between religion and ethnicity may be on the decline (although this varies noticeably from one ethnic group to another) – even at a time when communities in the USA are asserting their ethnic consciousness. Hammond and Warner speculate that neither religion nor ethnicity will disappear in the near future but the linkage between the two is almost certain to be weakened. Religion becomes more and more a matter of individual choice for members of ethnic minorities as it does for the host population. This, in a sense, is assimilation. Hammond and Warner also maintain that ethnicity, along with other background characteristics, will have a declining effect in determining religious identity. This process will be most obvious in suburban, non-denominational churches and in amorphous spiritual groups, but the inroads made by other religions into ethnic communities also signal further weakening of the link between religion and ethnicity. A sign of this is that Pentecostal Protestantism has made considerable inroads into Hispanic Catholicism, as has Black Islam into African American Protestantism.

What is the evidence to suggest assimilation? There is considerable indication, at least in the case of the USA, that those immigrants who entered at the beginning of the twentieth century – what is now at least the fourth generation – have jettisoned most of their minority cultural attributes. Over time, social and geographical mobility seems to have eroded the communal aspect of ethnicity. However, in the USA and elsewhere the picture is a complex one and no clear pattern emerges. Many of these complexities are evident in a consideration of some of the major ethnic groups which are discussed here with reference to Judaism, Islam, Hinduism and Sikhism.

Aspects of adaptation and cultural resistance

Judaism

Today, the largest communities of Jews outside Israel and the former Soviet Union are to be found in the West; in the USA, Britain and France. They also constitute the longest-established religio-ethnic constituency and for that reason it may be conjectured that they provide a useful case study for measuring levels of assimilation. The difficulty is that it is virtually impossible to draw conclusions given the variety of social and political contexts in which the Jewish community is located. Secondly, there have been different 'waves' of Jewish immigration into Western countries. In Britain, for example, there are Jews whose ancestors have had a presence for centuries. However, since the end of the Second World War successive influxes of migrants from different parts of the world have ensured that it is possible to speak of 'native' and 'immigrant' Jews.

There is good evidence, nonetheless, that Jewish communities exposed for a considerable length of time to the processes of social and geographical mobility have found their sense of identity slowly eroded. Social mobility, through occupation and wealth, brings ascribed status as defined by wider secular society, not by the religious community. Different lifestyles and life experiences, determined by income and social prestige, appear to undermine the cohesion of a unique ethnic–religious group which had previously been united by the same historical and collective experience. Although in the past the Jews had frequently constituted distinct ethnic enclaves, in modern Western states the Jewish community has tended towards assimilation as a deliberate strategy. Indications in Western Europe and the USA suggest that Jews are generally well integrated into economic and political life. Indeed, in the USA they constitute a powerful political lobby that has had considerable influence on successive government's international policy in respect of Israel and the Middle East.

As far as Judaism is concerned, evidence in Britain indicates a decline of attendance to synagogues especially by the young, a greater incidence of intermarriage with non-Jews and an increase in the divorce rate of Jewish marriages. If the young can be regarded as providing an index for the strength of Judaism, the future does not look promising. Evidence suggests that up to two-thirds of young Jews in Britain do not marry in a synagogue, preferring instead the simple ceremony of a secular registry office. Another indication is the results of Kosmin and Levy's (1983) study of religious ritual practice in Jewish schools compared to non-Jewish schools in Britain. Although the former scored higher, once home background was taken into account there was virtually no difference between the two groups in terms of the religious socialization of young people. According to this study, then, the next generation is not being rigorously inculcated with traditional religious values.

In the West far-reaching transformations have taken place in Judaism which do more than hint at on-going assimilation and point to the increasing effects of secularizing processes. In most countries the majority of Jews are still affiliated to one or other of the varieties of Orthodox Judaism. Even so, evidence points to transformations of the faith including profound changes within the Orthodoxy as the pressures of modern society become apparent. It is clear that Orthodox Jews have had to carve out strategies of survival, overcoming dissonance in their lives, through synthesis, transformation and the reinterpretation of beliefs. To be sure, in the USA especially, there has been something of a resurgence of expressions of religious Orthodoxy or even Ultra-Orthodoxy, but this sizeable revival can be interpreted as largely a form of fundamentalism that has emerged as a response to events in the Middle East and, more importantly, the liberalization of the faith in the West within the contours of an increasingly secular society.

It is the 'Progressive' section of Judaism, divided into Reformed and Liberal varieties, which is the clear marker of change. Reformed Judaism, beginning in the nineteenth century, attempted to provide a living faith, created in line with modern conditions and bringing certain liturgical changes and revisions in ritual which were designed to make the service of the synagogue more intelligible to the laity. Liberal Judaism is more radical in its theological formation and praxis. Here, Sabbath observance is frequently said to be a rabbinical creation, ritual circumcision denounced as barbaric, while other 'outdated' ritual has been criticized as crushing the 'true' spirit of religion. In their more progressive form, synagogues are so unconcerned with ritual that females attend services with their heads uncovered and where not even rabbis eat kosher foods.

Islam

The Islamic communities, since they are less well established, provide an interesting contrast. The broad picture suggests a paradoxical mixture of achievement and frustration, acceptance and alienation, and polarities of assimilation and isolation. In many respects these communities have been stricter in sustaining religious beliefs and practices than other faiths. Moslem children have been found to be more likely to favour the traditional arranged marriage than their Sikh and Hindu counterparts (Nielson, 1989), while Moslem parents also appear to be a good deal more stringent in their parental control of their children into the teenage years (Joli, 1984).

It would be wrong however, to produce a one-sided view of the Islamic community. Volt (1991) argues that while there are undoubtedly problems in fulfilling Islamic obligations in the midst of a secular society, these are not unresolvable. In fact, in a variety of respects Moslems are not essentially different from other minority groups.

Historically, Islam has always adapted itself to local conditions and has often proved to be tolerant of other faiths. There are also signs of assimilation. As Abdulla points out in the case of Germany, only slightly over half of the 1.7 million Moslems living there actually practice Islam (Abdullah, 1995, p. 77). Evidence in Britain shows that the younger generations of Moslems with a Western education have been inquisitive of their cultural roots and seek an earnest understanding of their cultural identity. At the same time, however, they have come to question some of the cultural and religious assumptions of their parents. While this may create certain dilemmas for the young, a challenge of traditional values may ultimately herald a greater assimilation (Ali, 1992, p. 113).

Hinduism

The broad range of teachings associated with Hinduism, the division of different waves of immigration from India and East Africa and internal divisions by caste have encouraged a fascinating combination of conservatism and innovation in the Western context. In the transplantation of Hinduism the demands of new locations, links with India and the length of residence away and particular geographical traditions have all influenced the significance of the faith at a local level in the West.

While it may be true that traditional ritual demands are not easy for the Hindu in dispersion, most Hindus have adapted, to one degree or another, to Western life (Thomas, 1993). At times there has been a simple cultural divergence expressed in religious terms. For instance, Hindus have traditions related to gender and sexuality which are at odds with the value orientations of mainstream society. However, perhaps above all is the significance of caste. In the West, communities and temples may be divided by linguistic and caste lines, not so much out of an ideological commitment to the caste system, but because they provide, amongst Indians, 'natural' communities and sources of identification. Nonetheless, the relevance of caste may be declining.

Adjustments are frequently made in the practices related to the issues of social and spiritual purity that are very much tied up with the central role of caste and there have sometimes been adaptations enabling the family and wider community to assimilate into the Western structure. However, change in the caste system for the

Hindu community is an uneven process. In some instances, especially in the case of a sect like the Swaminarayan, caste distinctions and distinctions of gender, as traditionally understood, are strictly maintained. Certainly, caste divisions are also fairly stringently upheld universally when they apply to the choice of marital partners and are frequently linked to the matter of ensuring the family line.

Sikhism

The origins of Sikhism in the Punjab and its adherence to the Punjab language in worship will ensure for the foreseeable future that it remains the religion of a particular linguistic and cultural grouping. Nonetheless, Sikhism retains a great diversity of culture from which it originates so that it is not useful to advance terms like 'popular Sikhism'. Nevertheless, the practice of arranged marriages and the rigorous division of the sexes are generally still upheld, while co-education is reluctantly accepted, and inter-caste marriages discouraged (Cole, 1989, p. 265). The matter of caste is particularly significant. For instance, Nesbitt (1997) examines the religious lives and attitudes of British-born children from two Punjab communities, the Valmikis and the Ravidasis. These are two castes traditionally associated with impure work (formerly known as 'untouchables'). Their stigmatization and marginalization is, to some extent at least, carried over into the British setting within the Sikh community and has proved to have far-reaching implications for individuals and family life.

Very often, practical and economic needs have eroded the boundary maintenance of the Sikh community (Jeffery, 1992, pp. 89–94). Central to the beliefs of Sikhism are the visible Khalsa symbols of the faith: the beard, uncut hair and related turban, wearing the Kirpan (ceremonial sword) and steel bracelet (Khara). How these traditions have been maintained or otherwise provides both a measure of assimilation on the one hand, and the attitude of the secular state to ethnic religions on the other.

In the early 1970s the British government had to modify its laws regarding the compulsory wearing of helmet protection for motorcycle riders which would have excluded Sikhs from wearing turbans. At the same time the general discarding of Khalsa symbols demonstrates a wish to assimilate to Western norms of dress and behaviour and, in more practical terms, to give a more 'favourable' impression when seeking employment (Helweg, 1991). Sikhs have discarded the Kirpan largely because they feared the British laws against carrying arms and also frequently discard the knee breeches usually worn as an undergarment. They have thus effectively broken their Khalsa vows. Of the five symbols it is usually the Khara which is retained since it is regarded as the least obtrusive.

Certain aspects of the Sikh faith have similarly lent themselves to assimilation. Sikhism is looked upon by its adherents as a progressive, reformed religion. Sometimes its radicalism and popularism have overspilled into the political arena. Hence, Sikhs have been very active in political campaigns and have frequently been overrepresented in labour organizations. Moreover, unlike some other religions, or divisions of some religion in which ancient traditions must be maintained, Sikhism, because of its reforming character, has not experienced as many difficulties as other faiths in being transplanted to an alien soil. Bhacha (1985), for instance, has shown that migrants to Britain predominantly belong to the Ramgarhia caste that migrated from East Africa during the 1960s and 1970s. They are highly educated, urbanized and motivated in terms of material and status aspirations. As a consequence adults have achieved a high degree of occupational success, while their children repeatedly perform well at all levels of education.

Summary

To the nations of the West, the religions of ethnic minorities appear to present a particular challenge. However, a complex picture remains with different levels of assimilation, state policy, and economic conditions all constituting important variables. The religions of ethnic communities are often perceived as being outside mainstream culture. Yet, if the post-modern theorists are correct, there is now less of a mainstream culture from which to deviate. Or, should it exist, it will incorporate aspects of other, more marginalized cultures. Hence, it is not surprising that many of the minority faiths have influenced Western societies in discernible and sometimes indiscernible ways. Such beliefs as reincarnation, although scarcely recognizable as a Hindu doctrine, are becoming increasingly popular in Western societies, while ethnic alternative medicines and therapies, cooking recipes and meditation techniques derived from non-Christian sources are now increasingly accepted as part of the contemporary Western way of life.

12 Popular Forms of Religiosity

This chapter considers the relevance of the more hidden expressions of religiosity in contemporary Western societies – those ranging from popular superstition, mysticism and the occult to the so-called quasi-religions that, in recent years, have increasingly attracted sociological interest. In this final chapter then, we recognize that many forms of popular religion today are not displayed via institutionalized or 'official' channels. Nor are they necessarily articulated through the new religions. Indeed, there are a vast range of religious beliefs and practices to be considered which are not easily discernible and rarely acknowledged by traditional religious authorities.

'Fringe' religions

It is clear that the rich variety of 'fringe' religions must be taken into account in any broad discussion of the so-called 'decline of religion'. In fact, it may be the case that such popular articulations of religiosity are possibly advancing at the same time that the more official and institutionalized forms appear to be in decline. This religious fringe, however, is far from new. The more esoteric and occultist types have historically constituted counter-cultural currents in Western societies and long competed with the more official forms for the allegiance of ordinary people. Hence, popular expressions of folklore and superstition have been detectable underneath the apparent domination of Roman Catholicism and the Protestant churches over the centuries and have tended to come to the fore when Christianity has been relatively weak and struggling for legitimacy, particularly among rural populations (Thomas, 1974). We might surmise, therefore, that far from being a cultural hangover from previous times, these aspects of religion function much like new religious movements (NRMs) in filling some kind of spiritual 'gap' left by conventional Christianity and can provide a focus of meaning and significance, if not belonging.

Superstition

'Superstition' is a term not easy to define. As with magic, it may simply be understood as representing an attempt to explain or even manipulate one's environment through various mystical or metaphysical means. In advanced industrial societies, where the primary means of understanding and controlling the world is through rational, scientific techniques, the level of superstition is, surprisingly, fairly high. For instance, a study in England (Abercrombie *et al.*, 1970) found that some 22 per cent of those sampled believed in lucky numbers and 18 per cent in lucky charms, while over 75 per cent 'touched wood' for protection. The study also showed that those who regarded themselves as 'religious' were more likely to be superstitious than those who claimed to be non-religious. Church-based people were however, noticeably less likely to be superstitious. There is tentative evidence here, then, that superstition may fill a spiritual need for those without Christian allegiance.

Contrary evidence nonetheless shows that many conventionally religious people also supplement their beliefs and practices with non-official religion such as astrology, extra-sensory perception (ESP), and psychic teachings (Bibby, 1987). Yet, whatever the spiritual mix, it is possible to see such displays of superstition as little more than a cultural left-over from previous generations since Abercrombie *et al.* found that there was little attachment to many beliefs with only around 6–8 per cent expressing a feeling of uneasiness if they did not perform the appropriate actions demanded by superstitious ideas.

Occultist practices

A related area to that of popular superstition is belief in the occult. Astrology, hexing, palmistry, numerology, amulets and charms, water divining and divination (by Tarot or pendulum) are included under this remit. A large body of literature has been produced in recent years which bears witness to their increasing popularity, or at least the exploitation of the marketability of aspects of the occult. If an interest in this area is increasing, it may therefore be as much to do with social change and cultural trends as the decline in Christianity. In the first instance, some observers have suggested that the 1960s and 1970s were periods of occult revival in countries like the USA which was discernibly linked to aspects of the counter-culture that developed at the time (Downton, 1979). Alternatively, since many related beliefs may be derived from the folk traditions of various ethnic groups, it could be argued that in the changing cultures of contemporary societies, occultist religiosity is spreading beyond its ethnic roots to the mainstream. Finally, to be added to the equation is the link with the contemporary preoccupation with health and healing. Occultist activities may be seen to be increasingly related to find-ing causes of illness and cures for illnesses, and providing herbal remedies (McGuire, 1992, 108). Whatever the exact origins, the belief in occultist practices would seem to be increasing as the data in Table 12.1 related to Britain indicates.

Astrology numbers among one of the more popular forms of superstition which involves a reading of the zodiac signs and incorporates a set of beliefs and practices concerned with the idea

Table 12.1 Belief in occultist practices, 1970s–1990s

	% of British population		
Belief in	1970s	1980s	1990s
Reincarnation	24	26	26
Horoscopes	23	26	23
Fortune telling	48	54	47
Lucky charms	17	19	18
Black magic	11	13	10
Spiritualism	11	14	14
Ghosts	19	28	31

Source: Adapted from Gill *et al.* (1998), p. 513.

that impersonal forces in the universe influence human life. Under the general category of astrology falls a wide range of practices from the highly sophisticated, complex speculations about the future to very crude newspaper horoscope columns. Such beliefs seem fairly widespread. The proportion of the US population believing in astrology seems to be somewhere between 15 per cent and 25 per cent (Gallop and Castelli, 1989, pp. 75–6), with some 25 per cent following their horoscope on a regular basis.

Although some people may be committed to astrology to the extent that they comprise a cultist movement, the great majority of those expressing interest do not embrace astrology as a central aspect of their lifestyle (Feher, 1994). In terms of social background, perhaps the most important variable when it comes to astrology is that of age. One study found that although the young were more likely to know more about astrology and be interested in it, a higher percentage of older people were actually committed (Wuthnow, 1976). In addition, while some elements of common religion, for example, herbalism are kept alive by distinct rural sub-cultural groups or ethnic minorities, it has been discovered that astrology is more prominent in an urban, rather than a rural context (Fischler, 1974, p. 287).

Witchcraft

The Old English term for witchcraft is 'Wicca'. It was adopted by practitioners to identify the cult of witchcraft which has enjoyed a renewed interest since the second half of the twentieth century. Today's craft is generally associated with Gerald Gardiner who, in the late 1940s, developed a mixture of beliefs drawn from ancient religious practices. These include Celtic beliefs to which has been added various elements of freemasonry and Rosicrucianism, as well as Egyptian and classical mythology. Wicca is essentially a mystery cult requiring initiation leading to a subsequent path of personal fulfilment and the development of psychic and magical ability. Advancement requires the passage through various grades of commitment. In nominally Christian cultures witchcraft has been regarded as particularly deviant. Interestingly, in Britain it was not until the Fraudulent Mediums Act of 1951 that individuals were legally allowed to practise witchcraft as long as they did not intentionally harm anyone.

Witchcraft beliefs and practices are followed with varying degrees of seriousness and involvement. At one end of the spectrum are people for whom witchcraft is probably something of a fad or form of entertainment. For others, there is an earnest belief in witchcraft, outwardly expressed in the performance of spells for health, protection, or success, or the ascription of special importance to astrological events such as solstices or eclipses. This greater involvement may also include belonging to a coven. The background of those who practice witchcraft is intriguing and, along with other occultist practices, there may have been something of a change in social profile. Once they were associated with the poorer and less educated sections of society. Lurmann (1989) has similarly shown how followers of witchcraft and magic in the London area are, for the most part, educated, well-qualified professionals many of whom are scientifically trained and employed in such industries as computers and pharmaceutical research. Witchcraft, he suggests, is an opportunity to indulge in the irrational and to thereby seek meaning from a radically different perspective of the world.

One of the interesting developments of witchcraft and paganism has been the adoption of some of their symbols and practices by a form of feminism which stresses the deviant heritage that the white witch represents (Culpepper, 1978). Although most Wicca covens are open to both sexes, the radically feminist Dianic covens, which are largely found in the USA, are exclusively female. Here, the head of the coven is a high priestess where, in rites of witchcraft, the power of the goddess is called down to possess her. Males, too, have their exclusive equivalent realm. The Ancient Druid Order, founded in 1717 by Kohn Tolland, has an almost exclusively male membership. It rejects the idea of a revealed deity which constitutes the dominant idea of Christianity. In contrast, the emphasis is on hermetic magic, theosophy and the ritual system of sun worship – the sun being the principal spiritual source – and includes, at its height, the summer Solstice rite. While some people may be devoted to certain expressions of the occult, it is clear that for others they are something of a fad or rather lacking in any true spiritual element. What is certainly evident is how older occultist practices are given a new direction and applied, especially through the vast amount of popular literature produced, with an appeal to human potential, healing and personal success. One example is numerology which is primarily concerned with adding and multiplying significant numbers to reveal likely outcomes in the future. Today, books such as *Numerology For Beginners* are mostly concerned with the importance of numbers in choosing a partner, moving house, changing job, or starting a business. How this works out in practical terms, to provide an illustration, is when moving house one is implored to be aware that towns and places can be converted into numbers and could be calculated to be a fortuitous event or otherwise.

There is little doubt that these ancient forms of the occult are undergoing a process of commodification. For Hawley (2001), this is exemplified by an advert for the internet on the London Underground:

> Thanks to excite.co.uk this woman found her astrologically ideal partner on-line. Amazingly, she also searched for her entire family tree, played backgammon with Christoph in Munich, found a local restaurant with an exclusively vegan menu, bid for an original Art Deco lamp and discussed spirituality with a Tibetan monk. All before her morning coffee. If she can, why can't you?

Another example of how ancient arts are applied to contemporary conditions is the increasing popularity of oriental occultist practices. One such is Feng Shui which means 'the Art of Living in Harmony'. It is a practice some 3000 years old which claims to enable individuals to find their ideal living environment and through this attain health, prosperity and happiness. The Chinese exponents of the art claim that where people live and how they allocate and arrange the rooms of their home can significantly influence the harmony of their life and general welfare. The attraction of this philosophy to a home-centred Western society is perhaps obvious but it also has the attraction of being concerned with a person's broader well-being.

Quasi-religion – problems of definition

So-called 'implicit' or 'quasi-religions' appear to be proliferating in contemporary Western societies and in doing so they have increasingly become of academic interest. In simple terms, they amount to a range of social phenomena which have at least some qualities in common, although often hidden or ambiguous, with more traditional forms of religion. By applying such criteria it is possible to group a great variety of social activity and belief together as being 'like religion' or, as defined by the *Oxford Dictionary*, 'implicit' as 'implied though not expressed' and 'quasi' as 'seemingly, not really, but almost'.

Among those which have been designated in this way by sociological studies are a whole range of sports, environmentalism, shopping, rock music, television, UFO cults, human potential movements, the 'cult' of Princess Diana, health fads and 'ethical' eating. The list is seemingly inexhaustible and, at first glance, appears to be stretching definitions of religion beyond any plausibility. For some sociologists, however, the implied religiosity in these diverse areas may suggest a resurgence of religion in the West. Although not particularly new, the growth of quasi-religions, seems to undermine the secularization thesis (Nesti, 1990). For others, arguing from a different perspective, they can be interpreted as yet another sign of the imminent demise of 'true' religiosity.

Clearly, there are a number of problems involved with definitions of implicit or quasi-religions in that they are commonly defined as a result of subjective interpretations. Hence, it might be argued that a social phenomenon is defined as a 'quasi' religion because it does not fall within either popular or common-sense views of what a religion is and/or what is officially defined as such by governments or other influential agencies including anti-cultist groups. There are obviously political and ideological overtones here. This is made clear by Eileen Barker's discussion of NRMs. Barker (1994) points out that the Unification Church, which adamantly describes itself as a religion, is viewed by both governments and popular opinion in very different ways. Frequently, it is seen as neither a 'real' nor genuine religion, indeed it is often interpreted as a quasi-religion because of preconceived ideas about its activities or alleged notorieties.

There is also the difficulty in establishing the boundaries between implicit or quasi-religions on the one hand, and supernaturalist religions or what might be called 'explicit' religions, on the other. The problem is what to place under the heading of 'quasi' as many groups, particularly 'holistic' movements with their emphasis on spirituality, health, personal growth and ecology, are difficult to clearly classify as either sacred or secular. It has also been suggested that many groups associated with the occult or astrology could be classified as quasi-religious (Cambell and McIver, 1974) and may be true for many strands of the New Age movement as well. At the same time, Bailey (1997, p. 7) points out that explicit or traditional forms of religion may themselves display aspects of implicit religion. We may cite neo-Pentecostalism which, while retaining many of the elements of conventional Christianity, has come to emphasize personal healing and human potential to such a degree as to make a virtual 'religion' out of this-worldly concerns.

The apparent dilemma regarding what is or is not a quasi-religion obviously opens up older debates as to what may be defined as religion. Greil (1993) believes that quasi-religions are a kind of compromise between functionalist and substantive defini-tions although it is probable that they can be qualified, depending on what criteria is chosen, as religions under many sociological definitions. This means, however, that they sustain a tension between the sacred and the profane, this-worldly and other-worldly, in such a way that no current definition of religion can satisfy what appears to be an ambiguity. Greil, however, identifies two key characteristics of quasi-religion which overlap with more traditional forms. First, they display organizational dynamics simi-lar to those of religious institutions, narrowly defined, but without the belief in the supernatural. Secondly, quasi-religions, in line with more orthodox forms, focus upon expressions of what might be termed the 'ultimate concerns' of human existence (Rudy and Greil, 1983).

In respect of the first feature, numerous writers have high-lighted some of the apparent religious aspects of secular organiza-tions. One of the more obvious parallels is with political organizations, particularly the political parties of the extreme Left and Right of the political spectrum, most notably those that are Marxist or Fascist. O'Toole's (1977) work, for instance, has described the process of 'conversion' and commitment in several political groups in Canada including the Internationalists and the Socialist Labour Party. Moreover, like similar studies it highlights the sectarian characteristics of political organizations. The cult that surrounds the leadership has accompanying uncompromising beliefs that border on a kind of religious dualism which divides the world into the forces of good and evil. There are also other forms of secular organizations which display the implicit characteristics of religious institutions. Among the less obvious are large-scale business enterprises. In this area Bromley and Shupe (1990) have described a number of large US corporations as having sectarian elements, while Peven (1968) has analyzed the use of what she calls 'religious revival techniques' to socialize sales personnel into the business ethic and to integrate them into the culture of the corporations.

Greil's second criteria for identifying quasi-religions suggests that while they do not focus on any specific supernatural dimension, such religions often centre around expressions of 'ultimate concern' in much the same way as orthodox religion (Rudy and Greil, 1983). This is because they provide a locus of meaning and significance to life. A similar point is made by Lemert (1975). Lemert is not concerned with similarities in the institutional basis of such social phenomena, but in exploring their relevance to Peter Berger's (1967) definition of religion. Hence, Lemert suggests that religious elements can be applied where there is evidence of a process of constructing and maintenance of a cosmic level of meaning in everyday life by the display of a sacred ethos, myth, ritual and symbol. In short, social phenomena may parade aspects of religiosity where what is held as 'sacred' reifies a way of life or culture. Lemert suggests that when people begin to apply a 'spirituality', seek significant meaning and sometimes moral dimension to their existence and concerns in this world which go beyond a mere material aspect, they are moving towards a religion of sorts. This is evident when they derive from life a desire for a harmony and balance and even a desire for simple contentment and happiness. Hence, for some people, the fanatical following of movie or rock stars and the near-obsession with bike clubs and trainspotting, for example, begins to take on implicitly religious dimensions.

The function of quasi-religions

More often than not, it is functional rather than substantive definitions which are utilized in categorizing quasi-religions. As we have seen (in Chapter 1), substantive definitions of religion tend to focus upon a belief in spiritual beings or the supernatural. Functionalist definitions centre upon what religion does, particularly in terms of reference to sacred practices. It is this latter approach which allows a far broader range of activities and beliefs to be described as religion. Here, Durkheim's functional definition of religion has proved popular since it involves a common set of beliefs and practices which unites a shared collective system of morality. There is, in Durkheim's definition, no mention of the supernatural. It is hardly surprising, therefore, that it has been seized upon to discuss such secular concerns as sporting activities to the extent that there is a 'complete identity' between religion and sport because they share beliefs, symbols and rituals in common (Prebish, 1984, p. 312).

Soccer has been a popular theme for discussion (either as an activity or spectator sport). For instance, Percy and Taylor (1997), emphasizing the fact that approximately the same number of people go to soccer matches in Britain as go to church, argue that there is a phenomenological relationship between rituals, performance and expectations of soccer crowds, as well as the dynamics of tribalism, 'popular' notions of masculinity and even shamanism in predicting match results.

In North America, the theme of sport as a quasi-religion has drawn a great deal of attention. Loy, McPherson and Kenyon (1978) conclude that, in recent years, sporting activities in the USA have helped fill the gap left by declining civil religion and have reinforced the American way of life. They do this by restructuring myths and values and creating a sense of history and tradition which subsequently fosters social integration. This kind of Durkheimien approach views religion in terms of a normative social functioning. All that has changed is its expression. Alternatively, sport may provide forms of 'folk' religion for certain sections of society and constitutes, especially for males, a distinct way of life and sub-culture (Demerath and Williams, 1985, p. 166). Some sports even appear to display aspects of religiosity which make reference to superhuman or possibly supernatural entities. Many popular sports elevate personalities to almost divine status. Famous soccer stars frequently assume a demi-god prestige, while the opposition's team may be designated as the 'forces of evil'.

Although Durkheim believed that religion would continue to

be pervasive in modern society he could not have anticipated all the forms that it has taken. At least this is the claim of Weinstein (1992) in her discussion of the religious dimensions of television. A key feature of contemporary society is its mode of integration: its solidarity is a function of the technological and organizational innovations of the mass media. Hence, national media such as television serves to depict society 'to itself and to celebrate it'. Television is not mere entertainment, according to Weinstein, but functions as the collective consciousness in society by imposing a common set of beliefs and morality. Television personalities become 'church leaders' and may even be conferred a sacred status as they are the embodiment of symbolic expressions of modern collective sentiments. This obviously takes quasi-religions beyond mere functional definitions in making overt references to the supernatural, to gods, spirits or any such supernatural force or some superempirical realm. Two other examples might be explored.

In his book *Elvis People: The Cult of the King* (1992), Ted Harrison describes the cult which was in embryo during Elvis Presley's life, and its substantial growth, after the singer's death in 1977, into what borders on a full-blown new religious movement. There is now a thriving market for 'relics', while Presley's former home at Graceland has become a site of pilgrimage for thousands of people. A 'priesthood' of impersonators preach the 'gospel' of Elvis throughout the USA and beyond. At the same time, Presley now has 'disciples' who claim to feel his presence especially in times of personal troubles. There are also a range of myths about the alleged supernatural events that attended his birth and his life-long quest for enlightenment which are not uncommonly interpreted as evidence that he was 'chosen' by a higher divine power.

A second example of quasi-religions that focus upon supernatural or near-supernatural entities is the various flying saucer societies. One of the most fascinating and entertaining works in this area is James Lewis' edited volume (1995) on UFO cults, *The Gods Have Landed*. Several contributors highlight the spiritual aspects of those such as the Raelian movement and Aetherius Society. These cults, which have become particularly popular since the 1950s, typically centre on communication with extra-terrestrial life forms who are believed to send messages to human beings through astral travelling or telepathy as well as physical contact. These alien beings frequently appear to border on supernatural entities since they are often perceived as far superior in every way to human beings and the 'salvation' to come is expected to arrive when the more advanced benevolent aliens show human beings the error of their ways. They may even take 'believers' away to some better place. The messages said to be sent by these extra-terrestrial beings often appear to be moral or 'spiritual' in content – calling on the human race to reconstruct the world it threatens to destroy through its ignorance and greed. Other contributors to Lewis' edited volume discuss such themes as those who claim a kind of 'religious' experience after being abducted by aliens, the cultist dimension of UFO cults in their conversion processes to a new worldview and theological questions raised by beliefs in extra-terrestrials.

So far, we have used various criteria to describe quasi-religions, but are these definitions sufficient? There is an important dimension yet to consider. Greil (1993) maintains that what might or might not be designated as 'quasi-religions' should largely depend on the actor's own definition rather than some template applied by the social scientist. This more phenomenological approach suggests that the principal question is whether a collective regards itself as a 'religion'. While some groups labelled as 'quasi-religions' by the so-called experts, such as Scientology (Barker, 1994, p. 105), are all too eager to be described in this way, it is probably the case that the majority undoubtedly are not.

We may consider one clear example. Sisking (1990) believes that the 'radical' psychotherapy group that she studied, the Fourth Wall Community (based in New York from the 1950s to late 1980s), displayed many of the characteristics of a religion. It was initially founded as an experiment in radical personality change and self-realization and included the following implicit elements of religion. First, a perfectionism and millenarianism – where a self-designated 'elect' or 'chosen people' intended to create perfect human beings in order to establish a new society. Secondly, apoc-alyptic beliefs such as the emphasis upon nuclear annihilation and the threat of AIDS. Thirdly, the unquestioning faith in an author-itarian leadership and the expulsion of 'heretics' from membership. Fourthly, a belief in absolute good and evil, the saved and unsaved, and the emphasis on 'confession' in the form of revelation made to one's therapist. Despite all these attributes of a religion, Sisking maintains that the community would have been horrified to have been depicted as such.

The rise of quasi-religions

If quasi-religions are becoming an increasing feature of life in the West, how might their growth be accounted for? There are clearly some explanations advanced in our discussion so far that answer this question, including the view that they may fill a vacuum left by the decline in civil religions. However, there are others to consider although they must be accompanied by some cautionary observations. First, such religions are not limited to the Western context. This means, of course, that there may be scope for comparative analysis as can be seen in the discussion between, for example, loyalties to a soccer team and aspects of 'primitive' tribalism. Secondly, there is something more basic to ponder. Wallace found that religion in most societies is not divided into a distinct sphere and that universally people have difficulty in separating religious belief from the secular aspects of their worldviews (Wallace, 1966). Western societies separate these spheres, and sociologists do likewise. The implications are significant in that they can be said to be discovering implicit religion in some social phenomenon which has perhaps long existed. Searching for some kind of new religiosity then, becomes the pastime of those who wish to refute the secularization thesis.

Quasi-religions, modernity and post-modernity

One of the most common explanations for the apparent growth of quasi-religions is that they are fulfilling some kind of social or human need. In line with a number of the studies considered above, Greil and Robbins (1994) believe that, at least in the USA, such religions are advancing in the space left by the decline of more traditional forms. They suggest that American 'folk' religion with its emphasis on the one God is losing its influence and they speculate that it may well be that traditional religions with transcendental worldviews are no longer satisfying or meaningful. At the same time, the link between the religious and non-religious is more difficult to discern as profound cultural changes continue to take place which blur the distinction between the two (Greil and Robbins, 1994, p. 16).

In discussing the proliferation of quasi-religions, other commentators prefer to stress aspects of post-modernity. Nesti

(1990), for example, sees implicit religion arising from the inability of the contemporary Western world to provide unitary systems of meaning. Rather, it fragments people into their own life experiences by weakening identity as well as perceptions of historical time, particularly perceptions of the past. Implicit religion includes the search for meaning and identity in a world which finds it increasingly difficult to provide them. This search originates in the individual's life experience, expressing itself by means of a complex system of symbols and practices. It may involve an attempt to transcend social isolation and join with others in a collective endeavour and integrate into a universe of meaning. Such religions allow for the primacy of a person's existence in the here and now. Hence, social forms and experience are translated into spiritual metaphors – giving secular phenomenon spiritual powers. It may also entail notions of a personal voyage or express itself in the form of escapism – crossing human borders and freeing individuals from social and psychological limitations.

What many of these explanations for the rise of quasi-religions have in common is the conviction that there exists a profound search for the meaning to life. However, it is one which is more this-worldly directed. This is perhaps most obvious in forms of quasi-religions which stress human potential and perfectionism. Many contemporary movements such as Gestalt training or Psychosynthesis give an emphasis on health and fitness. Here, 'salvation' of the body takes place over that of the salvation of the soul. It is significant in this respect that many overtly New Age and sectarian movements have recently begun to emphasize health and healing and carry doctrines and philosophies which integrate notions of wholeness, naturalness and purity – notions which, as Beckford (1983) has argued, dominate much alternative and counter-culture thinking.

Summary

What the 'fringe' and quasi-religions have in common is that they often constitute hidden forms of religiosity. Fringe, typically occultist, expressions tend to be hidden because if they are not practised in an individual capacity then they are represented by loosely organized groups typified by those representing neo-Paganism that constitutes a membership that, rather ironically, openly dislikes organized religion. Quasi-religions tend to be more 'hidden' in the sense that they are not obvious forms of religiosity and may only be described as such because they have been so defined by those sociologists who are prepared to take definitions of religion about as far as they will go. In doing so it is possible to suggest that there is perhaps a great deal more 'religion' to be observed in contemporary society than first appears to be the case. This does, of course, undermine traditional debates concerning secularization and vindicates those such as Herberg (1956) and Yinger (1965) who maintained that secularization might be viewed less in terms of the decline of religion and more in terms of religious change. In short, forms of religion anchored in supernatural views of reality have declined, and have been replaced by those which are more focused on this world. From this point of view, then, quasi-religions appear to be one of the most interesting and controversial expressions of religious life.

Conclusion – The Future of Religion in the West

This book has considered the nature, extent and consequences of contemporary religion in Western societies. It has attempted to do so by overviewing present sociological debates, by surveying contrasting theoretical frameworks and, through examining diverse forms of religiosity, discussing several principal issues pertinent to current religious belief and practice. The fact that it has engaged with so many themes is indicative of the complexity of religion in the West. Today, the sociology of religion focuses on a far wider range of concerns than merely tracing the alleged decline of religion. There are now numerous trends, intricacies and even contradictions to take on board, and all this makes it very difficult to predict the form and trajectory of religiosity in the future.

While it is the vogue to step aside from crude reductionist accounts of secularization, the broad theme is still an enduring one. It remains a useful means by which to proceed and it is explicitly or implicitly the continuing reference point for current debates and theorizing. To be sure, certain aspects of the 'hard' version of the secularization thesis are frequently rejected – particularly that which insists on the *inevitable* decline of religion. At the centre of the present sociological debate are the implications for religion in an increasing pluralist society. To put it succinctly, sociologists of religion now centre on the basic question: what is the relationship between religious pluralism and religious vitality? Earlier theories such as that of Peter Berger argued that the relationship was negative, that pluralism undermines vitality. At the beginning of the twenty-first century, sociologists of different schools are more inclined to argue that the relationship is a positive one – that pluralism increases vitality.

The major exponents of the 'pluralism equals religious revival' thesis are those that embrace one variety or another of the rational-choice model. They deny that an increasing rationalism and pragmatism is replacing a religious and superstitious view of the world. However, there is, so it is argued, an observable incursion of the dominant rational orientation into every aspect of social life which has repercussions for religion by way of its growth. The assumption is that a rational instrumentalism overspills into the realm of religion and allows choices for the 'spiritual seeker' who, free from social pressures, can opt for the religion of his or her choice. This can be expressed in private forms or, reflecting the move towards voluntary associations, sometimes more organizational expressions which are increasingly likely to be religious collectives constituted by people of similar background, life experiences and cultural styles.

A major strand of post-modernist theorizing also recognizes a revitalization of religion. This conviction of a resurgence of religiosity is at least partly based on the insistence that a rational view of the world has gone into reverse. From such an approach the loss of faith in rationality has opened a vacuum that religion can fill – providing a haven of meaning. Yet, along with the rational-choice theorists, there is an emphasis on the consumer dimension of religiosity and its commodification. Indeed, if there is any one theme which unites sociologists in the area today then it is the matter of choice and consumption in the field of religion.

If religion is being transformed, various questions must nonetheless be asked. One is, if religion is now becoming a matter of choice, what does this choice entail? In simple terms it would seem to involve choosing from an infinite variety of religions and the freedom to mix 'n' match according to one's spiritual, psychological and social needs in an 'open' spiritual marketplace to which a 'supply side' accordingly responds. It is evident however, that only certain types of religiosity are indicated as growth areas of religion. These are believed to be innovating forms of spirituality, with those involved now speculated to far outnumber the regular attenders of traditional Christian churches in some Western countries.

From the 1960s, this new religiosity was evident in the expansion of new religious movements (NRMs). However, their decline has been as rapid as their growth. Although of great sociological interest at the time, it is difficult to argue that they now have quite the same impact. Yet, their swift rise and fall does tell us something about contemporary religion. Above all, they are indicative of the tendency of religion to change swiftly – catering for the needs, albeit transitory, of specific social groups. For that reason they will tend to speedily come and go. This may also prove to be so in the future.

Of the different types of NRMs, the ones that have declined most rapidly are those with a world-rejecting tendency. The desire for communal life and experimentation now largely belongs to the past. Because of the extreme demands they make on their members, these NRMs are increasingly likely to be reduced to a small constituency. Choice in the level of commitment and individualism have eroded their appeal. On the other hand, those NRMs that have greater attractions are the world-affirming forms. Most are concerned with what they can do for believers in this world and where commitment is slight. These tendencies are now primarily observed in the New Age movement and related forms of mysticism founded on ancient religions ranging from the esotericism of the Eastern traditions, to the Western occultist and neo-Pagan strands. Added to these are numerous human potential client and audience cults which enhance the individual's well-being in this world through seemingly shallow spiritual expressions. Yet, even these have limited appeal. They are largely open to those who can afford to participate and have the time to indulge in the services they offer. Hence, they are, for the most part, the new spiritualities of the affluent middle-classes.

Current changes are exemplified by the New Age movement. There was much in its early stages that appeared to resurrect the spirit of the counter-culture of the 1960s. Yet, this more cultural resisting element has proved short-lived. The New Age is now primarily a movement which does not insist on 100 per cent commitment, although this may be the choice of some individuals. For the most part, the religious consumer will be as dedicated as s/he likes and takes out of the New Age what is to their advantage. This is essentially why the practices and beliefs are also extremely varied. It is thus the polar opposite of religious fundamentalism with its uncompromising dogma. The New Age, is perhaps, the ultimate mix 'n' match religion and this makes it a leading competitor in the religious marketplace. It is also a developing form of liberal and tolerant spirituality that is discernibly spreading in radically different dimensions – typically in the form of holistic spirituality or self-spirituality that has influenced different aspects of social life.

The New Age and esoteric and occult movements represent a particular form of religiosity. It is one that Fenn (1990) sees as entirely compatible with today's world in that it grants a restricted scope to the sacred and advances a low degree of integration between public and individual value systems. These forms of religion can be practised without coming into conflict with everyday occupational roles since they confine themselves to very particular times, places, objects and issues. Such religion provides an ecstatic and magical form of activity and an opportunity for the individual to indulge in the irrational against the enforced rationality of formal and bureaucratically structured organizations and roles of everyday life.

If the new spiritualities are predominantly a form of religiosity that may be marked by its transitory nature in the sense that they are constantly influenced by the fads and fashions of today's culture, the question may legitimately be raised as to its true level of spirituality. Some have doubted whether there is a great deal to be observed in these new religions. This is evident in Bryan Wilson's (1992, p. 96) much-quoted statement that the new forms of faith are so much 'pushpin, poetry, or pop-corn'. They thus tend to be void of all that is usually appraised as a true religiosity that adheres to an unchanging morality, belief and practice, and endures through the generations as an unquestioned 'rock of ages'.

What are the implications here for the pluralist–religious resurgence debate? If there is a major transformation of religion to individualistic and privatized forms, typified by the New Age, does this necessarily herald a resurgence of religiosity albeit outside of institutional structures? The answer is probably 'no'. The explicit and more implicit aspects of the new religiosity means that religion is taking a new direction and establishing new configurations. Nonetheless, if it is the case that fresh forms of religiosity are replacing the old, this may not effectively reverse the processes of the long-term decline of religion. It may well be that from a historical perspective the evidence still points towards an overall demise. The new religiosity, so it may be argued, does not make up for the decline of traditional Christianity, while the so-called revival of contemporary religion does not correspond, in any meaningful way, with the (Christian) revivals of previous generations (Bruce, 1996, pp. 272–3).

The new spiritualities are not the only forms of religion frequently advanced as proof of the revival of religion. The apparent growth of fundamentalism, particularly that of the Christian constituency in the USA, might suggest such a revival. However, it is difficult to argue that fundamentalism is foremost an integral part of consumer-style religion in the spiritual marketplace even if some individuals will 'buy into' a 'fundamentalist' way of life. Fundamentalist resurgence and sectarian schisms are scarcely new. They are primarily movements that have resisted certain tendencies of modernity and the relativism of post-modernity and are not ultimately a result of religious 'market forces'. In the West such movements of conservative Christianity are largely a reaction against an increasingly pluralist and secular society, the loss of the social significance of the faith, an increasing permissive culture and the decline of perceived sacred social institutions.

The emergence of Christian fundamentalism does not disprove the decline of religion thesis. Indeed, it may actually support it. The reality is that with each turn of the wheel such movements have less and less of a social impact and attract fewer adherents, while their momentum lasts for a shorter period of time. Today, there is the danger of overexaggerating the impact of fundamentalism in terms of the number of converts won and its influence on social and political life. The evidence suggests that it remains of far greater significance in North America than Europe. Yet, even in the USA, the fundamentalist element must be viewed as a relatively small, if vociferous minority that has made little real impact on public life.

In appraising the growth areas of today's religion that sector influenced by non-Christian global religions has also to be considered since they add to the increasing pluralism, religiously speaking, of advanced industrial societies. Historically, the West, as constituted by geographical region and the political frameworks of North America and Western Europe, has been united by a common cultural legacy – Christianity. To be sure, conflict between its major divisions, whether Protestant, Roman Catholic, or the Orthodox Church, have had profound repercussions. However, it is possible to speak of the Christendom of previous centuries. Whatever version of the faith prevailed at a particular time or place, it dominated social and cultural life and resisted incursions from outside – not just of military powers of conquest but of alien cultural and religious systems.

In the globalized context of the twenty-first century, the cultural boundaries of the West are increasingly penetrated. In an age when traditional religion seems to be declining, that of the ethnic minorities amounts to an important developing constituency. Their significance relates to the function of constituting cultural markers in a pluralist society. However, in the long run it may well be that the relentless process of assimilation and secularization will erode the religious life of many of these minorities, or at least blunt the more fundamentalist and militant inclinations of a few. Much will depend on that which cannot easily be discerned: political events elsewhere in the world. Globally, we are clearly in a new era of religion. Spiritual fervour is spreading in many parts of the globe, and it has become fashionable to label the believers – be they Moslem, Hindu, or Jewish – as 'fundamentalists' who frequently appear to be in conflict with the secular processes of modernization and global change. In some ways such world developments make the faiths of the ethnic minorities the least predictable area of religious life. One thing for sure, however, is that many of the doctrines and practices of the world religions will continue to have an impact on religious life in the West, whether they are or are not carried by ethnic communities. Above all, they will probably continue to enhance the mix 'n' match nature of contemporary religion and ensure that religious boundaries continue to disintegrate.

In predicting future social developments, the success of sociology has varied considerably. Once the discipline was assured of the inevitable decline of religion. This conjecture is now far from convincing. Given the current trends, it is difficult to forecast the future of religion in Western societies. No less easy to predict is the fate of the sociological specialism that surveys and analyzes this unique aspect of social life. It is obvious that the future of the latter is invariably entwined with the fortunes of the former. The decline of religion, as a social phenomenon, will mean the decline of the sociology of religion. There are important implications here for how religion is perceived today. It is evident that the emerging paradigms in the sociology of religion continue to extend definitions of religion. The problem remains, however, that such a broad definition appears to include too much of what has not historically counted as religion. Quasi-religions, holistic religions and self-spiritualities may in many respects depart from substantive definitions of religion. Today, practically anything can be regarded as religion by using a broad criterion and can even include social phenomena which categorically deny that they are religious in nature.

It may be, at the end of the day, that predictions about the future of religion depend on what is meant by the term. If religion continues to decline in Western societies then the sociology of religion will itself become increasingly marginalized. The sub-discipline may attempt to prolong its possible death throes by pushing back the frontiers of what is defined as religion. Above all, we might expect that for the sociology of religion, quasi-religions will become the growth area for study, as those based upon a supernatural frame of reference continue to recede. If there is no God, as Voltaire once claimed, man would have to invent one. It may be similarly said that if there is no religion in the Western world, then the sociology of religion will have to find it. For the meantime, however, it remains a vibrant part of the broad socio-logical discipline and possibly the most fascinating.

Bibliography

Abdullah, M. (1995) *Muslim Minorities in the West*, London: Grey Seal.

Abercrombie, N., Baker, J., Brett, S. and Foster, J. (1970) 'Superstition and Religion: The God of the Gaps', in D. Martin and M. Hill (eds), *Sociological Year-book of Religion in Britain*, 3, London: SCM.

Acquaviva, S. (1979) *The Decline of the Sacred in Industrial Society*, Oxford: Blackwell.

Adams, D. (1987) 'Ronald Reagan's "Revival": Voluntarism as a Theme in Reagan's Civil Religion', *Sociological Analysis*, 48: 17–29.

Aho, J. (1990) *The Politics of Righteousness: Idaho Christian Patriotism*, Seattle: University of Washington Press.

Akers, K. (1977) *Deviant Behaviour: A Social Learning Approach*, Belmont, CA: Wadsworth.

Albanese, C. (1993) 'Fisher Kings and Public Places: The Old New Age in the 1990s', *Annals*, 527: 131–43.

Albrow, M. (1995) 'Globalization', in R. Brym (ed.), *New Society: Sociology for the 21st Century*, Toronto: Harcourt Brace.

Alfred, H. (1976) 'The Church of Satan', in C. Glock and R. Bellah (eds), *The New Religious Consciousness*, Berkeley CA: University of California Press.

Ali, Y. (1992) 'Muslim Women and the Politics of Ethnicity and Culture in Northern England', in J. Sahgal and N. Yuval-Davies (eds), *Refusing Holy Orders*, London: Virago Press.

Ammerman, M. (1987) *Bible Believers*, London: Rutgers University Press.

Anthony, D. and Robbins, T. (1982) 'Spiritual Innovation and the Crisis of American Civic Religion', in M. Douglas and S. Tipton (eds), *Religion and America: Spirituality in a Secular Age*, Boston: Beacon Press.

Anthony, D. and Robbins, T. (1990) 'Civil Religion and Recent American Religous Ferment', in T. Robbins and D. Anthony (eds), *In Gods We Trust*, Cambridge, MA: Harvard University Press.

Anwar, M. (1981) *Young Muslims in a Multicultural Society*, Leicester: The Islamic Foundation.

Anwar, M. (1995) 'Muslim in Britain', in Abedin, S. and Z. Sardar (eds), *Muslim Minorities in the West*, London: Grey Seal.

Archer, A. (1986) *The Two Catholic Churches*, London: SCM.

Aries, P. (1974) *Western Attitudes to Death*, London: Marion Boyars.

Atchley, R. (1980) *The Social Forces in Later Life*, Belmont, CA: Wadsworth.

Bailey, E. (1997) *Implicit Religion*, Kampen: Kok Pharos Publishing House.

Bainbridge, D. (1997) *The Sociology of Social Movements*, New York: Routledge.

Barber, B. (1995) *McWorld versus Jihad*, New York: Times Books.

Barker, E. (1983) 'With Enemies Like That: Some Functions of Deprogramming as an Aid to Sectarian Membership', in J. Richardson (ed.), *Conversion Careers: In and Out of the New Religious Movements*, London: Sage.

Barker, E. (1984) *The Making of a Moonie*, Oxford: Blackwell.

Barker, E. (1985) 'New Religious Movements: Yet Another Great Awakening', in P. Hammond (ed.), *The Sacred in a Secular Age*, Berkeley, CA: University of California Press.

Barker, E. (1994) 'But is it a Genuine Religion?', in A. Greil and T. Robbins (eds), *Religion and the Social Order. Between Sacred and Secular: Research and Theory on Quasi-Religion*, 4, Greenwich, CT: JAI Press.

Barker, E. (1999) 'New Religious Movements: Their Incidence and Significance', in B. Wilson and J. Cresswell (eds), *New Religious Movements: Challenge and Response*, New York and London: Sage.

Barkun, M. (1986) *Crucible of the Millennium*, Syracuse, NY: Syracuse University Press.

Barr, J. (1978) *Fundamentalism*, London: SCM Press.

Barrett, D. (1998) *Sects, 'Cults' and Alternative Religion: A Survey and Sourcebook*, London: Cassell.

Barton, J. (1986) 'Religion and Cultural Change in Czech Immigrant Communities, 1850–1920', in R. Miller and T. Marzik (eds), *Immigrants and Religion in Urban America*, Philadelphia, PA: Temple University Press.

Bauman, Z. (1992) 'Postmodern Religion', in P. Heelas (ed.), *Religion, Modernity and Post-Modernity*, Oxford: Blackwell.

Bebbington, D. (1989) *Evangelism in Modern Britain*, London: Cambridge University Press.

Beckford, J. (1975) *The Trumpet of Prophecy: A Sociological Study of Jehovah's Witnesses*, Oxford: Blackwell.

Beckford, J. (1978) 'Conversion and Apostacy', in D. Anthony, J. Needleman and T. Robbins, *Conversion, Coercion and Commitment in New Religious Movements*, New York: Seabury.

Beckford, J. (1983) 'The World Images of New Religious and Healing Movements', in R. Jones (ed.), *Sickness and Sectarianism*, Aldershot: Gower.

Beckford, J. (1990) *Religion and Advanced Industrial Society*, London: Unwin Hyman.

Beckford, J. (1992) 'Religion, Modernity and Post-Modernity', in B. Wilson (ed.), *Religion: Contemporary Issues*, London: Bellew Publishing.

Bellah, R. (1964) 'Religious Evolution', *American Sociological Review*, 29(3): 358–74.

Bellah, R. (1967) 'Civic Religion in America', in R. Richey and D. Jones (eds), *American Civic Religion*, New York: Harper & Row.

Bellah, R. (1971) 'Between Religion and Social Science', in R. Caporale and A. Grumelli (eds), *The Culture of Unbelief*, Berkeley, CA: University of California Press.

Bellah, R. (1975) *The Broken Covenant*, Berkeley, CA: University of California Press.

Bellah, R. (1976a) 'Reflections on the Protestant Ethic in Asia', *Journal of Social Issues*, 19(1): 52–60.

Bellah, R. (1976b) 'New Religious Consciousness and the Crisis of Modernity', in C. Glock and R. Bellah (eds), *The Consciousness Reformation*, Berkeley, CA: University of California Press.

Ben-Yehuda, N. and Goode, E. (1994) *Moral Panics: The Social Construction of Deviance*, Oxford: Blackwell.

Berger, P. (1967) *The Sacred Canopy*, Garden City, NY: Doubleday Anchor.

Berger, P. (1970) *A Rumour of Angels: Modern Society and the Rediscovery of the Supernatural*, London: Allen Lane.

Berger, P. (1973) *The Social Reality of Religion*, Harmondsworth: Penguin.

Berger, P. (1979) *The Heretical Imperative*, London: Penguin.

Berger, P. and Luckmann, T. (1967) *The Social Construction of Reality*, Garden City, NY: Doubleday Anchor.

Beyer, P. (1994) *Religion and Globalization*, London: Tavistock.

Bhacha, P. (1985) *Twice Migrants*, London: Tavistock.

Bibby, R. (1978) 'Why Conservative Churches are Really Growing. Kelley Revisited', *Journal for the Scientific Study of Religion*, 17(2): 127–38.

Bibby, R. (1987) *Fragmented Gods: The Poverty and Potential of Religion in Canada*, Toronto: Irwin.

Bibby, R. (1993) *Unknown Gods: The Ongoing Story of Religion in Canada*, Toronto: Toronto University Press.

Bibby, R. and Brinkcroff, W. (1983) 'Circulation of the Saints Revisited', *Journal for the Scientific Study of Religion*, 22, 153–62.

Bird, F. and Reimer, B. (1982) 'Participation Rates in New Religious and Para-Religious Movements', *Journal for the Scientific Study of Religion*, 21(1): 1–14.

Bloul, R. (1996) 'Engendering Muslim Identities: Deterritorialization and the Ethnicization Process in France', in B. Metcalf (ed.) *Making Muslim Space in North America and Europe*, Berkeley, CA: University of California Press.

Bocock, R. (1993) *Consumption*, London: Routledge.

Boudin, A., Dain-Cricq, A. and Hirschhorn, M. (1982) 'The Wood and the Trees: Reflections on "The Return of the Sacred" ', *Social Compass*, 31(4): 297–310.

Bourdieu, P. (1977) *Outline of a Theory and Practice*, London: Cambridge University Press.

Bowman, M. (1993) 'Reinventing the Celts', *Religion*, 23, 147–56.

Brierley, P. (2000) *Religious Trends*, London: Marc Europe.

Bristow, J. (1977) 'Vice and Vigilance', Dublin: Gill & Macmillan.

Bromley, D. and Shupe, A. (1979) 'The Tnevnoc Cult', *Sociological Analysis*, 40(4): 361–6.

Bromley, D. and Shupe, A. (1981) *Strange Gods: The Great American Cult Scare*, Boston: Beacon Press.

Bromley, D. and Shupe, A. (1990) 'Rebottling the Elixir: The Gospel of Prosperity in America's Religio-Economic Corporations', in T. Robbins and D. Anthony (eds), *In Gods We Trust: New Patterns of Religious Pluralism in America*, New Brunswick, NJ: Transaction.

Brouwer, S., Gifford, P. and Rose, S. (1996) *Exporting the American Gospel*, Routledge: New York.

Bruce, S. (1988) *Rise and Fall of the New Christian Right in America*, Oxford: Clarendon Press.

Bruce, S. (1990) *A House Divided: Protestantism, Schism and Secularization*, London: Routledge.

Bruce, S. (1992) 'Religion in the Modern World', in M. Haralambos (ed.), *Developments in Sociology*, 8, Ormskirk: Causeway Press.

Bruce, S. (1993) 'Religion and Rational Choice', *Sociology of Religion*, 54(2): 193–205.

Bruce, S. (1996) 'Religion in Britain at the Close of the Twentieth Century', *Journal of Contemporary Religion*, 11(3), 261–74.

Bruce, S. (1997a) 'The Pervasive World-View: Religion in Pre-Modern Britain', *British Journal of Sociology*, 84(4).

Bruce, S. (1997b) 'Zealot Politics and Democracy: The Case of the New Christian Right', in R. Barker (ed.), *Political Ideas and Political Action*, Oxford: Blackwell.

Bruce, S. (1999) *Choice and Religion: A Critique of Rational Choice Theory*, Oxford: Oxford University Press.

Buchanan, T. and Conway, M. (1996) *Political Catholicism in Europe, 1918–65*, Oxford: Clarendon Press.

Budd, S. (1973) *The Sociology of Religion*, London: Penguin.

Cambell, C. (1999) 'The Easternization of the West', in B. Wilson and J. Cresswell (eds), *New Religious Movements: Challenge and Response*, New York and London: Sage.

Cambell, C. and McIver, S. (1974) 'Cultural Sources of Support for contemporary Occultism', *Social Compass*, 34: 41–60.

Carey, S. (1987) 'The Indianization of the Hare Krishna Movement', in R. Burghart (ed.), *Hinduism in Great Britain*, London: Tavistock.

Carrol, J., Hargrove, B., and Lummis, A. (1983) *Women in Cloth*, New York: Harper & Row.

Casanova, J. (1994) *Public Religions in the Modern World*, Chicago: University of Chicago Press.

Castles, S. and Kosack, G. (1973) *Immigrant Workers and Class Structure in Western Europe*, Oxford: Oxford University Press.

Christiano, K. (1987) 'Church as a Family Surrogate', *Journal for the Scientific Study of Religion*, 25(3): 339–54.

Cohen-Sherbok, D. (1991) 'Jews and Europe', *Religion Today*, 6(2): 3–5.

Cole, W. (1989) 'Sikhs in Britain', in P. Badman (ed.), *Religion, State, and Society in Modern Britain*, Lampeter: The Edwin Mellen Press.

Coleman, S. (1991) 'Faith Which Conquers the World. Swedish Fundamentalism and the Globalization of Culture', *Ethnos*, 56(1/2): 6–18.

Cook, G. (2000) *European Values Survey*, Gordon Cook Foundation.

Cox, H. (1994) *Fire From Heaven*, Reading, MA: Addison-Wesley.

Crippen, T. (1988) 'Old and New Gods in the Modern World: Towards a Theory of Religious Transformation', *Social Forces*, 67(2): 316–36.

Crowley, V. (1994) *The Phoenix from the Flame*, London: Aquarian.

Culpepper, E. (1978) 'The Spiritual Movement in Radical Feminist Consciousness', in J. Needleman and G. Baker (eds), *Understanding the New Religions*, New York: Seabury.

Cupitt, D. (1998) 'Post-Christianity', in P. Heelas (ed.), *Religion, Modernity and Post-Modernity*, Oxford: Blackwell.

Davie, G. (1994) *Religion in Britain Since 1945: Believing Without Belonging*, Oxford: Blackwell.

Davies, C. (1999) 'The Fragmentation of the Religious Tradition of the Creation, After-life and Morality: Modernity Not Post-Modernity', *Journal of Contemporary Religion*, 14(3): 339–60.

Davies, R. and Richardson, J. (1976) 'The Organization and Functioning of the Children of God', *Sociological Analysis*, 37(4): 321–39.

Demerath, N. (1965) *Social Class in American Protestantism*, Chicago: Rand McNally.

Demerath, N. and Williams, R. (1985) 'Civic Religion in an Uncivil Society', *Annals of the American Academy of Political and Social Science*, 480: 154–66.

Derks, F. (1983) *Uittreding Uit Nieuwe Religieuze Bewegingen*, report in *Psychology of Religion*, Katholieke Universieit Nijmegen, unpublished research.

Dobbelaere, K. (1981) 'Secularization: A Multi-Dimensional Concept', *Current Sociology*, 29(2): 3–21.

Dobbelaere, K. (1992) 'Roman Catholicism: Function Versus Performance', in B. Wilson (ed.), *Contemporary Religious Issues*, London: Bellew Publishing.

Dolan, J. (1998) 'Immigrants and the American Experience', in J. Butler and H. Stout (eds), *Religion in American History: A Reader*, New York: Oxford University Press.

Douglas, M. (1966) *Purity and Danger*, London: Routledge.

Douglas, M. (1973) *Natural Symbols*, Harmondsworth: Penguin.

Douglas, M. (1983) 'The Effects of Modernization on Religious Change', in M. Douglas and S. Tipton (eds), *Religion in America*, Boston: Beacon Press.

Downton, J. (1979) *Sacred Journeys*, New York: Columbia University Press.

Durkheim, E. (1915) *The Elementary Forms of the Religious Life*, London: Allen & Unwin.

Eade, J. (1993) 'The Political Articulation of Community and the Ismalization of Space in London', in R. Barot (ed.) *Religion and Ethnicity: Minorities and Social Change in the Metropolis*, Kampen: KOK Pharos Publishing House.

Ebaugh, H. (1988) 'Leaving Catholic Convents: Towards a Theory of Disengagement', in D. Bromley (ed.), *Falling from the Faith*, Newbury Park, CA: Sage.

Eliade, M. (1969) *The Quest: History and Meaning in Religion*, Chicago: University of Chicago Press.

Ellul, J. (1976) 'Hermeneutique de la secularization fictive', in *Hermeneutique de la secularization fictive: actes du colloque de Rome*, Paris: Aubier.

Ellwood, R. (1973) *One Way: The Jesus Movement and Its Meaning*, Engelwood Cliffs, NY: Prentice-Hall.

Engels, F. (1963) *The Peasant War in Germany*, Moscow: Progress Publishing.

Esposito, J. and Watson, M. (2000) *Religion and the Global Order*, Lampeter: University of Wales Press.

Featherstone, M. (1982) 'The Body in Consumer Culture', *Theory, Culture and Society*, 1(2): 18–31.

Featherstone, M. (1990) 'Introduction', in M. Featherstone, *The Global Culture*, London: Sage.

Feher, S. (1994) 'The Hidden Truth: Astrology as Worldview', in A. Greil and

T. Robbins (eds), *Religion and the Social Order. Between Sacred and Secular: Research and Theory on Quasi-Religion*, 4, Greenwich, CT: JAI Press.

Fenn, R. (1990) 'Pre-modern Religion in the Postmodern World', *Social Compass*, 37(1): 96–105.

Festinger, L., Riecken, H. and Schachter, S. (1956) *When Prophecy Fails*, Minneapolis: University of Minnesota Press.

Finke, R. (1997) 'The Consequence of Religious Competition: Supply-Side Explanations for Religious Change', in L. Young (ed.), *Rational Choice Theory and Religion: Summary and Assessment*, New York: Routledge.

Fischler, C. (1974) 'Astrology and French Society: The Dialectic of Archaism and Modernity', in E. Tiryakian (ed.), *On the Margins of the Visible*, New York: Wiley.

Flanagan, K. and Jupp, P. (eds) (1996) 'Introduction', in K. Flanagan and P. Jupp (eds), *Postmodernity, Sociology and Religion*, London: Routledge.

Fox, R. and Adams, R. (1972) 'Mainlining Jesus: The New Trip', *Society*, February, 56.

Freud, S. (1938) *Totem and Tabu*, Harmondsworth: Penguin.

Gallop, G. and Castelli, J. (1989) *The People's Religion: American Faith in the 1990s*, New York: Macmillan – now Palgrave.

Gee, P. (1992) 'The Demise of Liberal Christianity?', in B. Wilson (ed.), *Contemporary Religious Issues*, London: Bellew Publishing.

Gellner, E. (1993) *Postmodernism, Reason and Religion*, New York: Routledge.

Gennep, A. Van (1908) *The Rites of Passage*, London: Routledge & Kegan Paul.

Gerami, S. (1989) 'Religious Fundamentalism as a Response to Foreign Dependency: The Case of the Iranian Revolution', *Social Compass*, 36(4): 45–80

Gerard, D. (1985) 'Religious Attitudes and Values', in A. Abrams, D. Gerard and N. Timms (eds), *Values and Social Change in Britain*, Basingstoke: Macmillan – now Palgrave.

Gerlach, L. and Hine, V. (1970) *People, Power and Change: Movements of Social Transformation*, Indianapolis, IND: Bobbs-Merrill.

Giddens, A. (1991) *The Consequences of Modernity*, Cambridge: Polity Press.

Gifford, P. (1990) 'Prosperity: A New and Foreign Element in African Christianity', *Religion*, 20(4): 373–88.

Gill, R., Hadaway, C. and Marler, P. (1998) 'Religious Belief in Britain', *Journal for the Scientific Study of Religion* 37, 507–16.

Glock, C. (1958) *The Role of Deprivation in the Origin and Evolution of Religious Groups*, Survey Research Centre, A-15, Berkeley, CA: University of California Press.

Glock, C. and Bellah, R. (1976) *The New Religious Consciousness*, Berkeley, CA: University of California Press.

Glock, C. Ringer, B. and Babbie, E. (1967) *To Comfort and To Challenge*, Berkeley, CA: University of California Press.

Glock, C. and Stark, R. (1969) 'Dimensions of Religious Commitment', in R. Robertson (ed.), *Sociology of Religion*, Harmondsworth: Penguin.

Goddijn, W. (1983) 'Some Religious Developments in the Netherlands (1947–1979)', *Social Compass*, 30(4): 409–24.

Goffman, E. (1961) *Asylums*, Garden City, NY: Doubleday.

Goode, W. (1963) *World Revolutions and Family Patterns*, New York: The Free Press.

Goodridge, R. (1975) 'The Ages of Faith – Romance or Reality?', *Sociological Review*, 23: 381–96.

Gordon, D. (1974) 'The Jesus People: An Identity Synthesis', *Urban Life and Culture*, 3(2): 159–78.

Gordon, M. (1964) *Assimilation in American Life: The Role of Race, Religion and National Origins*, Oxford: Oxford University Press.

Gray, R. and Moberg, D. (1977) *The Church and the Older Person*, Grand Rapids: MI: Eerdmans.

Greely, A. (1981) 'Religion and Musical Chairs', in D. Anthony and T. Robbins (eds), *In Gods We Trust*, Cambridge, MA: Harvard University Press.

Greil, A. (1993) 'Explorations Along the Sacred Frontier: Notes on Para-Religions, Quasi-Religions, and Other Boundary Phenomenon', in D. Bromley and J. Hadden (eds), *Religion and the Social Order*, 3, Part A, Greenwich, CT: JAI Press.

Greil, A. and Robbins, T. (1994) 'Introduction: Exploring the Boundaries of the Sacred', in A. Greil, and T. Robbins (eds), *Religion and the Social Order. Between Sacred and Secular: Research and Theory on Quasi-Religion*, 4, Greenwich: CT: JAI Press,

Greil, A. and Rudy, D. (1984) 'What Have We Learned From Process Models of Conversion? An Examination of Ten Case Studies', *Sociological Focus*, 17(4), 305–21.

Gusfield, R. (1963) *Symbolic Crusades: Status Politics and the American Temperance Movement*, Urbana, IL: University of Illinois Press.

Hadaway, C., Marler, P. and Chaves, M. (1993) 'What the Polls Don't Show', *American Sociological Review*, 58 (December): 741–52.

Hamilton, M. (1995) *The Sociology of Religion*, London: Routledge.

Hammond, P. (1976) 'The Sociology of American Civil Religion: A Bibliographic Essay', *Sociological Analysis*, 37(2): 169–82.

Hammond, P. (1986) *Making Sense of Modern Times*, New York: Routledge & Kegan Paul.

Hammond, P. (1988) 'Religion and the Persistence of Identity', *Journal for the Scientific Study of Religion*, 27(1): 1–11.

Hammond, P. and Warner, K. (1995) 'Religion and Ethnicity in Late-Twentieth-Century America', in W. Roof (ed.), *The Annals of the American Academy of Political and Social Sciences*, 572 (May): 55–66.

Hanf, T (1994) 'The Sacred Marker: Religion, Communalism and Nationalism', *Social Compass*, 41(1), 9–20.

Harder, M. (1974) 'Sex Roles in the Jesus Movement', *Social Compass*, 21: 345–53.

Harding, S., Phillips.D. and Fogarty, K. (1985) *Contrasting Values in Western Europe*, London: Macmillan – now Palgrave.

Harper, C. (1974) 'Spirit-Filled Catholics. Some Biographical Comparisons', *Social Compass*, 31: 311–24.

Harris, C. (1999) 'The Cult of Princess Diana: Sociological Perspectives' in T. Walter (ed.), *Mourning for Diana*, Oxford: Berg.

Harris, M. (1990) *America Now*, New York: Simon and Schuster.

Harrison, M. (1974) 'Sources of Recruitment to Catholic Pentecostalism', *Journal for the Scientific Study of Religion*, 13(3): 49–64.

Harrison, T. (1992) *Elvis People. The Cult of the King*, London: HarperCollins.

Hartman, P. (1976) 'Social Dimensions of Occult Participation', *British Journal of Sociology*, 27(2): 199–213.

Hawley, S. (2001) 'Finding God in Consumption', in S. Porter, M. Hayes and D. Toms (eds), *Faith in the Millenium*, Sheffield: Sheffield Academic Press.

Heelas, P. (1996) *The New Age Movement: The Celebration of Self and the Sacrilization of Modernity*, Oxford: Blackwell.

Heelas, P. (1998) 'Introduction', in P. Heelas (ed.), *Religion, Modernity and Post-Modernity*, Oxford: Blackwell.

Heelas, P. (2000) 'Expressive Spirituality and Humanistic Expressivism', in S. Sutcliffe and M. Bowman (eds), *Beyond the New Age*, Edinburgh: Edinburgh University Press.

Heinman, S. (1990) 'Constructing Orthodoxy', in T. Robbins and D. Anthony (eds), *In Gods We Trust*, New Brunswick, NJ: Transaction.

Helwig, A. (1991) *Sikhs in England: The Development of a Migrant Community*, Delhi: Oxford University Press.

Herberg, W. (1956) *Protestant–Catholic–Jew: An Essay in American Religious Sociology*, Garden City, NY: Anchor Doubleday.

Hervieu-Leger, D. (1998) 'The Transmission and Formation of Socioreligious Identity in Modernity: An Analytical Essay', *International Sociology*, 13(2): 213–28.

Hiebert, P. (1982) 'The Flaw of the Excluded Middle', *Missiology*, 10(1): 35–47.

Hill, M. (1971) 'Typologie sociologique de l'ordre religieux', *Social Compass*, 18: 45–64.

Himmelstein, J. (1986) 'The Social Basis of Anti-Feminism: Religious Networks and Culture', *Journal for the Scientific Study of Religion*, 25(1): 1–15.

Hobart, C. (1974) 'Church Involvement and the Comfort Thesis in Alberta', *Journal for the Scientific Study of Religion*, 13: 463–70.

Hofstadter, R. (1955) *The Age of Reform*, New York: Vintage Books.

Hoge, D. (1987) *Women in Ritual and Symbolic Roles*, New York: Plenum.

Holt, J. (1940) 'Holiness Religion: Culture Shock and Social Reorganization', *American Sociological Review*, 5: 740–7.

Hornsby-Smith, M. (1987) *Roman Catholics in England*, Cambridge: Cambridge University Press.

Hornsby-Smith, M. (1992) 'Believing Without Belonging. The Case of Roman Catholics in England', in B. Wilson (ed.), *Religion: Contemporary Issues*, London: Bellew Publishing.

Hunt, S. (1993) 'Racism in Europe', *Talking Politics*, 6(1): 52–6.

Hunt, S. (1998) 'The Radical Kingdom of the Jesus Fellowship', *Pneuma*, 20(1): 21–42.

Hunt, S. (2000) ' "Winning Ways": Globalisation and the Impact of the Health and Wealth Ministries', *The Journal of Contemporary Religion*, 14(2): 36–48.

Hunt, S. (2001) 'The British Black Pentecostal "Revival": Identity and Belief in the "New" Nigerian Churches', *Ethnic and Racial Studies*, 24(1): 104–30.

Hunter, J. (1987) *Evangelicalism: The Coming Generations*, Chicago: Chicago University Press.

224   *Bibliography*

Inglehart, R. (1997) *Modernization and Post-Modernization*, Princeton, NJ: Princeton University Press.

Jacobs, J. (1989) *Divine Disenchantment: Deconverting from New Religions*, Bloomington, IND: Indiana University Press.

James, W. (1902) *The Variety of Religion Belief*, New York: Longman.

Jarman, N. (1997) *Material Conflicts: Parades and Visual Displays in Northern Ireland*, Oxford: Berg.

Jeffery, P. (1992) *Migrants and Refugees. Muslim and Christian Pakistani Families in Bristol*, Cambridge: Cambridge University Press.

Johnson, B. (1961) 'Do Holiness Sects Socialize in Dominant Values?', *Social Forces*, 39: 301–16.

Johnson, B. (1985) 'Liberal Protestantism: The End of the Road?', *Annals*, 480: 39–52.

Johnson, S. and Tamney, J. (1989) 'Support for the Moral Majority', *Journal for the Scientific Study of Religion*, 23(2): 183–96.

Joli, D. (1984) 'The Opinions of Mirupi Parents in Saltley, Birmingham about Their Children's Schooling', *Research Papers: Muslims in Europe*, 24 (December).

Judah, J. (1974) *Hare Krishna and the Counter Culture*, New York: John Wiley.

Kelley, D. (1978) 'Why Conservative Churches are Still Growing', *Journal for the Scientific Study of Religion*, 17(2): 165–72.

Kemp, A. (1993) *Witchcraft and Paganism Today*, London: Michael O'Mara Books.

Kepel, G. (1994) *The Revenge of God*, Cambridge: Polity Press.

Khasala, K. (1986), 'New Religious Movements Turn to Worldly Success', *Journal for the Scientific Study of Religion*, 25(2): 233–47.

Kim, A. (1993) 'The Absence of Pan-Canadian Civil Religion', *Sociology of Religion*, 54(3): 257–75.

Kokosalakis, N. (1986) 'The Political Significance of Popular Religion in Greece', unpublished paper presented to the 11th World Congress of Sociology, International Sociological Association, Los Angeles.

Kosmin, B. and Levy, C. (1983) *Jewish Identity in an Anglo-Jewish Community*, London: Board of British Jews.

Kuusela, K. (1996) 'Mosque of Our Own. Turkish Immigration in Gothenburg: Facing the Effects of a Changing World', in R. Barot (ed.) *Religion and Ethnicity: Minorities and Social Change in the Metropolis*, Kampen: Kok Pharos Publishing House.

Lang, K. and Lang, G. (1960) 'Decisions for Christ: Billy Graham in NYC', in A. Vidich and D. White (eds), *Identity and Anxiety*, New York: The Free Press.

Larkin, G. (1974) 'Isolation, Integration and Secularization: A Case Study of the Netherlands', *Sociology Review*, 22(1): 401–18.

Leach, E. (1967) *Culture and Communication*, Cambridge: Cambridge University Press.

Lehman, E. (1985) *Women Clergy: Breaking Through the Barriers*, New Brunswick, NY: Transaction.

Leibman, R. (1983) 'Mobilizing the Moral Majority', in R. Liebman and R. Wuthnow (eds), *The New Christian Right*, New York: Aldine.

Lemert, C. (1975) 'Defining Non-Church Religion', *Review of Religious Research*, 16(3), 186–97.

Levine, E. (1980) 'Rural Communes and Religious Cults', *Adolescent Psychiatry*, 8: 138–53.

Lewis, J. (1989) 'Apostates and the Legitimation of Repression', *Sociological Analysis*, 49(4): 386–96.

Lewis, J. (ed.), (1995) *The Gods Have Landed. New Religions from Other Worlds*, New York: State University Press.

Lewis, R. and Bromley, G. (1987) 'The Cult Withdrawal Syndrome', *Journal for the Scientific Study of Religion*, 26(4): 508–22.

Lincoln, C. (1989) 'The Muslim Mission in the Context of American Social History' in G. Wilmore (ed), *African American Studies*, Durham, NC: Duke University Trust.

Loftland, J. (1979) 'White Hot Mobilization: Strategies of Millenarian Movements', *Journal for the Scientific Study of Religion*, 20(2): 375–85.

Loftland, J. and Skonovd, N. (1981) 'Conversion Motives', *Journal for the Scientific Study of Religion*, 20(2): 375–85.

Loftland, J. and Stark, R. (1965) 'Becoming a World-Saver: A Theory of Religious Conversion', *American Sociological Review*, 30: 862–74.

Loy, M., McPherson, B. and Kenyon, G. (1978) *Sport and Social Systems*, Reading, MA: Addison-Wesley.

Luckmann, T. (1967) *The Invisible Religion*, New York: Macmillan – now Palgrave.

Luckmann, T. (1990) 'Shrinking Transcendence, Expanding Religion', *Sociological Analysis*, 50(2): 127–38.

Luhrmann, T. (1989) *Persuasions of the Witch's Craft: Ritual Magic and Witchcraft in Present Day England*, Oxford: Blackwell.

Lyons, D. (1996) 'Religion in the Post-Modern World. Old Problems New Perspectives', in K. Flanagan and P. Jupp (eds), *Post-Modernity, Sociology and Religion*, London: Macmillan – now Palgrave.

Lyotard, J. (1984) *The Post-Modern Condition*, Manchester: Manchester University Press.

Mandel, R. (1996) 'A Place of Their Own. Contesting Places in Berlin's Migrant Community', in B. Metcalf (ed.) *Making Muslim Space in North America and Europe*, Berkeley: University of California Press.

Martin, B. (1998) From Pre- to Postmodernity in Latin America: The Case of Pentecostal', in P. Heelas (ed.), *Religion, Modernity and Post-Modernity*, Oxford: Blackwell.

Martin, D. (1965) 'Towards Eliminating the Concept of Secularization', in J. Gould (ed.), *Penguin Survey of the Social Sciences*, Harmondsworth: Penguin.

Martin, D. (1978) *A General Theory of Secularisation*, Oxford: Blackwell.

Martin, D. (1982) 'Received Dogma and New Cult', *Daedelus* (Winter): 53–71.

Martin, D. (1990) *Tongues of Fire: The Explosion of Pentecostalism in Latin America*, Oxford: Latin America.

Martin, D. (1991) 'The Secularization Issue: Prospect and Retrospect', *British Journal of Sociology*, 42: 465–74.

Martin, D. (1996) *Forbidden Revolutions*, London: SPCK.

Marty, M. (1978) *Fundamentalism*, Boston: Beacon Press.

Marty, M. (1987) 'Fundamentalism', Boston: Beacon Press.

Marx, J. and Ellison, D. (1975) 'Sensitivity Training and Communes:

Contemporary Quests for Community', *Pacific Sociological Review*, 18(4): 442–62.

Mathisen, J. (1989) 'Twenty Years After Bellah: Whatever Happened to American Civil Religion', *Sociological Analysis*, 50(2): 129–46.

Mauss, A. and Perrin, R. (1989) 'Saints and Seriousness', *Review of Religious Research* 34: 176–8.

McGuire, M. (1992) *Religion: The Social Context*, Belmont, CA: Wadsworth.

McLuhan, M. (1962) *The Guttenberg Galaxy*, Toronto: Toronto University Press.

Melton, G. (1987) 'How New is New? The Flowering of the "New" Religious Consciousness Since 1965', in D. Bromley and P. Hammond (eds), *The Future of the New Religious Movements*, Macon, GA: Mercer University Press.

Milbank, J. (1990) *Theology and Social Theory: Beyond Secular Reason*, Oxford: Basil Blackwell.

Miller, D. (1997) *Reinventing American Protestantism*, Los Angeles: University of California Press.

Mosqueda, L. (1986) *Chicanos, Catholicism and Political Ideology*, New York: University Press of America.

Neitz, M. (1990) 'Quasi-Religions and Cultural Movements: Contemporary Witchcraft as a Churchless Religion', in A. Greil and T. Robbins (eds), *Religion and the Social Order. Between Sacred and Secular: Research and Theory on Quasi-Religion*, 4, Greenwich, CT: JAI Press.

Nelson, G. (1968) 'The Concept of Cult', *Sociological Review*, 16(3): 351–62.

Nesbitt, E. (1997) ' "Splashed with Goodness", The Many Meanings of Amrit for Young British Sikhs', *Journal of Contemporary Religion*, 12(1): 17–34.

Nesti, A. (1990) 'Implicit Religion; The Issues and Dynamics of a Phenomenon', *Social Compass*, 37(4): 423–38.

Newport, F. (1979) 'The Religious Switchers in the United States', *American Sociological Review*, 44: 258–52.

Niebuhr, H. (1929) *The Social Sources of Denominationalism*, New York: World Publishing.

Nielson, S. (1989) 'Islamic Communities in Britain', in P. Badman (ed.), *Religion, State, and Society in Modern Britain*, Lampeter: The Edwin Mellen Press.

O'Toole, R. (1977) *The Precipitous Path: Studies in Political Sects*, Toronto: Peter Martin.

Palmer, S. (1994) *Moon Sisters, Krishna Mothers, Rajneesh Lovers*, Syracuse, NY: Syracuse University Press.

Parsons, T. (1951) *The Social System*, New York: The Free Press.

Percy, M. (1995) 'Fundamentalism: A Problem for Phenomenology', *Journal of Contemporary Religion*, 10(1): 83–91.

Percy, M. and Taylor, R. (1997) 'Something for the Weekends, Sir? Leisure, Ecstasy and Identity in Football and Contemporary Religion', *Leisure Studies*, 16: 37–49.

Peven, D. (1968) 'The Use of Religious Revival Techniques to Indoctrinate Personnel: The Home Party Sales Organization', *Sociological Quarterly*, 20: 97–106.

Poloma, M. (1989) *The Assemblies of God at the Crossroads*, Knoxville: University of Tennessee Press.

Porter, D. (1992) 'Some Recent Developments in Seventh-day Adventism', in B. Wilson (ed.), *Religion: Contemporary Issues*, London: Bellew Publishing.

Prebish, C. (1984) ' "Heavenly Father, Divine Goalie": Sport and Religion', *The Antioch Review*, 42(3): 306–18.

Puttick, E. (1995) 'Sexuality, Gender and the Abuse of Power in the Master–Disciple Relationship: The Case of the Rajneesh Movement', *Journal of Contemporary Religion*, 10(1): 29–40.

Puttick, E. (1999) 'Women in New Religious Movements', in B. Wilson and J. Cresswell (eds), *New Religious Movements. Challenge and Response*, London: Routledge.

Rabinowitz, J. (1992) 'The Effects of Demographic Dynamics on Jewish Communial Participation in the United States', *Sociological Analysis*, 53(3): 39–54.

Richardson, E. (1981) *Islamic Cultures in North America*, New York: Pilgrim Press.

Richardson, J. (1980) 'Conversion Careers', *Society*, 17: 47–50.

Richter, P. (1994) 'Seven Days Trading Make One Week? The Sunday Trading Issues as an Index of Secularization', *British Journal of Sociology*, 45(3): 333–48.

Richter, P. and Francis, L. (1998) *Gone But Not Forgotten*, London: Darton, Longman & Todd.

Ritzer, G. (1996) *The McDonaldization of Society*, Newbury Park, CA: Pine Forge Press.

Robbins, T., Anthony, D. and McCarthy, J. (1983) 'Legitimating Repression', in D. Bromley and J. Richardson (eds), *The Brain-Washing-Deprogramming Controversy: Sociological, Psychological, Historical and Legal Perspectives*, New York: Edward Mellin.

Roberts, R. (1994) 'Power and Empowerment', *Religion Today*, 9(3): 3–13.

Robertson, R. (1970) *The Sociological Interpretation of Religion*, Oxford: Blackwell.

Robertson, R. (1979) 'Religious Movements and Modern Societies', *Sociological Analysis*, 40, 297–314.

Robertson, R. (1993) 'Community, Society, Globality, and the Category of Religion', in E. Barker, J. Beckford and K. Dobbelaere (eds), *Secularization, Rationalism, and Sectarianism*, Oxford: Clarendon.

Rochford, E. (1985) *Hare Krishna*, New Brunswick, NJ: Rutgers University Press.

Roof, W. (1976) 'Traditional Religion in Contemporary Society: A Theory of Local-Cosmopolitan Plausibility', *American Sociological Review*, 41: 195–208.

Roof, W. (1994) *A Generation of Seekers: The Spiritual Journey of the Baby Boom Generation*, San Francisco: Harper & Row.

Roof, W. and McKinney W. (1985) 'Denominational America and the New Religious Pluralism', *Annals*, 480: 24–38.

Roof, W. and McKinney W. (1987) *American Mainline Religion: Its Changing Shape and Future*, New Brunswick, NJ: Rutger's University Press.

Rudy, D. and Greil, A. (1983) 'Conversion to the Worldview of Alcoholics Anonymous', *Qualitative Sociology*, 6: 1–28.

Sargant, W. (1957) *Battle for the Mind*, London: Heinemann.

Sarna, J. (1978) 'The American Jewish Experience and the Emergence of the Muslim Community in America', *American Journal of Islamic Social Sciences*, 9 (Fall): 370–82.

Schoenfeld, E. (1992) 'Militant and Submissive Religions: Class, Religion and Ideology', *British Journal of Sociology*, 43(1): 111–40.

Sharot, S. (1992) 'Religious Fundamentalism: Neo-Traditionalism in Modern Societies', in B. Wilson (ed.), *Religion: Contemporary Issues*, London: Bellew Publishing.

Shiner, L. (1966) 'The Concept of Secularization in Empirical Research', *Journal for the Scientific Study of Religion*, 6: 207–20.

Shupe, A. and Bromley, D (1980) *The New Vigilantes: Deprogrammers, Anti-Cultists and the New Religions*, Beverley Hills: Sage.

Shupe, A., Spiermann, R. and Stigall, S. (1977) 'Deprogramming: The New Exorcism', *American Behavioral Scientists*, 20(6): 941–56.

Sihvo, J. (1988) 'Religion and Secularization in Finland', *Social Compass*, 35(1): 67–90.

Simpson, J. (1983) 'Moral Issues and Status Politics', in R. Liebman and R. Wuthnow (eds), *The New Christian Right*, New York: Aldine.

Sisking, A. (1990) 'The Sullivan Institute/Fourth Wall Community: "Radical" Psychotherapy as Quasi-Religion', in A. Greil and T. Robbins (eds), *Religion and the Social Order. Between Sacred and Secular: Research and Theory on Quasi-Religion*, 4, Greenwich, CT: JAI Press.

Smark, P. (1978) 'Mass Marketing God', *Atlas*, 25: 19–20.

Smelzer, N. (1962) *Theory of Collective Behaviour*, London: Routledge & Kegan Paul.

Smith, A. (1990) 'Towards a Global Culture?', in M. Featherstone (ed.), *Global Culture: Nationalism, Globalization and Modernity*, London: Sage.

Smith, W. (1989) *Lecture on the Religion of the Semites*, Edinburgh: Black.

Snow, D. (1976) *The Nichiren Shoshu Buddhist Movement in America*, Los Angeles: University of California, unpublished PhD thesis.

Snow, D. and Machalek, R. (1983) 'The Convert as a Social Type', in R. Collins (ed.), *Sociological Theory*, San Francisco: Jossey Bass.

Snow, D. and Machelek, R. (1984) 'The Sociology of Conversion', *Annual Review of Sociology*, 10: 167–90.

Snow, D. and Phillips, C. (1980) 'The Loftland–Stark Conversion Model: A Critical Reassessment', *Social Problems*, 27: 430–47.

Solomon, T. (1981) 'Integrating the "Moonie" Experience', in T. Robbins and D. Anthony (eds), *In Gods We Trust*, Cambridge, MA: University Press.

Stacey, W. and A. Shupe (1982) 'Correlates of Support for the Electronic Church', *Journal for the Scientific Study of Religion*, 21: 291–303.

Staples, C. and Mauss, A. (1987) 'Conversion and Commitment', *Journal for the Scientific Study of Religion*, 26(2): 83–147.

Stark, R. and Bainbridge, W. (1980) 'Secularization, Revival and Cult Formation', *Annual Review of the Social Sciences of Religion*, 4: 85–119.

Stark, R. and Bainbridge, W. (1985) *The Future of Religion*, Berkeley, CA: University of California Press.

Stark, R. and Bainbridge, W. (1987) *A Theory of Religion*, Berkeley, CA: University of California Press.

Stark, R., Finke, R. and Guest, A. (1996) 'Mobilizing Local Religious Markets: Religious Pluralism in the Empire State, 1855–1865', *Sociological Review*, 61(2): 203–18.

Stark, R. and Iannaccone, L. (1993) 'Rational Choice Propositions About Religious Movements', in D. Bromley and J. Hadden (eds) *Handbook on Cults and Sects*, Greenwich, CT: JAI Press.

Stark, R. and Iannaccone, L. (1994) 'A Supply-Side Reinterpretation of the "Secularization" of Europe', *Journal for the Scientific Study of Religion*, 33(1): 230–52.

Stark, R., Kent, L. and Doyle, D. (1982) 'Religion and Delinquency: The Ecology of a "Lost" Relationship"', *Journal of Research in Crime and Delinquency*, 19: 4–24.

Stauffer, R. (1974) *Radical Symbols and Conservative Functions*, unpublished paper presented to the Society for the Scientific Study of Religion, Los Angeles, 1974.

Steinitz, L. (1980) 'Religiosity, Well-being, and Weltanschauung Among the Elderly', *Journal for the Scientific Study of Religion*, 19(1): 60–7.

Stoeltzel, J. (1983) *Europe at the Crossroads*, Paris: Presses Universitaire de France.

Strauss, R. (1976) 'Changing Oneself: Seekers and the Creative Transformations of Life Experience', in J. Loftland (ed.), *Doing Social Life*, New York: Wiley.

Tabor, J. and Gallagher, E. (1995) *Why Waco?*, Berkeley, CA: University of California Press.

Tatla, D.S. (1993) 'The Punjab Crisis and Sikh Mobilization in Britain', in R. Barot (ed.), *Religion and Ethnicity: Minorities and Social Change in the Metropolis,* Kampen: Kok Pharos Publishing House.

Thomas, K. V. (1974) *Religion and the Decline of Magic*, London: Weidenfeld & Nicolson.

Thomas, T. (1993) 'Hindu Dharma in Disperion', in G. Parsons (ed.), *The Growth of Religious Diversity. Britain Since 1945*, 1, London: Routledge.

Thompson, J. (1974) 'La participation catholique dans le mouvement du renouveau charismatic', *Social Compass*, 21(2): 325–44.

Thompson, W. (1997) 'Charismatic Politics: The Social and Political Impact of Renewal', in S. Hunt, M. Hamilton and T. Walter (eds), *Charismatic Christianity*, London: Macmillan.

Tilly, C., Tilly, L. and Tilly, R. (1975) *The Rebellious Century*, Cambridge, MA: Harvard University Press.

Tippet, A. (1973) 'The Phenomenology of Worship, Conversion and Brotherhood', in W. Clark (ed.), *Religious Experience*, Springfield, IL: Thomas.

Tipton, S. (1982) *Getting Saved From the Sixties*, Berkeley, CA: University of California Press.

Tiryakian, E. (1974) 'Towards the Sociology of Esoteric Culture', in E. Tiryakian (ed.), *On the Margins of the Visible*, New York: Wiley.

Towler, R. and Coxon, A. (1979) 'The Fate of the Anglican Clergy, London: Macmillan – now Palgrave.

Tracey, M. and Morrison, D. (1979) *Whitehouse*, London: Papermac.

Troeltsch, E. (1931) *The Social Teachings of the Christian Churches*, London: Allen & Unwin.

Tschannen, O. (1991) 'The Secularization Paradigm: A Systematization', *Journal for the Scientific Study of Religion*, 30(4): 395–414.

Turner, B. (1983) *Religion and Social Theory: A Materialistic Perspective*, Atlantic Highlands: Humanities Press.

Turner, V. (1974) *The Ritual Process*, Harmondsworth: Penguin.

Tylor, E. (1903) *Primitive Culture*, London: Mowbray.

Umansky, E. (1985) 'Feminism and the Revaluation of Women's Roles Within American Jewish Life', in Y. Haddad and E. Findly (eds), *Women, Religion and Social Change*, Albany: State University of New York Press.

Vance, N. (1984) 'Sport is a Religion in America', *The Chronicle of Higher Education*, 28(12): 25–7.

Victor, J. (1992) *Satanic Panic*, Chicago: Open Court Publishing.

Volt, J. (1991) *The Muslims of America*, New York: Oxford University Press.

Wald, K., Owen, D. and Hill, S. (1989) 'Evangelical Politics and States Issues', *Journal for the Scientific Study of Religion*, 18: 1–16.

Wallace, A. (1966) *Religion: An Anthropological View*, New York: Random House.

Wallerstein, I. (1980) *The Capitalist World Economy*, Cambridge: Cambridge University Press.

Wallis, R. (1974) 'The Aetherius Society: A Case Study in the Formation of a Mystagogic Congregation', *Sociological Review*, 22(1): 27–44.

Wallis, R. (1982) 'Charisma, Commitment and Control in a New Religious Movement', in R. Wallis (ed.), *Milleniallism and Charisma*, Belfast: Queen's University Press.

Wallis, R. (1984) *The Elementary Forms of New Religious Life*, London: Routledge & Kegan Paul.

Wallis, R. (1986) 'Figuring Out Cult Receptivity', *Journal for the Scientific Study of Religion*, 25, 494–503.

Wallis, R. (1993) 'Introduction' in R. Wallis (ed.), *Sectarianism*, Oxford: Clarendon.

Walter, T. (1990) 'Why Are Most Church-goers Women?', *Vox Evangelica*, 95: 599–625.

Walter, T. (1999) *On Bereavement: The Culture of Grief*, Buckingham: Oxford University Press.

Warner, R. (1993) 'Work in Progress Towards a New Paradigm for the Sociological Study of Religion in the United States', *American Journal of Sociology*, 98(5): 1044–93.

Waughn, E., Abu-Laban, B. and Oureshi, J. (1983) *The Muslim Community in North America*, New York: The Free Press.

Weber, M. (1958) 'The Protestant Sects and the Spirit of Capitalism', in H. Gerth and C. Mills (eds), *From Max Weber: Essays in Social Theory*, London: Routledge.

Weber, M. (1965) *The Sociology of Religion*, London: Methuen.

Weigert, A. (1971) 'An Emerging Intellectual Group Within a Religious Organization', *Social Compass*, 18(1): 101–15.

Weinstein, D. (1992) 'Television as Religion: The Reemergence of the Conscience-Collective', *Listening: Journal of Religion and Culture*, 20(1): 6–16.

Westley, F. (1978) 'The Cult of Man: Durkheim's Predictions and Religious Movements', *Sociological Analysis*, 39: 135–45.

Willoughby, W. (1981) *Does American Need a Moral Majority?*, Plainfield: Haven Books.

Wilmore, G. (1983) *Black Religion and Black Radicalism*, Maryknoll, NY: Orbis.

Wilson, A, (1978) *Finding a Voice: Asian Women in Britain*, London: Virago.

Wilson, B. (1966) *Religion in a Secular Society*, London: Weidenfeld & Nicolson.

Wilson, B. (1968) 'Religion and Churches in Contemporary America', in W. McLoughlin (ed.), *Religion in America*, Boston: Beacon Press.

Wilson, B. (1970) *Religious Sects*, London: Heinemann.

Wilson, B. (1976) *Contemporary Transformations of Religion*, London: Oxford University Press.

Wilson, B. (1982) *Religion in Sociological Perspectives*, Oxford: Oxford University Press.

Wilson, B. (1992) 'Reflections on a Many Sided Controversy', in S. Bruce (ed.) *Religion and Modernization*, Oxford: Clarendon Press.

Woodhead, L. and Heelas, P. (eds) (2000) *Religion in Modern Times*, Oxford: Blackwell.

Wright, S. (1987) *Leaving Cults: The Dynamics of Defection*, Washington, DC: Society for the Scientific Study of Religion.

Wright, S. (1988) 'Leaving New Religious Movements', in D. Bromley (ed.), *Falling From the Faith*, Newbury Park, CA: Sage.

Wuthnow, R. (1976) *The Consciousness Reformation*, Berkeley, CA: University of California Press.

Wuthnow, R. (1988) *The Restructuring of American Religion: Society and Faith Since World War II*, Princeton, NJ: Princeton University Press.

Wuthnow, R. (1993) *Christianity in the Twenty-First Century*, Oxford: Oxford University Press.

Yinger, T. (1965) *The Invisible Religion*, New York: Macmillan – now Palgrave.

York, M. (1995) K. Flanagan and P. Jupp (ed.), 'The Church Universal and Triumphant', *Journal of Contemporary Religion*, 10(1): 61–72.

York, M. (1996) 'Post Modernity, Architecture, Society and Religion: A Heap of Broken Images, or A Change of Heart?', in M. York, *Post-modernity, Sociology and Religion*, London: Macmillan – now Palgrave.

Zurcher, L. and Kirkpatrick, R. (1976) *Citizens for Decency: Anti-Pornography Crusades as Status Defence*, Austin: Texas University Press.

Index

Rise of Capitalism (Market Economy)

The Enlightenment

- Authoritive ethics, aesthetics and knowledge, new forms in a modern context
- Progress away from irrationality, tyranny and towards a brave new world.
- "Have courage to use your own intelligence."
- Away from identity communities toward enlightened communities → determinism
- Are we ever autonomous?
  ↳ full maturation
- emphasis on individualism

French Revolution

- Old Regime → hedgemony of power
  ↳ Breaking open old order

Industrial Revolution

- Socio-economic form of change
- Steam power for industry

Overall Themes

From small scale to large scale
Local   Global

Characteristic of Western History
Since 1400's
- communication was the crucial aspect
- ✓ multi-faceted change in modernity
  - political - NGO's, EU, UN
                liberal democracy
  - economic - urban, industry
                globalism
  - social
  - religion

Science and technology
Culture - Mass production
            Mass consumption
            Mass marketing
            Mass Communication
            Mass Literacy
            Mass Media
            Global Travel
            Information Society
            Popular Culture

23386932R00132

Made in the USA
Lexington, KY
08 June 2013